Mohamed's Ghosts

Mohamed's Ghosts

*An American Story of
Love and Fear in the Homeland*

STEPHAN SALISBURY

NATION
BOOKS

NEW YORK

Published by Nation Books, A Member of the Perseus Books Group
116 East 16th Street, 8th Floor
New York, NY 10003

Nation Books is a co-publishing venture of the Nation Institute and the Perseus Books Group.

Books published by Nation Books are available at special discounts for bulk purchases in the United States by corporations, institutions, and other organizations. For more information, please contact the Special Markets Department at the Perseus Books Group, 2300 Chestnut Street, Suite 200, Philadelphia, PA 19103, or call (800) 810-4145, ext. 5000, or e-mail special.markets@perseusbooks.com.

Designed by Trish Wilkinson
Set in 9.5 point Utopia

Library of Congress Cataloging-in-Publication Data

Salisbury, Stephan.
    Mohamed's ghosts : an American story of love and fear in the homeland / Stephan Salisbury.
        p. cm.
    Includes index.
    ISBN 978-1-56858-428-7 (alk. paper)
    1. Ansaarullah Islamic Society. 2. Muslims—Pennsylvania—Philadelphia. 3. Terrorism—United States—Prevention—Social aspects. 4. Islamophobia—Pennsylvania—Philadelphia. 5. Philadelphia (Pa.)—Ethnic relations. I. Title.
F158.9.M88S25 2009
305.6'970974811090511—dc22   2009050469

10 9 8 7 6 5 4 3 2 1

For Jennifer

Contents

Introduction: How to Take Down a Mosque   1

ONE
Since When Is Being Muslim a Crime?   29

TWO
A Snake with Its Head Raised   63

THREE
They, Like, Attacked This Neighborhood   111

FOUR
We Don't Know If He Was an Informer   133

FIVE
Brothers   169

SIX
Nothing to Hide   203

SEVEN
Literally and Figuratively a Cesspool   219

EIGHT
Nobody Wants a Terrorist Case   247

NINE
What's the Use of Me?   269

Acknowledgments   291
A Note on Sources   293
Index   299

How to Take Down a Mosque

*I*T SEEMED LIKE A *long sleep, and when I woke, I found myself in an-other country, a shadow country running parallel to where I thought I'd been living for decades. This was a land where everything was the same, but not the same. Here was a country at war, but not at war; a country at peace with arrests and investigations carried out in the sinking light of dawn; a country keeping tabs and comfortable with the busy work. You don't know what you don't know, they liked to say these days. And no one said much more. What did I know? When I was a student at Columbia University back in the late 1960s, I lived in a country at war, and everyone knew it; a country of arrests and bellicose investigations; a country of records and files and inter-rogations and violence. It was a country of anger and resentments, a country that hunkered down to protect itself from enemies within, and ultimately a country so powerful, so magnanimous, so enfold-ing, it could absorb millions of alienated opponents and transform them into the engines of the future. And here I was, the future was now, and I felt we had slept for twenty years, only to awake back at* *the beginning, back when you didn't know if your conversation was being recorded, if your wanderings were being tracked, and if your name graced endless sheets of paper silently filed away in a government cabinet. A cold, ineffable presence now filled the air. What I thought was dead was not dead, simply transmogrified. This was a country of ghosts, apparitions that once seemed vanquished, but that had reappeared and reappeared and reappeared, each time with a different face, a different story, and greater, more secret ruthlessness. There may be anger here, but it was stashed out of the way, folded and stored in an attic.*

I remember driving with my father one day, back in the summer of 1967, following a sophomore year in which I grew more and more fiercely opposed to the Vietnam War. The government is hopelessly corrupt, I said. It's hopelessly dictatorial, slaughtering millions in Southeast Asia, ignoring or jailing anyone opposed to the war and willing to take action over it. The government only understands force. Only force will end the killing. No, he said, that is never the answer. We were driving down First Avenue in Manhattan on a hot night. There were days, he said, and I remember them, when children lived over here along the East River starving to death. They lived on the banks of the river and picked at garbage. Old people starved. Families were thrown out of their homes. There were people sleeping on the street, thousands, maybe tens of thousands dying of hunger and disease. There were campfires in Central Park and tents and lean-tos. It's better now; slowly it has improved. You proceed with small steps.

My father was tough, but the most gentle of men. And in this brief conversation, street lights flickering across his face, reflecting off his wire-rimmed glasses, he distilled his philosophy into one short sentence: He believed in perfectibility. Governments, for the most part, harbor no such belief. They are about sustainability. The governed are always a threat to that. In my father's view, the way to perfect was to expose. Show the difference between what is said and what is done, between what we think we are and what we actually do. Open up that wound for all to see and cauterize it. On this hot summer night— perhaps Detroit was burning at the time or Newark or East Harlem— he told me that patience was required, patience and information. There are many questions, he said, and what you see at any moment offers up answers. My father was an American newspaperman to the core, and even though the government had secretly burglarized our suburban house at the onset of World War II in the ludicrous belief he was a German spy; even though he had lived in Moscow as a correspondent under constant surveillance, watched at all times, bugged, shadowed, and censored; even though he had seen friends disappear into the Soviet penal system and later saw American friends bugged and arrested and beaten in the South during the civil rights movement; and even though he was clandestinely watched and listened to by the CIA and National Security Agency when American authorities were annoyed by his Soviet reporting and infuriated by his Vietnam reporting for the New York Times, *even after all of this repetition, this drumbeat of cynical deceit, he believed in the power of truth and reason, the power of change, and the bedrock fact of human decency. Perfectibility. As the Vietnam War continued in its ferocity year after year, he believed that bringing the raw facts to light would ultimately overpower deception. The war would be stopped because people would finally grow sick of the prevarications—but only if they knew about them. I remember being stupefied by this almost serene stubbornness, this willingness to accept less as enough, even for a moment. But despite people dying in the streets of Detroit and Newark that very summer, shot on the spot by our own government, he had seen far more ghosts than I had.*

Deep into another war, I stood on a forlorn corner in Philadelphia and found myself asking the most basic questions of any war at any time: Who is friend, and who is foe? Who is being attacked and for what reasons? What is defeat, and what is victory? Am I an enemy? Strange questions, really, after so many years of killing. Shouldn't a nation at war have clear answers after so many deaths and so much disruption? I had similar questions a generation ago, as did millions of other Americans; the absence of plausible answers was one reason so many took to the streets in opposition to the war in Southeast Asia.

What did this corner, tucked away in a forgotten pocket of the city, have to do with war? On one side of Wakeling Street, fronted by a sweeping, empty asphalt parking lot, stood the low-slung Baptist Worship Center and Excell Christian Academy—a formidable box that in earlier times served as a giant Super Fresh market and Eckerd drugstore. Directly across the street, east of the church, the Risque and Excitement video emporiums offered a "Hot Summer Sale— Twice the Fun!" Down the block, a pink billboard poked up over Aramingo Avenue: "Can you sell mud to a pig?" it asked, in the name of sales-employment.com. Looming over all, just beyond the hum and rattle of elevated I-95, the Allied Chemical complex sprawled— mainstay, lifeline, and sometimes explosive threat to the neighborhood; at night, the outlines of its intricate maze of pipes and girders and tanks covering forty-five acres near the Delaware River flickered in a tracery of bright white lights, an otherworldly outline of the toxic workaday world.

Cars streamed past, and the sidewalks were empty. I was alone here and probably unobserved. No video cameras jutted from the front of an AOH clubhouse down the block, where a couple of afternoon drinkers sat at the bar and a green, white, and orange Irish flag drooped from a second-floor pole. No camera was suspended over the intersection. I had no cell phone emitting its silent tracking signal. My car was an old company car. No GPS chips were lodged anywhere in its battered body. No E-Z pass marked my passage through any tolls to get here. No neighbors leaned on their sills, watching. No black SUVs with darkened windows sat still as cats in the Baptist parking lot.

I was drawn to this spot, the corner of Wakeling Street and Aramingo Avenue in Philadelphia's old working-class community of Frankford Valley, by an easily overlooked whitewashed cinderblock building across from the Baptist Center—a one-time auto body and repair shop, in recent years converted to a mosque. There were no worshippers on this day, however. The central bay door was pulled shut. A chain-link fence, tangles of weeds growing up through its interlacing loops, surrounded building and parking lot. A dirty yellow Abco Auto Body sign teetered over the barbed wire atop the fence, and a metal gate stood chained and padlocked shut. The windows were boarded up.

Next door was a seriously weathered three-story stucco house with a brick-front first floor and a rickety high porch. A red crayon, a small toy truck, a green squirt gun, several yellowed newspapers, and a pot of ashen flowers were strewn across porch and steps. The first-floor windows were partially covered with plywood. A battered white chest of drawers leaned on garbage cans at the foot of the porch stairs. The house was empty.

Emptiness spread now like a durable stain down Wakeling, but for a moment, an instant in the life of Frankford Valley, this spot had been one of the dramatic focal points of the Global War on Terror.

Federal agents, primed and ready, watched this house and the old body shop, now so quiet and still and forgettable, for months. Many evenings and Fridays they would sit in dark unmarked sedans across Wakeling in the Baptist parking lot, making no effort to hide—promoting themselves, in fact—observing the comings and goings of people at prayer. Infiltrators were dispatched to the mosque to gather information on any terrorist plots budding on the poor streets of Frankford Valley. Informers sucked up all manner of gossip and rumor and whispered it to any congregant who might listen and then on to federal agents who, in turn, laid it down as fact in reports that wended their way to the Philadelphia office of Immigration and Customs Enforcement and the Philadelphia Office of the FBI, to the immigration and criminal courts, and on through the federal bureaucracy to Washington and perhaps even to John Ashcroft himself.

And it is here, on May 27, 2004—a day after Ashcroft sternly warned once more of terrorists among us—that a hundred agents from the Joint Terrorism Task Force (JTTF) and the IRS, not to mention local police, armed with automatic weapons, protected by body armor and employing bomb-sniffing dogs, descended in the early morning to round up a thick-bodied Egyptian imam who had overstayed his visa and married an American citizen, possibly to gain American citizenship for himself and—though this thought was hardly entertained by authorities—possibly for love.

In retrospect, it seems that marriage and family were surrogates for fraud and dark designs, and religion and nationality had once again become the very essence of threat in America. The war on terror burst at the corner of Aramingo and Wakeling like a mine, roiling and scattering everyone in its wake, and then moved on. The waters of urban life closed quickly. But what happened here goes beyond protective zealousness in the wake of 9/11. It is more than a metaphor for countless engagements in the war on terror, the many raids in the murk of dawn, the innumerable arrests for purported marriage fraud or minor visa irregularities. It demonstrates more than an anti-Islamic or anti-immigrant predicate undergirding much of "homeland security." What Frankford Valley reveals is a disturbing paradox that has moved to the heart of an increasingly conflated public and private life. What isn't there suggests what could be, and what could be, is. Absence of evidence is evidence itself. What can be imagined has replaced the actual. And the generally messy essences of daily life are not seen for what they are—mistakes or foolishness or hubris or even misguided helpfulness; rather, they are masks of a grim intent deliberately obscured.

Nothing seems to be what it appears; be is not finale of seem. And the only constant is anxiety and fear. Fear is the clay of power and of reality itself.

SEEING THIS MOSQUE, A house of worship, ultimately obliterated by a federal raid following the onset of the Iraq War finally shattered a kind of cultural sleep for me—a child of the Cold War, McCarthyism, and the subversions of COINTELPRO. Walking through Frankford Valley and speaking with those members of the congregation I could find, I was forced to continually reflect on past periods of national threat and on my own experience. What at first seemed an anomaly on Wakeling Street was, I realized, a refashioned political drama in a skein of such dramas leading back far into my past and into the past of my country. What is here has been here before; it has been repeatedly reworked and reborn, regardless of partisan politics. Wakeling Street, rough edged and out of the way, was a road through an old and menacing landscape of domestic and political trauma.

Not that there weren't differences. The past was the same and not the same. A generation ago, for those involved in civil rights or antiwar politics, government intrusion and disruption was a fact of life. At Columbia we knew the university was involved with the Defense Department and war research; we knew that federal agents and police were disguised and undercover on campus; we knew informants were sprinkled among our fellow students and even within the faculty, passing information about student antiwar and political activities to New York police and federal authorities. Wiretaps, informers, surveillance, disruption—those were the particulates of poisoned water. None of it mattered at the time. None of it served as a political deterrent. Such subversions were merely obstacles. Yes, many of my friends and classmates were watched, consigned to secret police files, targeted by undercover agents and government informers and, ultimately, included on illicit government lists of dangerous and subversive persons in need of monitoring and even preemptive arrest. My own father was on such a list and in such files, and I was too. And yes, acts of informants, undercover police, and agents provocateurs yielded arrests, violence, and even death. Then, as now, "freedom" was invoked by the government to justify war and all manner of questionable domestic activity.

But freedom also had a concrete meaning, spelled out for us in the nation's founding documents and hammered into us daily as schoolchildren as we came out from under our desks following atom bomb drills. The Soviet Union was totalitarian. America was free. Freedom was what defined us as a nation and bestowed on us our moral certitude. It's all right there in the U.S. Constitution. The woeful children living under Communism had no rights. Our fathers had triumphed over Hitler and the Nazis. Our leaders would triumph over Communism. Why? Because we are a free people.

As I look back, it seems that this rhetoric had some unexpected consequences: It lent legitimacy and possibility to the civil rights movement. It's what ultimately drove the anti–Vietnam War movement as well. We had a right to damn the government and push it and challenge it, and the government had no right to undermine our fundamental liberties to maintain its power and control. And if the wise men in charge intended to scoop us up and ship us off to fight and perhaps die in Vietnam, we had a fundamental right to say no, not here, not now, not ever. In fact, we were powerless and voiceless: We were expected to kill or be killed at the behest of the government, we were expected to follow the orders of our elders, but we had no say, no vote, no part in deciding who those leaders were and what went into their orders. Those active in the civil rights movement faced the same stark contradictions. What alternative to the street did we have? In the street, we exercised our freedom and found a voice. We gained strength and fearlessness—whatever the faults and tragic results of our actions—from our youth, our numbers, and our ideals. Freedom was not a rhetorical device; it formed the core of political life—even in the absence of voting rights, even in a world controlled by white men, even in the coddled world of academic in loco parentis. We acted. That was our America: We were children growing up in a republic of ideas, and our freedom was in the street and in our actions.

IN THE SUMMER OF 1967, when my father sought to tamp down my political impatience and naiveté, we traveled to the Soviet Union with a small army of *New York Times* reporters preparing special coverage of the fiftieth anniversary of the Bolshevik revolution. I was along just soaking it all up, and I remember one day we drove with Ray Anderson, the *Times*' Moscow bureau chief, out to Zagorsk— center, even then, of the Russian Orthodox Church. Motoring along a beautiful country road, we decided on the spur of the moment to stop at a grassy town square for a picnic. It was peaceful and green, and the Cold War was far away, frigid in the wake of the Six Day War. We parked and were spreading a blanket when two cars full of KGB agents raced up and slammed to a stop. Not allowed, they shouted. It was not on our approved itinerary. We could not sit in the grass and eat bread and cheese and drink wine. Absolutely forbidden. We had been followed all the way from Moscow. And after we packed up and headed off, we were followed all the way to Zagorsk. And then all the way back to the National Hotel, across from the Kremlin and St. Basil's Cathedral. To Anderson and my father, this was typical; to me, it was shocking.

Later that fall, as I returned to school for my junior year at Columbia, a major antidraft demonstration was held in lower Manhattan. Antiwar protestors sought to block access to the Selective Service center on Whitehall Street, an important intake point for military inductees and a symbol of the arbitrary nature of the war. As the crowd became more and more boisterous and demonstrators sat down blocking the entrance, New York City police on horseback rode directly into them. Large numbers of people were unable to avoid flailing hooves, and panic and blood spilled across the sidewalk. I was planning to participate in this demonstration, but I was late, and by the time I arrived, demonstrators had fanned out through the financial district, disrupting traffic. As I watched, I struck up a conversation with a friendly bearded kid who said he had seen horses smash into crowds of people, scattering everyone and leaving some lying on the street, too injured to move. He said it was fucked up. I agreed. He said it required action. I said yes. And then, as a patrol car moved past us on the street, the bearded kid grabbed me, twisted my arm behind my back, and called out to the car, and before I knew even what was happening, I was shoved against the patrol car, surrounded by uniformed police, pushed in, and whisked away directly to the Criminal Courts Building on Centre Street, known as the Tombs. I should have expected undercover agents trolling the streets. People were challenging the law and the draft. We had deviated from our approved itinerary. Mayor Lindsay praised police for the respect shown the rights of demonstrators.

The daily world of the old Soviet Union and the daily world of America in the 1960s were hardly equivalent. What was revealed, however, on the country road to Zagorsk and at curbside on Broad Street in lower Manhattan was the unsettling and threatening duplicity of a covert police presence. Whether on that town square in Russia or in the New York Financial District, police were secretly operating within the ordinary space of daily life. And in both cases, the message delivered was identical: Don't step out of line. Tell your friends and neighbors not to step out of line. You are being watched, and you don't know who or where we are. You don't know what you don't know. God knows what the poor peasants in that beautiful Russian village had to go through in the wake of our aborted picnic. God knows how many others were busted for nothing by that friendly and earnest kid near Whitehall Street.

At least I was a conscious actor in Manhattan on that day long ago. I meant to be at Whitehall. What about the Muslims attending services on Wakeling Street? Almost all were immigrants. Some were full-fledged citizens. Some had overstayed their visas. Some were in the process of obtaining green cards that would bestow long-term residency. Some already had green cards. All of these people were simply trying to live their lives. Yet it didn't matter how long they had been in the United States. It didn't matter what their formal immigration status was. All feared the government. All feared the murk of immigration. All feared the specter of Guantanamo. All believed they were on the high edge of America balanced over a black maw. They had no defense, no protection but anonymity. They feared the knock on the door in the night. And they all understood, in the wake of September 11, 2001, what I failed to realize as a kid: the friendly guy on the corner, eager to strike up a chat and pass the time talking about comings and goings, might not be what he appeared to be. The street did not represent freedom for them; it threatened with exposure, attack, arrest, detention, deportation.

After decades, with another war mounted and Whitehall Street largely forgotten, with no draft, and barely any images of the battlefield penetrating into the public realm, with government agents and undercover cops again moving out invisibly into local communities, with arrests, with invocations of freedom coming from Washington, and with deep, deep fear suffusing many immigrant enclaves, I looked around and wondered, What country is this? What is a "homeland?"

THE ABCO BODY SHOP was, as I said, not an Abco Body Shop and hadn't been one for years. It was the home of the Ansaarullah Islamic Society, a small mosque established in January 2002 by Mohamed Ghorab, a mechanical engineer, mediocre businessman, passionate student of Islam, and Egyptian national who had dreamed of starting his own mosque since before he came to the United States from Alexandria in 2000.

The building wasn't disguised; it wasn't posing as Abco to obscure some mysterious and sinister agenda. The congregation simply could not afford to remove the old Abco sign post, and besides, they were only tenants and given the huge monthly rental for the property, over $4,000, there always seemed to be more pressing needs. That became increasingly the case as 9/11 receded and the war on terror ground its way across the American battlefield, sowing apprehension daily. By late 2003, more often than not, congregation bail and legal matters needed immediate attention, sucking up the financial resources of everyone connected with the mosque. Why bother with the Abco sign?

The bedraggled house next door served as the imam's residence. He lived there with his first American wife, or at least they lived there together part of the time. But life between them became difficult, and after their divorce, Mohamed Ghorab lived there with his much-loved second American wife, Meriem Moumen, a Morocco-born U.S. citizen. They settled in, even as the house, with its porous, failing roof and kitchen ceiling, gradually collapsed around them—like much else in their world.

I looked up at the house and tried to imagine Ghorab and Moumen coming out the front door. She is dark and veiled, holding their baby; he wears a white galabiya and whispers something funny in her ear. She laughs as he pulls the door closed. But Ghorab had hardly a chance to begin his ministry and life with Moumen when, in March 2003, he was arrested for his supposedly fraudulent first American marriage. Then, a year after he posted a $50,000 bond, Ghorab was again arrested in the massive May 2004 raid. He was never released after that, never charged with any criminal wrongdoing, kept in solitary confinement for long periods of time, never granted bail. He was simply held, first at York County Prison, south of Harrisburg, where the federal government leases a huge wing to hold immigration violators and terrorism suspects, and then at Pike County Prison, in northeastern Pennsylvania, far from Philadelphia, an untenable drive. He was alone. Meriem was alone.

In November 2005, after enduring one disappointing and incomprehensible hearing after another, after getting repeatedly ineffective and costly legal advice, Ghorab gave up his fight to remain in the United States and was deported to Egypt in December. Moumen went too, taking their American-born eighteen-month-old daughter. But her thirteen-year-old daughter by a previous marriage, also American-born, refused to leave the United States, rending the family like brittle paper and rocking Moumen to her psychic core. Husband or daughter? America or Egypt? Depression or death-in-life? Meriem's choice. By that time, not surprisingly, the Ansaarullah Islamic Society had closed, unable to pay its bills, unable to retain its congregation, unable to function at all. The mosque shut down, itself a victim and, in the eyes of many, a target of the war on terror.

Did Ansaarullah represent anything more than a battered old city corner revived by the devout? Did it embody some kind of inchoate threat, a threat invisible to all but those who knew what no one else seemed to know? What is known and incontrovertible is that months after the mosque was incorporated in January 2002, congregants began to face waves of legal troubles as the federal antiterror campaign fired up. At least half a dozen members were arrested for purported immigration violations. A half dozen more were detained and released. Still more were questioned. Some were told their immigration problems might disappear if they provided the right kind of information to authorities. They began working with immigration and law enforcement officials, reporting back on the daily life of the mosque. Several congregants found themselves in deportation proceedings, unable to meet bond, unable to help their families, unable even to understand the labyrinthine and increasingly hostile immigration system.

The president of the mosque, a U.S. citizen, confronted by extensive scrutiny from law enforcement and federal revenue agents, finally sold his house and left the country for Dubai. He was never charged with any violations or crimes. Other members of the mosque, fearing the taint of this fated place, simply vanished. As late as the fall of 2006, long after the mosque had closed, long after Ghorab had left the country, federal authorities were still pursuing former Ansaarullah members, forcing them out of the country. Even in 2008, the mosque, so obscure during its functioning life, was invoked in immigration papers as the site of threats and intimidation directed against a man seeking American citizenship.

I once asked a savvy federal prosecutor why authorities showed such obsessive concern with Ansaarullah.

"Don't you wonder why so many bad guys are hanging around the place?" the prosecutor responded.

"Why do you say 'bad guys'? Scratch the surface of any immigrant group, and you're going to find immigration violations. They aren't crimes," I said.

"That's probably true. But are we supposed to ignore them?"

"But why go after these guys? They probably represent a tiny fraction of immigration violations around the city," I said. The conversation ended in a circle.

"Immigration goes in there. They find one guy, then another and another and another. We can't ignore them."

Besides, the prosecutor said, eerily echoing many anti-Communist prosecutors in the early 1950s and many other prosecutors in supposed U.S. terror cases of the twenty-first century, "You don't know what we know."

What is the essence of "knowing"? Is something true if all believe it is true? If something hasn't happened, does that mean it has been prevented? Is the absence of an event proof that it was stopped, erased before written? When is nothing something? What shadows are cast by nothing?

Secretary of Defense Donald Rumsfeld pondered the question in February 2002 at a Defense Department press briefing: "Reports that say that something hasn't happened are always interesting to me, because as we know, there are known knowns; there are things we know we know. We also know there are known unknowns; that is to say, we know there are some things we do not know. But there are also unknown unknowns, the ones we don't know we don't know."

By THE TIME GHORAB was deported, Ansaarullah existed only in memory, a dead dream that left no visible trace on the Frankford Valley landscape. In the lives of those associated with it, however, the mosque and the federal onslaught on it left a scarred trail of crushing debt, broken families, bitterness, psychological dislocation, bewilderment, and abiding fear. Mosque members lost their homes and their livelihoods. They mistrusted each other. Native-born American citizens—children and teenagers—were driven from their country and from their parents. The neighborhood, not rich in social resources to begin with, lost a safe haven for children and a source of charity freely given to poor families, Islamic and non-Islamic alike. Anxieties and rumors were stoked by what happened at Aramingo and Wakeling—even though details of what actually happened were not widely known—and spread far beyond the narrow Frankford Valley streets.

I began stopping in at Ansaarullah during Friday prayers in June 2005, drawn by conversations I had been having with Muslims in Philadelphia and with immigration attorneys. After writing extensively for the *Philadelphia Inquirer* about the impact of 9/11–inspired security measures on the physical landscape of the city, I now wondered how the war on terror had affected ordinary people in the Muslim community. You should visit that mosque up in Frankford or someplace up there, people said. There's something going on there. A big raid. Taliban or terror. Don't really know. There was some problem with the imam. Maybe there still is. Maybe you'd better keep away from him.

No one seemed to know, though vague rumors abounded. In a large city, a small dying dream barely stirs the waters, but ripples of rumors spread endlessly. And since Islam lacks a priestly hierarchy and a bureaucracy—each congregation operates independently—information about a mosque and its doings is often a matter of what gets passed along by word of mouth, sometimes a dark exercise in whisper down the lane. No central authority issues statistics or totes up congregants. Large mosques with hundreds and hundreds—even thousands—of members are publicly visible, but many congregations are much smaller, and except for those in attendance, news of their activities and fates exists in the grey of rumor and gossip. What was this Ansaarullah, I wondered, after learning the name of the mosque, and I made my way to its pulled-up bay door.

What I found, just a few months before the mosque closed, was the remnant of what had once been a lively and fairly substantial multinational congregation of two hundred or so. The first Friday I visited, twenty-four worshippers showed up—Somali cab drivers, Jordanian ice cream truck vendors, Palestinian workers on break who hurriedly kicked off their shoes and rushed in a few minutes after 1:00. That June afternoon was hot, and half a dozen ceiling fans turned slowly, stirring the humid air. I was welcomed by Meriem, completely covered in grey with a black veil and *hijab*, a cell phone constantly in her hand, conversations continuously on-going in English, French, and Arabic. She was too busy to talk to me as she arranged for afternoon prayer, spoke with a congregant about appeals for donations, and cajoled what I took to be creditors on the phone. After prayer it was the same: more phone conversations, multiple languages, a creased, grim brow. The next week, attendance was down to nineteen. At the end, perhaps half a dozen men turned out on the last Friday in July—and as many children. No matter what seemed to be transpiring in the adult world, no matter what the sorrows or the drama, there were always children at Ansaarullah, hopping on bouncy balls, playing with foam blocks, rolling on the mismatched green and grey and brown carpet remnants covering the concrete floor.

"We will miss it," said Oma, a reedy, friendly girl of nine who lived in the neighborhood and had no other indoor place to go, really. Moumen and Ghorab had befriended her family and helped them with food and child care, and Oma and her playmates often wandered through the raised bay door during Friday prayer and in the evenings.

"Who are you?" she asked me. I told her I was a reporter simply visiting the mosque.

"What are you reporting? Are you a policeman?"

"No, I'm just visiting the mosque, and I may write about it. That's all."

"Do you like it?"

"Yes," I said. "Everyone is very friendly. Do you like it?"

"Of course I do! We come here all the time. I can play basketball!" She picked up a small yellow ball, tossed it at a tattered net leaning next to a wall, and ran over to pick it up, only mildly encumbered by her long grey *abaya*. A little boy grabbed the ball, and they both came over to me.

"The mosque is closing," I said. "Will you miss it?"

A look of concern passed over her small face. The little boy just stared at me.

"Yes, we will all miss it. Everyone will."

HOW COULD ANSAARULLAH CONTINUE? Imam Ghorab was in prison. The president of the mosque had fled the country. Atef Idais, a young Palestinian who stepped in to lead prayers following the imam's arrest, had been arrested himself. A helpful imam from New Jersey had come to lead Friday prayers—Meriem drove an hour to pick him up and an hour to take him home—but he was no longer able to spend the time, and there was no pay. The arrests came in drumbeats. Congregants were importuned to become informers. If they refused, they found themselves deported. At least one congregant was detained and began providing information on everyone else; when his usefulness was exhausted, federal agents refused to grant him promised naturalization as a U.S. citizen. Whom was he going to complain to?

None of these members of Ansaarullah were charged with any violations unrelated to immigration. Certainly none had been arrested on any terror-related charges (although Atef Idais was portrayed in court as a lying member of Hamas, a characterization that he denied flatly, eliciting exasperation and scorn from prosecutors). They had all spoken openly to federal agents—commonly saying they had nothing to hide—only to find that immigration regulations cast a wide and indiscriminate net, one that could be artfully deployed.

Authorities took virtually everything these congregants said in court and in interviews as a lie, a misrepresentation, a deception, a feint. Were two arrestees actually brothers? Was Ghorab really married? Was Idais really in love? Was Ansaarullah really a mosque?

The last few Fridays, a thin Somali cabdriver, who profusely apologized to his fellow worshippers for his faulty knowledge of the Quran, tried haltingly to lead prayers. Another congregant pleaded for donations to stave off the inevitable.

Then there was no one to lead at all.

The landlord—in neighborhood legend the owner of vast tracts of Frankford Valley, including Risque Video and the Baptist center across the street—evicted the mosque, which was at least three months in arrears on its rent, about $12,000. He evicted Meriem and her children, amid many tears and angry shouts, from their home next door. The doors and the gates were locked. Everyone vanished, melting into the city, leaving the country, or disappearing into the penal complex.

THERE WAS NO ONE on the street the day I stood in front of the mosque, flipping the padlock on the gate and taking inventory of the imam's old porch with its children's castoffs and dead plants. Was this place a battlefield? Did Sheik Ghorab, as his congregants called him, represent an enemy? Was his house an outpost for some kind of radical cell? What was a cell, anyway? A group of worshippers angry over American foreign policy? Quakers certainly fit that description—and they have found themselves targets of law enforcement investigations and surveillance in recent times as well— just as they had during the 1960s and 1970s and 1980s. Were Quaker cells in our midst for decades? In Philadelphia?

How do you prove you are who you are? How do you prove you are a simple citizen in a war that posits simple citizens as deadly enemies? And why do you need to make these proofs at all?

"IN THIS NEW WAR, our enemy's platoons infiltrate our borders, quietly blending in with visiting tourists, students, and workers," Attorney General John Ashcroft proclaimed at a June 2002 Washington press conference. "They move unnoticed through our cities, neighborhoods, and public spaces. They wear no uniforms. Their camouflage is not forest green, but rather it is the color of common street clothing. Their tactics rely on evading recognition at the border and escaping detection within the United States. Their terrorist mission is to defeat America, destroy our values, and kill innocent people."

Government officials have rarely deviated from this message. It could be anyone. The enemy is relentless and invisible and everywhere, like the air or a child's bogeyman.

"We pay a price for being such a free country. People move, are able to move in and out. They're able to burrow into our society. We're doing a better job of understanding who's coming in and who's leaving. But if there is a sleeper cell here, we're doing everything we can to find them and disrupt them," George W. Bush told Diane Sawyer of ABC News at the end of 2003. "How many Arab sleepers do we have now?" wondered Sawyer. "I can't answer the question," the president replied.

What is the measure of freedom? What is the price to defend it? What denotes an Arab sleeper? What kind of society have we become when the ordinary is suspect and the mundane is seen as a ruse and a cover?

"I am concerned," FBI Director Robert S. Mueller III told the Senate Select Intelligence Committee in February 2005, "about what we are not seeing."

With the nation's highest law enforcement officials, the greatest concern is expressed over what they are "not seeing." What kind of war is waged against what is not seen? How is the invisible made visible?

The demise of Ansaarullah suggests at least partial answers—similar events have played out like a fugue with variations over and over across the United States since September 11, 2001. New York City, Detroit, Chicago, Los Angeles, Miami, Columbus, Denver, Cleveland, Albany, Toledo, and Lodi, California. Dozens of Middle Eastern

and South Asian mosques and communities have found themselves
infiltrated by informers and subjected to surveillance and much-
publicized arrests, detentions, and trials. In virtually every case, the
charges have deflated, largely flattening into immigration-related
technicalities or petty criminal accusations, such as credit card fraud,
or into the amorphous catch-all, material support for terrorism.
Where terror-related convictions have been obtained, they have almost invariably involved aggressive use of informants, leading to bitter complaints of government entrapment and provocation.

There has been a wider, lingering effect of all of these charges and
criminal cases, the same in city after city, town after town. Money
has been diverted from mosque and charity and groceries and rent
to legal defense. Anxiety has been aroused in the population at large.
Families have broken. Communities have become riddled with suspicion from without and within. People don't know if their good
friend or their neighbor, their fellow worshipper or their boss is
passing along gossip and rumor to immigration or law enforcement
authorities. They don't know if angry words will be interpreted as
dire threats. They don't know if they can talk with each other on the
telephone without some charged word triggering vast electronic
scrutiny. They don't know if some derisive comment will serve as an
invitation for an informer to embroider a tale and pass it along—
often in the hope of receiving something in return. Whatever else
may be said about America in the post–9/11 world, informing is wo-
ven deeply into many aspects of life. From law enforcement to the
media, informers drive much of the action.

"If we don't know you, we won't talk to you," one Muslim congregant said to me. "Even if we know you, we won't talk. How do we
know who you really are?"

That congregant at least had a community. There are places in
America, in Philadelphia and in other cities, that no longer exist:
whole communities scattered by the war on terror, neighborhoods
destroyed for the greater good.

No one knows how many mosques have melted away in the heat of America in the twenty-first century. Islamic organizations have not attempted to track the rise and fall of congregations around the country. Nor has the federal government. But as far as I have been able to determine, no large, very public mosque has shut its doors as a direct result of post–9/11 law enforcement investigations—though many have come under intense financial pressure as donations have dried up and congregants have stayed away. This is true even years after September 11. Ansaarullah was not a large mosque, and even in Philadelphia, its demise went unnoticed. In that city, I found no other mosque forced to close as a result of law enforcement pressures in recent years. In New York City, which has a much larger Muslim community, I uncovered one small mosque forced to close as a direct result of police scrutiny. At least two small New York mosques closed due to financial problems—indirect victims, perhaps, of the war on terror. Probably the numbers are similar in other major population areas around the country.

There also have been thousands of interrogations, detentions, and deportations of imams—mosque spiritual leaders—all over the country. Again, no one is certain how many imams have had encounters with authorities, but a substantial percentage of investigations involve mosque leaders. Based on numbers culled from thousands of news accounts over the years, I estimate at least 1,000 imams have been interrogated, arrested, detained, or deported since 9/11. No federal official I spoke with acknowledged a directed campaign, but the numbers speak for themselves. As Richard Nixon once remarked, go after the leadership—the "teachers, preachers, and politicians," as he put it—and followers will evaporate.

Islamic charitable organizations and foundations, at the same time, have been major targets of informers and investigations. The federal government has closed seven Muslim charities since 9/11, freezing at least $16 million in assets. Charges of terrorism or support of terrorism have proven difficult to prosecute, however, and investigators have moved very slowly. In the high-profile 2007 Dallas trial of the Holy Land Foundation, federal prosecutors failed to convict any of the five leaders of the foundation on any terrorism or related charges. One man was acquitted, and jurors were deadlocked over charges against the other four. The government retried the case and, the second time around in 2008, achieved sweeping convictions. The defendants said they would appeal. In the meantime, federal authorities continued to arrest and jail people on charges related to the foundation. None of the other charities have been prosecuted on terrorism or criminal charges as of mid-2009, but their assets are frozen nonetheless. Such law enforcement scrutiny has strangled contributions to individual mosques and larger Islamic organizations across the country, undermining the charitable giving that is an essential tenet of the Islamic faith and straining mosques and other Muslim institutions in need. "Why invite trouble?" one woman said to me, explaining her reluctance to give. "I am ashamed, but how can I know if something I give now, if somebody is going to look at that next year and say, 'Well, she's giving to this terrorist organization'?" I had no answer. Many now give in cash and skip the tax deductions.

As the roots of the war on terror have reached deeper into American soil, the fears and difficulties growing in immigrant communities have crept like thick, entangling vines into other parts of American society. Political groups opposed to war in Iraq or environmental degradation or animal experimentation or globalism or administration policies in general or even the death penalty have discovered infiltrators in their midst, their communications monitored, their members detained, questioned, and sometimes arrested. Gay organizations and even artists have been subjected to surveillance and arrest. Perhaps a place like Ansaarullah served as training ground not for would-be terrorists but for counterterrorism and immigration task forces. How deep into religious and community life could intelligence gathering go? How disruptive could it be? Ansaarullah could provide some answers.

What my experience during the 1960s showed, what was made clear by 1970s congressional investigations of domestic intelligence abuse, and, indeed, what is obvious from even the most cursory review of political police activity anywhere and anytime is that such activity is inherently expansive and endlessly inventive. What begins in the monitoring of one group leads to broader and broader monitoring. Monitoring leads to disruption, arrests, and sometimes fatal violence. A desire to keep tabs on one group leads to an efflorescence of files focusing on an ever-growing number of groups and individuals further and further removed from the original target. Fear of the Soviet Union and a concern over its ideology lead to arrests of U.S. labor organizers, loyalty oaths for public school teachers, blacklists in Hollywood and in academia, and on and on. Concern about a rogue band of radical Saudis, largely U.S.-funded opponents of Soviet aggression in Afghanistan in the 1980s, leads to monitoring of American mosques, charities, nonprofit organizations, journalists, citizens, and dissident groups. Almost always the surveillance and information gathering start with a swarthy group of strangers— American blacks, Italian immigrants, Jews, Arabs. Ethnicity and race are infused with a "foreign ideology"—anarchism, socialism, Communism, black nationalism, "jihadism." Fear fertilizes the public soil; governmental power drives the plow.

"There is a continuum between those who would express dissent and those who would do a terrorist act," the FBI's Mueller said in a remarkable 2002 speech at Stanford Law School. "Somewhere along that continuum we have to begin to investigate. If we do not, we are not doing our job. It is difficult for us to find a path between the two extremes."

Difficult indeed. On April 7, 2003, less than a month after the start of the Iraq War, several hundred antiwar protestors milled around and picketed gates at the busy and gritty Port of Oakland, where war profiteers were supposedly doing business. Massed police fired directly into the crowd with wooden bullets—"dowels" they called them. They fired concussion grenades and tear gas. Nearly sixty people were injured, including eleven longshoremen, and about twenty-five protestors were arrested. Dockworkers, who had been simply watching the protest unfold and were debating whether to cross the picket lines to work, said they were given no more than a minute or two to get away. People were shot as they scrambled to disperse. Police said the shootings were inspired by "agitators" in the crowd. But picketers and longshoremen alike said there were no such agitators, whatever they might be, and no violence until police opened fire.

This is a point on the continuum, a continuum that appears more and more like a billowing miasma.

As it happens, police were primed for trouble, even expecting it. The California Anti-Terrorism Information Center, a $7-million-a-year creature of the war on terror, an agency designed to collect and distribute antiterror-related information to local authorities throughout the state, had secretly alerted the Oakland Police Department a week before the demonstration that violence could be in the cards. Officers should be ready for anything. The center, as part of its routine, was monitoring dissident political activities, including the planning of the port protest.

"If we receive information that 10,000 folks are going to a street corner and going to block it, that's breaking a law," Ed Manavian, head of the center, told a reporter for the *Oakland Tribune*. It was necessary, he said, to gather such information about perfectly legitimate political groups and distribute it to law enforcement authorities. "That's the kind of information that we're going to relay."

But the prospect of protest itself (which in this case involved 500, not 10,000), the mere fact of organized, focused dissent, was clearly enough to justify law enforcement surveillance and action in the eyes of California authorities. The antiterror center—one of fifty-eight such state and local centers that have sprouted across the country since 9/11—was systematically monitoring ordinary political activity. It wasn't investigating probable terrorist planning. It wasn't focusing on what even remotely could be characterized as potential terrorist threats. The fact of the matter was that the center didn't know what it didn't know. It wasn't seeing anything. That was the concern. Something must be there, like a picture in a cloud.

"You can make an easy kind of a link that, if you have a protest group protesting a war where the cause that's being fought against is international terrorism, you might have terrorism at that [protest]," Mike Van Winkle, a California Justice Department spokesman, told the *Oakland Tribune*. "You can almost argue that a protest against that is a terrorist act."

"Terrorism," he continued, "isn't just bombs going off and killing people."

It used to be, before 9/11 changed everything, that the job of the Justice Department and state and local law enforcement, theoretically at least, was to investigate crimes, terrorist or not. That's how the FBI managed to capture Timothy McVeigh, the white Christian Oklahoma City bomber. Authorities investigated, searched, and arrested. The continuum ranged from probable cause to a crime. The continuum ran from real information to real acts.

Now, as more than one federal and local law enforcement official said to me in recent years, as Osama bin Laden remains at large and terrorism continues to erupt with virulence in Iraq, Afghanistan, and Pakistan and across the Middle East, it is too dangerous to wait for the crime or the probability of a crime about to be committed. "Our job is to prevent, not arrest after the fact," a U.S. attorney said to me. Attorney General Ashcroft declared that policy immediately after 9/11. Once he did, virtually any arrest or detention, any use of informers, any surveillance could be justified. Federal authority now embraced domestically what the Bush administration embraced in its foreign policy—preemption. It is too dangerous to wait for the smoking gun to become a mushroom cloud, according to the mantra of at least half a dozen administration officials in the Iraq War run up. Within the homeland, the focus is on what used to be the fictional dystopian world of "pre-crime." Not only immigrants and foreigners—such as Ansaarullah congregants—are capable of pre-crime. In a time of a potentially endless war—another formerly fictional dystopian notion—with an unlimited battleground, the enemy lurks within, and in order to find and stop him, robust enforcement "tools" are needed. The plain fact is that if there is no "enemy within," if "homegrown" cells are not simply elusive but an illusion—as appears increasingly to be the case—then the entire apparatus of the war on terror crumbles in the homeland. We need Ansaarullah and its sinister band of worshippers. We need their clutches. We need vigilance. We need protectors.

A month after the Oakland shootings, demonstrators held another protest, this time to denounce the violence of the police that April day at the docks. A meeting was held; leaders for the march and protest were elected; plans for the action were discussed and ratified. The two men elected to lead dissidents were, as it happened, undercover police officers assigned to monitor local political activity. "Two of our officers were elected leaders within an hour," Deputy Police Chief Howard Jordan told a civilian review board probing the matter, the *San Francisco Chronicle* reported. Why? he was asked. "To gather the information and maybe even direct them to do something that we want them to do," Jordan replied.

The year following the shootings, the Oakland police force, faced with a class-action lawsuit brought on behalf of the dockworkers' union by the ACLU of Northern California, agreed to forego the use of the supposedly nonlethal firepower on display in April 2003. Willow Rosenthal, one of the plaintiffs in the suit, who was shot in the leg and faced many subsequent surgeries and a skin graft as a result, took some solace from the police agreement. At least, she said, "what happened to me will never happen again in Oakland."

By then, the war on terror had moved on. And the fact still remains: The California Anti-Terrorism Information Center is still in business, still on guard, still searching and collecting and distributing "reliable information that meets . . . stringent guidelines for intelligence gathering and civil rights protections," as the agency puts it on its website. Shortly after Willow Rosenthal made her statement, a California Highway patrolman gave his assessment of the battleground on the West Coast. "You don't really know what a terrorist looks like, what kind of car they drive, or anything else," he said. "So it's basically everything and everybody and anything out here."

Who can predict when a Quaker or Pakistani or environmental or gay or black organization might turn on the country? So-called fusion centers—such as California's and the fifty-plus others that have sprouted in every state—are in the business of identifying those groups, pinpointing those individuals, uncovering plans, and sharing the information with, ultimately, thousands of agencies from coast to coast. A vast continuum.

I LEFT THE PADLOCKED gate of Ansaarullah and walked beneath an old stone railroad viaduct and up Wakeling Street, stopping at a small grocery at the corner. A Korean woman at the counter inside, separated from her customers by inch-thick bulletproof glass, said she knew nothing about a mosque. "No, no, no," she said, waving her hands.

A woman was sitting on a chair at the corner of Worth Street eating a hot dog and talking to a friend. A mosque, she said, you mean like a club? No, no, her friend said, he means like a church. No, she said, I don't know anything about it. Her friend looked thoughtful and then said, no, he didn't know anything. "I have my own issues," he explained.

A man in a nearby park, drinking a beer and watching his boy play hopscotch, shook his head. "A mosque?" he asked. "What's that?"

A stunning question, but an interesting one. What is a mosque but a place of worship? Not any more, apparently. Not in Philadelphia. Not anywhere.

It was a sunny day. There were no black SUVs in view. A few little children played on a jungle gym. A man shadowboxed in a small area off the playground. This was the wake of battle. No one seemed to notice, and only I seemed to feel the haunting.

"What happened at Ansaarullah was an exercise in how to take down a mosque," one man who knew the mosque and knew Ghorab told me later. "They wanted to see if they could find an efficient way to do it. And they did."

ONE

Since When Is Being Muslim a Crime?

THE RAID CAME ON the hazy Thursday morning of May 27, 2004. Mohamed Ghorab rose early—the sky just streaking with light—cleansed himself, as he always did, and prepared for prayer. His wife, Meriem Moumen, brewed a pot of strong dark coffee, and when her husband returned from the mosque next door, she put out a cup for him in their small kitchen and then helped their elder daughter, Eliza, gather her papers and homework for school. Nothing unusual seemed to be going on outside their sagging house on Wakeling Street in the unassuming working-class neighborhood of Frankford Valley in Philadelphia. Aramingo Avenue was busy, as always. Traffic streamed by on Wakeling. A normal morning.

Out their front windows, across Wakeling, they could see the vast field of asphalt stretching up to the Baptist Worship Center and Excell Christian Academy. There were no cars in the parking lot this early morning, but on Sundays it was packed, and Ghorab often considered the irony that his house and his little mosque next door fronted a colossal Baptist conclave operating from a converted supermarket, a Philadelphia megachurch with thousands of devotees. He would smile to himself. That was America. Who could fathom its contradictions? Besides, some worshipper seeking solace or salvation might one day wander across the street to his white-washed cinder-block mosque—carved out of a humble old auto body shop—wander through the open gates, venture through the open bay door, and there meet a welcoming group of worshippers and discover the truth of Allah and his messenger, Mohammed, peace and blessings be upon him. Instead, the Baptists mostly complained that visitors to Ghorab's mosque—the Ansaarullah Islamic Society—were parking in their lot. Such are the roots of religious conflict in a crowded city.

The Baptists were so touchy about their parking. They even installed bollards, slender metal poles, along the sidewalk to block cars from pulling haphazardly off the street. No matter—Ansaarullah marked the modest fulfillment of a dream nurtured since Ghorab arrived in the United States from Egypt, penniless and without prospects, in 2000. Maybe there were not thousands attending; maybe no television broadcast beamed Ghorab's bearded face and passionate voice to viewers across the region. But Ansaarullah was young, and here, at last, in the unlikely city of Philadelphia, Ghorab was an imam able to minister to his own congregation, elaborate his own teachings and understanding of the Quran, impart his own view of the proper and pious life. This was no one else's house of God. No one else was guiding the flock. Ghorab was imam and acknowledged leader, and it was all bound up in what had been a well-used, abandoned Abco Body Shop. Cars and religion, he thought: This was America. From the porch of his house, immediately next door to the mosque, Ghorab glanced at the precarious Abco signpost angling over the cracked cement auto body yard. The sign was now a flag rising over Ansaarullah's small weedy landscape. Surely it was testimony to God's indifference to his worldly surroundings and man's ability to make something of anything.

Hᴀᴍɪᴅ, ᴛʜɪɴ ᴀɴᴅ sᴀʟʟᴏᴡ, a fellow Egyptian who helped the imam, arrived early, as always, that Thursday morning, opening the fence gate and pulling up the central bay door of the building. A few worshippers had arrived for the day's first prayers, and some remained. Hamid was sweeping the front of the lot. His gangly body, all elbows and sharp shoulders, reminded the imam of a mantis, a thought he kept to himself but chuckled at all the same.

After a few words with Hamid—make sure the fans are on if it becomes hot; have some tea if you like—the family got into their old silver Honda and headed for the Greenberg School in Bustleton, a twenty-minute drive. Eliza, a seventh grader, was in the back seat. Ghorab drove. Meriem sat beside him in the passenger seat.

These were the last settled and familiar moments of the day.

Wʜᴇɴ ᴛʜᴇʏ ᴀʀʀɪᴠᴇᴅ ᴀᴛ Greenberg, Ghorab pulled over and stopped. Children and teachers thronged the sidewalks. Eliza got out of the car, and Meriem watched as she mounted the building's broad front steps, already talking with friends.

"Okay, we can go," Meriem said, turning to Ghorab.

Then the familiar vanished.

"Stop!" yelled someone, Meriem recalled. "Stop!"

Confused, she looked around and saw a police officer staring at the car.

"What are all these lights?" Ghorab asked, craning his neck and peering left and right, looking at cars with flashing lights.

"Stop!"

Ghorab saw an immigration officer he recognized, and then armed agents and police seemed to pour in from everywhere.

"Get out of the car! Hands up! Hands up!" officers shouted as they converged on the bewildered couple. Moumen was paralyzed.

"My brain went blank," she said. "Frozen." She remembers seeing Eliza standing twenty feet away at the top of the steps, shock and fear washing over her face as the everyday world fell apart on the street below.

Children and parents arriving at school were terrified by the scene. A little girl screamed. Parents rushed inside, away from the street, away from the chaos.

What is happening? Meriem wanted to know. What is going on?

"All I can remember is everybody shouting at us," she said later. Standing in the middle of Sharon Lane, no shoes, she felt smothered by agents. "We couldn't get an answer." Ghorab was equally bewildered. His minimal English failed him. None of the agents responded to any questions, Moumen said. Ghorab was engulfed, placed in handcuffs, and hustled away. He would never return home.

While this was taking place, as many as a hundred agents stormed the Ansaarullah Islamic Society, seven miles away. They deployed bomb-sniffing dogs and primed their automatic weapons as they fanned through the ramshackle building. Hamid was struck dumb by the tide of police, helpless in the face of the onslaught; only later did he snap to with cries of no, no. He shuddered at the sight of dogs padding into the holy space. Neighbors and passers-by gathered to watch while agents pushed into Ghorab's tumbledown house. Moments later, officers, with Meriem in tow, arrived and joined the raid.

At the same time, yet more agents stormed the home of Jabi Khatut, president of Ansaarullah and owner of a pizza parlor and other businesses around town. Crowds formed outside his pleasant house on Covered Bridge Path.

The war on terror had arrived at the poor streets of Frankford Valley and the quiet, winding roads of Bustleton.

THE TELEPHONE RANG SOON after in the Philadelphia office of John J. Taylor, state representative for Frankford Valley and surrounding neighborhoods. Kathleen Zoladek, his local aide, answered. On the line was a woman who lived near the mosque in Frankford Valley. Tessie and her husband had just been out on Wakeling Street. "She's a pretty sharp older woman, her husband and her," Kass Zoladek told me later.

"Guess what's going on right now," Tessie whispered over the phone.

"I don't know, Tessie, what's going on?" Kass said.

"That place is getting raided on the corner," Tessie told her.

"No!"

"I went down, but I'm not talking to nobody," Tessie said with finality.

"No, don't talk to nobody."

Tessie was not surprised that a nest of Muslims was routed by the police. She didn't exactly know what they were or where they came from or what they were doing here or anything else. But the country was at war, don't you know? And weren't those strange people the reason? She knew they were trouble, even if she didn't exactly know what kind of trouble. It was a relief to see police taking care of the problem, whatever it was.

Meriem Moumen was infuriated. The raid, which seemed to be led by the IRS, was based on a search warrant seeking financial records for some reason, she told me. Agents tore apart her house. They emptied out drawers, upended bedding, jabbed holes in mattresses, pulled apart sofas, ransacked closets. They removed cartons of bills and papers, indiscriminately it seemed. A computer was carted away. They demanded to know who she was in reality. I am Meriem Moumen, she said. I am Sheik Ghorab's wife. No, you are not, she said they responded. You are Aafia Siddiqui. Admit it. Moumen was even more confused. Who is this Aafia Siddiqui? she wanted to know. She's all over the news, agents replied. We're looking for her. That's who you are. No, no, she said. I don't know what you are talking about.

Siddiqui had indeed been in the news. On that day, the *Philadelphia Inquirer* hit the street with an alarming story, announced with a four-column banner headline across the front page: "U.S. Seeks 7 in Terror Alert." Above the headline the paper displayed small mug shots of seven Middle Easterners, six men and a woman, collectively described as "armed and dangerous"—a characterization taken from comments made by Attorney General John Ashcroft. Siddiqui was one of the seven. She is a Pakistani woman with an MIT doctoral degree in neurological science. Photographs show her with large, round eyes, wide mouth, and curving, Picasso-esque lips. Moumen, a Morocco-born American citizen, tall and lithe with delicate, dark features, has been in this country for many years; she looks nothing like Siddiqui, who disappeared in Pakistan in 2003 and was arrested in Afghanistan in 2008.

Where does the money come from? Moumen was asked. What does the mosque do with the money? Where does Ghorab stash his funds? Where are the guns? Where are the assault rifles? Where is the terror room? Where do you train the hijackers? She said she had no idea what they were talking about.

"The mosque doesn't have anything to do except worshipping God," Moumen maintained, as she later did with *Inquirer* reporters. There is no money. There are only bills. Debts. What are you talking about?

In the mosque, armed agents and dogs searched everywhere and picked over everything. Papers, computer disks, cassette tapes with the sheik's sermons, books—all were carted away. Moumen could not get the image of her daughter's fear-stricken face out of her mind, she said to me. Why? she asked an immigration agent. Why? Why did you do that to us at the school? Why did you do that to us? Why not here? If you have to arrest, if you have to search, why not at our house? The agent, she remembered later, only shrugged and said, "It wasn't my call."

Not long after the raid began, one Ansaarullah congregant received a call on his cell phone, he told me. Are you all right? the caller asked. "Yes, of course. Why do you ask?" The mosque is being raided, the caller said, his voice rising in urgency.

"For what?"

"I don't know."

Disturbed by the call, the congregant got in his car and headed for Ansaarullah. When he was a block away on Aramingo Avenue, he saw what seemed like dozens of flashing lights on police cars. Crowds spilled off of the sidewalk and out into the street. The congregant decided he would do well to avoid the scene. Who knew what was going on? All the way back home he glanced in his rearview mirror. Were those cars following him? Surely they were. He made an unexpected turn right. The cars also turned. What is going on?

At Jabi Khatut's house, in Bustleton, a similar raid and search took place. Papers were collected and carted off, but no arrests were made. Khatut, not surprisingly upset that his home had been ransacked, kept a very low public profile in the days that followed. Laconic with reporters, he said agents asked many questions, but there was "nothing to worry about." He had no more to say in public, although privately he was seething.

Meriem Moumen was not so willing to roll over in public. She was enraged by the raid and the arrest of her husband.

"He is a loving person," she told my colleagues at the *Inquirer*. "He is peaceful." In a comment that foreshadowed remarks made by other mosque members many months later, she said: "He's the one who told us: 'Your visa—it's a contract of peace. You cannot go bombing people. You can't. You can't go hurting children. You can't hurt old people.'"

Agents cared nothing about this, she said.

"They crossed the line," she said. "Since when is being Muslim a crime?"

Siddique was at work when he got a call on his cell phone.

"One of the brothers, a brother who's a police officer, a Muslim, he called me," Siddique said. "'Where you at?'

"'I'm at my job.'

"'You know what's going on at the *masjid*?'

"I said, 'What?'

"He said, 'The police is at the *masjid*.'

"'Yeah? Why?'

"'I don't know, but it's all over the place, all over the news, all over everywhere.'

"'Okay. I'm gonna go there now.'

"He said, 'I'll meet you there.'"

By the time Siddique arrived, the raid was more or less over, and only "remnants of people"—a handful of investigators—remained. They finished packing and left. Several Ansaarullah members had come to the mosque, appalled at what was taking place, and many, many reporters and other media people were milling about seeking scraps of information. Congregants eyed them with mistrust and kept their distance. Television vans, long satellite poles thrusting up into the sky, dominated Aramingo Avenue. Clusters of neighbors watched from across Wakeling Street, in front of the Baptist center's parking lot.

Several people told Siddique, a tall African American with a friendly but serious demeanor, what had happened. "They came in," he said to me. "Seventy policemen came in with dogs, agents with dogs inside the mosque, search dogs. They came in, went all over the place, took what they wanted to take—there was nothing to hide anyway, so they could take what they wanted to take. They went and took everything."

Siddique said he was more or less resigned to the situation. "They did everything they're supposed to do—whatever their job requires, when you come to ascertain, to take information," he said. "That's their job. By the time I got here it was all newspaper reporters. Channel 10, 3, 6, 57, 29—plenty of them. And a lot of people, they was defensive, you know, the Muslims was defensive, some of them. It was like, 'Man, they took the sheik, why they bothering us? Why they bothering us? We didn't do anything here.'"

Siddique felt bombarded with complaints. He had no official position at the mosque, which he had been attending for about two years, but he was savvy and unafraid, and in the post–9/11 world, those were qualities in short supply around Muslim communities. Now Ansaarullah congregants were scared, really scared. They were angry, utterly perplexed, and offended by the media, too—the crowds of reporters waiting to capture any scrap of information, any quote, any energetic or arresting visual image.

"Why are they filming our families?" one man wanted to know. "Why?" Siddique tried to calm him, explaining that "they were showing people arriving; everybody was being filmed." The man was not appeased. "We don't want them inside the *masjid*," he said. "This is not a place for a party." Siddique suggested inviting everyone in. "Show them we have nothing to hide," he said. "Let's invite them in, and they can come in and film and see whatever. We can delegate two or three people to interview with them, and the rest of us—we'll just go about our normal activity."

And that's what they did. Nothing to hide.

Jerri Williams, the Philadelphia FBI spokeswoman, denied that the raid—conducted by the federal Joint Terrorism Task Force—had any connections with a terrorism investigation, although in doing so, she managed to use the word terrorism several times. "We have no information connecting activities or individuals involved with terrorism-related matters," she said. "But as part of our support, we'd be reviewing items obtained to see if there is any terrorism connection."

Nor did the raid have any connection with the Ashcroft press conference the day before, said Rich Manieri, spokesman for the Philadelphia U.S. Attorney's Office. "The timing was unfortunate and coincidental," he said. What a coincidence.

In that morning's paper, beneath the "Terror Alert" banner headline, the attorney general's scowling face was featured in an enormous photograph. He stood next to a stern Robert S. Mueller III, FBI director, in front of a poster of mural-like proportions. More mug shots of the seven suspects were plastered on the poster beneath the heading "Seeking Information Alert," which seemed, when I looked at it early in the day, an odd kind of locution, a long way from the cowboy rhetoric of demand—"Wanted: Dead or Alive"—favored shortly after the 9/11 attacks by President Bush. The president had aimed his rhetoric at a domestic audience, invoking an attitude of swagger and confidence, but getting what he wanted dead or alive was a job for the military or clandestine forces overseas, thousands of miles away—not next door or down the block. In this case, Mueller and Ashcroft were seeking to mobilize ordinary Americans, asking them to look around at their neighbors and neighborhoods right here. They were sewing suspicion in what everyone in Washington was now calling "the homeland"—a label that I associated with the Rhineland but that actually had been pulled from the bowels of old Pentagon reports by Bush speechwriters and slapped on the nation of immigrants, a branding of sorts.

The "Terror Alert" story, by Shannon McCaffrey, a reporter in Knight-Ridder's Washington bureau, detailed Ashcroft's warnings of an imminent terror attack, plots in the making, and new intelligence that showed "al Qaeda's specific intent to hit the United States hard." Again, in an odd detail, Ashcroft attributed some information to an "al Qaeda spokesman"—lending the terror network a familiar, faintly corporate aura. Such a conveniently organized construct, so familiar, served to domesticate the nebulous war on terror—a war against a tactic, not a nation or even an organization—and citizens were being told anyone could be involved anywhere at any time. We were all soldiers now.

Ashcroft ticked off a string of upcoming high-profile events stretching out over the summer and fall and leading up to the 2004 presidential elections. Al Qaeda could not resist the prospect of an attack during this period, he said. McCaffrey's story also mentioned the possibility of "mass casualties" as the result of an attack, attributing that scary potential to an anonymous federal law enforcement official. Tom Ridge, secretary of Homeland Security, however, declined to raise the nation's color-coded threat level from its now-routine elevated yellow status—not even to orange. In fact, Ridge did not attend the "Seeking Information Alert" announcement at all. What is going on here, I wondered, reading the story. Mass casualties, seven armed terrorists roaming the countryside, plots forecast, the nation still jittery in the wake of the Madrid train bombings—yet Ridge feels no need to attend the press conference or even to raise the nation's threat level, something he had been quick to do in the past. In fact, earlier in the day, as I later discovered, Ridge had appeared on television and suggested that homeland residents faced "significant threats" for sure, but they should nonetheless "go about living their lives and enjoying living in this country," as he said on CBS. A year later, after Ridge stepped down as secretary, he complained that Ashcroft was hyping intelligence.

Officials in John Kerry's presidential campaign immediately tied the Ashcroft announcement to President Bush's flagging poll numbers in the face of deepening difficulties in Iraq. The attorney general just as quickly brushed such talk aside. While the election season might form the backdrop to this alert, Ashcroft maintained there was nothing political in the announcement. And Mueller reassured citizens that thousands of FBI agents and local police would be working to protect the country in the months ahead. He urged citizens to report suspicious behavior and persons and announced that vast numbers of Middle Easterners in the United States would be interrogated, again.

Apart from the potential play of partisan politics and interdepartmental rivalries, one thing seemed obvious at the time: Nebulous fears were being stoked. Several, if not all, of the seven Middle Easterners thrust into the spotlight had been publicized and wanted by the FBI for months; Aafia Siddiqui had even been reported taken into U.S. custody in Pakistan a year earlier (American officials at first equivocated and then denied the accounts). Why such a high-profile media event now? Could it be that administration officials were concerned that citizens were shifting their focus—that the war on terror was losing its edge in the public mind? It appeared that the announcement and its visuals were designed to rekindle any flagging embers of anxiety, while at the same time reminding people that the government's organized defenses were managing the continuing crisis in an efficient manner. Everyone across the country needed to help, however, because the person next door could be a danger indeed. The enemy has the shadowy face of these seven men and women; the enemy is everywhere; the enemy is nowhere; the enemy is what we do not know; the enemy is what we think we know but actually don't.

In the wake of the "alert," media accounts immediately linked the Philadelphia raids and arrest of Ghorab with the simultaneous arrest in London of a Muslim cleric accused of al Qaeda support and efforts to establish a terror training camp in Oregon and the San Diego arrest, also on the same day, of Hasan Saddiq Faseh Alddin, a Saudi supposedly associated with friends of the September 11 hijackers. With arrests on both coasts bracketing the country and another arrest in Europe, Tom Ridge told reporters, "There's not a consensus within the administration that we need to raise the threat level."

No consensus, according to the top federal terror chief. No terror, according to the lead domestic terror investigative agency. Mixed signals from the highest levels of the terror bureaucracy. Yet hundreds of gun-toting authorities proceeded to invade a house of worship and private homes in Philadelphia. What brought it on? What dark transgression had prompted such a harsh and dramatic response? Or looked at another way: What manner of public acquiescence allowed or even encouraged the raids? It wouldn't take much given the climate of war in the homeland. Neighbors could have reported groups of "Arabs" gathering in the parking lot. A wave of greeting could have been interpreted as a coded signal. Perhaps someone angry with the imam sought a little payback. Or a debtor with no resources was seeking a way out by selling "information." Or maybe it was simply all inspired by an unsophisticated, mercurial Muslim free in a time of fear, an imam unwilling to bend in a time of heavy wind. The FBI, characteristically, won't discuss the raid or Ghorab, even after his deportation for supposed marriage fraud. The Philadelphia police won't discuss the reasons for the raid—and probably aren't sure themselves, given how tightly federal authorities hold information. Immigration and Customs Enforcement won't discuss it, either.

In fact, what seems clear now, several years later, is that the liberal presence of eager and creative informers operating in an environment where ordinary, forgettable, daily events have become highly combustible brought Mohamed Ghorab and everyone around him under intense federal scrutiny beginning in late 2002 and ultimately precipitated the massive raid on his home and mosque in May 2004.

Ghorab inspired talk.

MOHAMED GHORAB, FORTY-FIVE in 2004, is a stocky man, powerfully built and heavyset—his wife calls him "big boned"—with a pouffy, dark auburn beard now dotted with grey, a broad face, and a barrel chest. To his supporters, he is welcoming, witty, charismatic, authoritative; to federal agents, those same qualities appear threatening, too clever by half, and certainly an invitation for a closer look. Ghorab was born and raised in Alexandria, Egypt, where he first became so fascinated with Islam that at the age of thirteen he began intensive religious studies with Sheik Salem. The sheik was deeply impressed by the boy's diligence and his aptitude for understanding the many layers of the Quran, and within a year Ghorab had committed the holy book to memory, a prodigious feat. Sheik Salem encouraged him to stay the course, and that same year, when Ghorab was fourteen, he was invited to lead prayers at the Society

El Shariaa mosque—a great honor. Ghorab's father, however, was adamant: The boy must also continue his secular academic studies and attend university to study some form of engineering. His father was a practical man, and, he argued, the world is a practical place. Ghorab told U.S. authorities that he "respected my father's wishes and studied engineering." But the young man wanted more. "I really wanted to become well versed in Islam, so I studied with many different imams." He was indeed a dutiful son. His father died in 1977, but the son followed paternal direction as solemnly promised, attending El Monofiah Engineering and Technology College in Shebeen El Koum, eventually graduating with an honors degree in electrical engineering in 1991, according to accounts written up by federal agents and submitted to immigration court. But his real interest lay with the Quran.

For ten years, until the old imam died, Ghorab studied with Sheik Salem, pursuing insight into the way the Quran could be applied to contemporary life and how life could be lived according to wisdom and insight drawn directly from the book. He became the principal imam of El Mftah Mosque in Alexandria, leading daily worship and Friday services and providing "spiritual and moral guidance and other assistance" for his flock, as he told investigators. His wife Meriem Moumen says simply, "He fell in love with his religion." In love with his religion or not, Ghorab still had to eat and provide for his family after marriage. In 1985, at the age of twenty-seven, Ghorab married Soima Said in Egypt, and three children followed quickly, with more to come. Faced with such burgeoning responsibilities, he gathered up his inheritance from his father and launched a textile business, importing and exporting cotton and other kinds of cloth used for robes, veils, and various items of clothing.

Ghorab, however, was not a great entrepreneur. His heart was not in business; his heart, as Meriem said, was with Islam. Sheik Salem, Ghorab's mentor, was a Salafist, a man who sought insight and guidance directly from the Quran, and Ghorab followed his path.

Salafists are perceived in the West as deeply conservative, but the movement began as a progressive force early in the last century. It is not synonymous with harshly conservative Wahhabi beliefs originating in Saudi Arabia, and it is even less a stand-in for any ideas or ideology emanating from al Qaeda and its various apologists. The U.S. government recognizes this subtlety and complexity—in theory anyway—as noted in a 2003 report from the nonpartisan Congressional Research Service: "Modern Salafi beliefs have their roots in a reform-oriented movement from the early twentieth century, which progressively grew more conservative. In line with puritanical Islamic teachings, Salafis believe that the ultimate religious authority is located directly in the Quran and in the Prophet's practices, and not in commentaries which interpret these sources. . . . The Salafiyya is not a unified movement and there exists no single Salafi 'sect.' However, the Salafi interpretation appeals to a large number of Muslims worldwide—in Africa, Asia, North America, and throughout the Middle East."

Much has been made of connections between various terrorists— such as shoe bomber Richard Reid and the 9/11 hijackers—and an extremist worldview said to be rooted in Salafism. Salafism, as a result, has been characterized as an ideology of brooding violence. This is a profound distortion. The Office of the Inspector General in the Justice Department, in a 2004 report on the Bureau of Prisons religious service providers for Muslims, noted that "most Muslims who adhere to Wahhabism refer to themselves as 'Salafis,' meaning 'Unitarians,' because al-Wahhab emphasized the transcendental unity of God. The term 'Salafi' literally means 'one who follows the Prophet Muhammad and his companions,' and also can be used to describe all Muslims, not just Wahhabis." Wahhabism is a particular kind of Salafism, the report argues; while all Muslim "puritanical groups" may arguably be Salafist, not all Salafists are Wahhabi.

The report goes on to say that fifteen of the nineteen September 11 hijackers were from Saudi Arabia—all believed to be Wahhabis.

"In the United States, Wahhabism has been equated with radicalism and terrorism in some newspaper articles, books, and public discourse," the report says. "However, not all experts agree that 'Wahhabism' and 'Salafism' are inherently synonymous with violence, terrorism, or radicalism. For example, FBI counterterrorism officials told us that Wahhabism is not inherently violent or terroristic, but has been manipulated for violent or terroristic ends."

Salafists, it should be noted—before every distinction is lost in a tangle of distinctions—gave birth to the first feminist movements in Muslim countries and assigned weight and authority to the practice of science and the scientific method—not only to the parsing of the Quran. Mohammad Abduh (1849–1905), chief mufti of Egypt and one of the Salafist movement's founders, for instance, deplored the abject status of women in Egypt and argued forcefully for their educational and legal rights. He circumscribed polygamy, granted women the right to initiate divorce actions, and supported their political rights. At least some scholars now believe that Abduh is the anonymous author of parts of Qasim Amin's groundbreaking *The Liberation of Women*, published in 1899.

There is within the Salafist tradition, then, a pragmatic side, which allows life to be lived in the twenty-first century. Nevertheless, it is safe to say that Ghorab sought his grounding in the Quran. While a pragmatic approach to life may not be foreclosed to Salafists, success in daily affairs is hardly assured. For Ghorab, that proved to be the case. In the 1990s, his family expanded—he now had six children—and his business faltered badly. His marriage became a crucible of tension as debts mounted.

In 2000, with his affairs in a state of financial collapse, his marriage ended by divorce, and with Egyptian security and intelligence forces making daily life increasingly perilous for the religious, Ghorab decided to leave Alexandria and come to the United States. On many occasions in the late 1990s, Ghorab later told friends and associates in this country and as he stated in court documents,

Egyptian security forces hauled him in for questioning. The questions did not seem aimed at him specifically, he told friends and investigators. Rather, jittery authorities would regularly round up many, many imams and bring them in for interrogation. Sometimes the sessions would last a few hours; sometimes they would last for days on end. What had he heard on the street and in the market? Who was criticizing the government? What did he have against Mubarak? Whom did he know in Egyptian Islamic Jihad? What did he know about the radical group Al-Gama'a al-Islamiyya? What did he know of the Luxor massacre? Who was making antigovernment remarks of any kind? Egypt became more and more violent in the 1990s, and pressures mounted on security agencies. Searching for those they could not see, they brought in the visible.

Ghorab, however, has adamantly denounced violence whenever questioned by friends as well as federal agents. He was never charged with anything in Alexandria, and security forces never told him that he was considered a suspect for any specific crime in Egypt. Nevertheless, he was ordered by government authorities not to preach on occasion, and then, like several other imams, he found his mosque seized by anxious security forces, who had been ineffective in preventing terrorist violence throughout the country in the 1990s. As allowed by Egyptian law, ownership of the mosque was transferred to the government, and Ghorab was adrift without a base.

"They interrogated me on numerous occasions for extended lengths of up to one week, yet charges were never filed," Ghorab later reported to U.S. authorities. "During the interrogations I would be kept without any food, to use starvation as a tactic. I am a member of Dawaa Salafia, a peaceful religious organization. Myself and others who belong to this organization have been persecuted by the Egyptian police force. I and other members of the organization have been arrested, tortured and harassed by the Egyptian police force for being suspected terrorists, yet no charges were ever filed." A leader from Ghorab's Alexandria mosque, since reconstituted, confirmed

Ghorab's recollections in a statement submitted to immigration court. "He was persecuted by the Egyptian government," the leader said, adding that authorities barred him from "lecturing, providing lessons, and . . . preaching, as well as performing Eid [or holiday] ceremonies based on direct imperatives from the country's national security and bureau of investigation." Yet Ghorab was always released. Neither the repeated interrogations nor the seizure of the mosque is an uncommon occurrence, Egyptian human rights advocates told me. And Egyptian authorities, who have had a great deal of experience with terrorism suspects, beginning with widespread arrests following the assassination of Sadat in 1981, ultimately were uninterested in this imam.

But as Ghorab's statements imply, it is not for nothing that the United States has "rendered" its own terrorist suspects to Egypt, where information can be boiled out of an unwilling man, like fat. Egyptian security forces are hardly constrained by nettlesome legalities. Since the 1981 assassination of President Sadat, a state of emergency has been in effect in the country, granting sweeping powers to security forces. The International Federation for Human Rights estimated in 2005 that 16,000 people were being held without charge in "administrative detention" by Egyptian authorities; some had been in custody for a decade. The situation remains the same, rights workers told me. An act of violence in Egypt, simple political dissent, vague suspicions, sexual orientation, a whim—all can lead to arrest. Sometimes even being a child is hazardous: The government makes mass arrests of children—to clear the streets and to extract information. In 2001, according to Human Rights Watch, 11,000 children were arrested in street sweeps.

Often detainees are taken into custody for simply being in the wrong place at the wrong time—a practice many immigrants hoped to escape when they came to the United States, but experience has proven those hopes misguided. In North Sinai, for instance, in October 2004, five men were arrested and charged with terrorist attacks in the area, the International Federation for Human Rights reported. Subsequently, 3,000 people were arrested in sweeps carried out by Egyptian security forces around Arish, hometown to one of the five men charged. Wrong place. Wrong time. "During investigations by Egyptian security forces detainees were tortured," the federation stated in a report to the UN High Commissioner on Human Rights submitted in 2005.

The report summarized the current situation in Egypt with regard to torture:

> Torture is endemic and has become a routine tool of investigation in police stations and prisons. Between 1993 and April 2004, 412 torture cases were recorded, 120 of which resulted in the death of the victim, almost certainly due to the torture or mistreatment. The state of emergency in Egypt facilitates the occurrence of torture. Under the Emergency Law, individuals can be detained for thirty days (renewable once) before being charged and before they have the right to challenge their detention. . . . There is a lack of safeguards to prevent acts of torture. Several sources reported widespread use of torture in connection with the 2003 antiwar demonstrations [sparked by the U.S.-led invasion of Iraq]. Torture practiced in Egyptian prisons and detention centers takes many forms, including electroshocks, being hung upside down for extended periods of time, cigarette burning all over the body, strip searching of men and women, sexual harassment and rape. Egyptian prison legislation codifies humiliating and degrading treatment by allowing foot-chaining in order to prevent escape.

All human rights organizations agree that Islamic groups of every stripe are most often targets of Egyptian security measures—detentions, arrests, disappearances, torture.

That the United States would be flying detainees incognito all over the world to find congenial environments, like Egypt, for questioning was a publicly unknown practice when Ghorab made his decision to leave for America. In fact, at least in part, he immigrated because of a desire for, and a love of, freedom. In the United States, Ghorab later told many people, one is free to practice one's faith without interference from the government, without fear, without secrecy, without security forces defiling the house of worship. The United States is a free country, he said; no one spits on your faith. It was a momentous move to be made and one not undertaken lightly. Ghorab had been outside of his country only twice previously, once on a pilgrimage to Mecca, an obligation of every Muslim, and once on a failed 1999 business venture to Kuwait. He knew virtually no English and had only a few friends when he arrived at Newark Airport at the end of March in 2000—a man seeking freedom, fleeing religious persecution, hoping for economic opportunity; it is a classic tale of immigration to the New World.

FOLLOWING HIS TUMULTUOUS AND bewildering arrest in front of the Greenberg School in Bustleton, Mohamed Ghorab was taken directly to York County Prison south of Harrisburg, about three hours from Philadelphia, and his attorney, Anser Ahmad, tried to figure out what was going on. It wasn't easy. Federal authorities were vague about the raid and reluctant to give Ahmad any information at all, he said. The immediate jailing of the imam, Ahmad learned, was triggered by an earlier immigration charge. In 2003, Ghorab had been accused of marriage fraud, jailed, and held on $50,000 bail. He appealed, and members of Ansaarullah banded together, raised the money, and managed to get their leader released. The bail had been revoked on the spot at Greenberg, and Ghorab had been whisked away. Yet no criminal charge was filed against him. Why? Why was bail revoked? Why was Ghorab jailed? No answers.

In the early days following the raid, Ahmad speculated that Ghorab may have come under scrutiny for his politics—he opposed both the Afghanistan and the Iraq invasions, hardly unique positions even among non-Muslims. "One or two of his sermons may have touched on supporting Muslims around the world who are going through troubled times," Ahmad told a reporter the day after the raid. "But nothing in the matter of supporting uprisings." He suggested to another reporter that maybe Ghorab's ability to post the $50,000 bail imposed in his marriage fraud case sparked federal interest.

Two local law enforcement officials very familiar with the Muslim community told me that police had never had any complaints about or problems with Ansaarullah. One of these law enforcement officers—who had not been consulted prior to the raid—said he was not surprised that a congregation composed of ice cream truck vendors, lunch-wagon operators, and taxi drivers could pull together substantial amounts of cash in a short period of time. "Those Mr. Softee trucks can knock down a thousand dollars a day," he said. "Can they raise the money? Sure they can. It's perfectly viable to raise the money to help the imam out."

Despite his public ruminations, Anser Ahmad had no idea why Ghorab had been taken into custody. "At that point I was also speculating because I didn't really know what was the driving force," Ahmad told me. He first contacted Immigration and Customs Enforcement, known as ICE, and they said, no, they did not organize the raid. The FBI said the IRS led the raid. The IRS wasn't talking. And still isn't.

"It was a dribble and pass," said one attorney familiar with the case. "ICE can use the IRS and try and develop evidence of not paying taxes. The IRS can use the FBI. The FBI can use ICE." The ball goes around until what? "Jail or deportation."

Several sources told me that federal prosecutors first claimed that the raid on the mosque was part of a tax-fraud investigation, and when that proved utterly unproductive, rather than back off, federal officials determined the case amounted to a national security matter. The mere mention of national security was enough to put a damper on any public information. Ghorab's court hearings were closed. Records were sealed. Authorities said details of the case could not be shared. No press. No public. No family. No talk.

What national security issues could be raised? The FBI and the U.S. Attorney's Office both said publicly that the case was not about security or terror. Yet a June 2, 2004, FBI report submitted to immigration court within a week of Ghorab's arrest tells a different story. In it, an agent asserted that "Ghorab had established a 'training room' in the main floor of an Islamic mosque where Ghorab was Imam or spiritual leader of the mosque. A seat similar to an airplane passenger seat was placed in the middle of the training room." If that wasn't disturbing enough, the report went on flatly to state: "2 AK-47 rifles were in the basement of the same mosque concealed in a blanket underneath the training area."

This was alarming without a doubt, yet, for some reason, the FBI was not prepared to move on these dramatic finds—even after examining every inch of Ghorab's home and mosque. "At the present stage of this investigation the FBI is gathering and culling information that may corroborate or diminish our current suspicions of Ghorab. The FBI has been unable to rule out the possibility that Ghorab may be a threat to the national security of the United States due to his possible connections to terrorist and extremist organizations." Attached to this document was a decade-old article from the *New York Times Sunday Magazine*, titled "Street Guns."

No bail for Ghorab.

The problem with this report is that none of it appeared to be based on fact—except the suggestion that federal agents were unwilling to let go of the case. There was no "training room." There were no AK-47 rifles. It is true that an old cushioned chair was stashed somewhere in the basement of the mosque, piled with the belongings of a former lessee of the old body shop building. The chair even had his name on it. But no guns or seats were ever produced by government attorneys in any of the numerous hearings held in Ghorab's case. No testimony was given confirming that guns were ever located in the basement of the mosque or that a "training room" ever existed. This information, initially presented to immigration court as hard fact, was apparently passed to the FBI by an Ansaarullah informant who heard it from someone else, according to congregants who also were aware of the rumor—and knew it was simply talk, possibly even planted talk. Planted by whom? No one could say with certainty, but more than one congregant told me informers were everywhere inside the mosque, inside the Muslim community, all over Frankford Valley. Everywhere.

A few days following the raid, another congregant of Ansaarullah, a Jordanian, was hauled in by federal authorities after a coworker identified him as one of the Ashcroft-Mueller group of seven terrorists furtively plotting somewhere in America. It was obvious that the Jordanian had nothing to do with the seven—he bore no resemblance to any of them and had worked steadily in Philadelphia for quite some time, but federal agents questioned him extensively about airplane seats and training rooms, the man's attorney told me later. What did he know about the radical cleric Ghorab? What kind of training went on at Ansaarullah? What kinds of weapons were kept under wraps in the homes of worshippers? Where did Ghorab get the money? The Jordanian was simply befuddled by what appeared to him utter fantasies, and authorities eventually ran out of questions and let the man go.

He never returned to the mosque.

WHEN GHORAB FIRST ARRIVED at Newark in 2000, lack of language and unfamiliarity with the United States and its loose customs hardly presented problems. He quickly picked up a job driving a taxi based at the airport. Through a few acquaintances already here, he made contact with some mosques in the New York City area and met an African American Muslim woman, Hajrah Alakbar, whom he married in due course in June of the same year. It is this marriage, to a woman he met through preaching, that would ultimately lead to

Ghorab's arrest. His friends and associates, indeed Alakbar herself, maintain that the couple married in good faith and legitimately—even though they were later divorced. Based on the marriage, Ghorab applied, in August 2000, to the Immigration and Naturalization Service (INS) for permanent residency in this country. His temporary visa had expired in June—the month of his marriage.

"He was so sweet, so, so sweet—just a good guy," Alakbar told me several years later. "He had problems in Egypt, but I swear to God, you could never find a sweeter, more loving person. He was the kind of person who would always say yes to what you wanted. No matter what, he would never say no. And they went after him like he was responsible for 9/11."

Alakbar was introduced to Ghorab by her stepfather and, she said, fell in love with him. Though the sheik knew minimal English and their "cultures clashed," she said, she found him to be devoted to her. "He would do anything for you," she said, and their relationship blossomed. "I will always love him to the day I die." Yet a year later, in September 2001, days before the attacks on the World Trade Center and the Pentagon, the INS terminated Ghorab's residency application. It's unclear from the record what the basis for this termination might have been—failure to provide proper documentation was the most likely factor, but immigration officials declined to discuss the matter.

Alakbar said there was also a problem with tax documents that accompanied Ghorab's application. A Muslim acquaintance had filled out the forms and gathered the information needed to support Ghorab's application, she said, and he apparently added a tax form for Alakbar that was false. During an INS interview, she was asked about it and said she had no idea what it was. Neither, she said, did Ghorab.

"The INS took a long time to give us a meeting on the application," Alakbar said. "I wasn't working then, and Mohamed was not working at a real job—you know, he was under the table, and he was driving the taxi."

"Someone trying to help Mohamed put a tax form in with Mohamed's papers," she continued. "They asked me if I filled it out, and I told them, 'No, I didn't file taxes.' Mohamed said he didn't know anything about it either. Somebody was trying to help us, and I think they suspected Mohamed was lying. Mohamed didn't realize what the brother was doing. He didn't even understand the IRS."

This issue may have caused a problem with immigration authorities, but it was never explicitly raised afterwards, as far as I can determine. None of Ghorab's attorneys who would discuss the case with me ever mentioned this personal tax issue. And Alakbar, whose name was affixed to the form, was never questioned about it. Neither the INS, ICE, the FBI, nor the IRS ever brought the matter up with her, she said. "They never asked me anything later."

Authorities did seem confused about Alakbar, however. In various immigration documents, her name is spelled "Alkabar," "Alkobar," and "Elkebre"—probably phonetic renderings. But a September 3, 2003, letter to "Hajrah Alkabar" from the Department of Homeland Security Bureau of Citizenship and Immigration Services laid the blame at Alakbar's feet and informed her that the various confused spellings cast "doubt as to the bona fides of your marriage."

While the application was terminated, no INS action was imminent, so Ghorab planned to appeal but put the matter of marriage and residency aside for the time being. He had started yet another business, this time seeking to import and export textile-related machinery, and things were, not surprisingly, going poorly. Indeed, the business failed quickly. Driving a cab was again his financial mainstay. More importantly, though, he was increasingly involved with a variety of different mosques—leading prayers, teaching classes, preaching, and offering "guidance." He spread his message at two mosques in Brooklyn and one on Staten Island. Alakbar and her two teenage sons lived in New Jersey, and that fact, along with some helpful friends in New York, led Ghorab to preach at Dar-Ui Islam in Elizabeth, New Jersey, and eventually at Masjid Taha Islamic Society in Philadelphia and Masjid Ibrahim in Newark, Delaware, where he delivered sermons.

Ghorab, said Alakbar, was comfortable in all mosques, whether the congregation was African American or Arab or a diverse mix. "He was a pretty cool guy like that," she said. "Mohamy was basically cool."

What did he preach?

"Every Muslim preaches peace; every Muslim preaches that you obey Allah and Mohammed, his messenger, peace and blessing be upon him. I never saw or heard him preach fighting or hurting anybody. Never. Never. You know, God does not like suicide. You don't commit a crime against someone who hasn't committed a crime against you. People loved him as a sheik, and that's why the feds went after him. I was scared because I thought they was going to arrest me for marrying him. But they never did."

Alakbar did not mean that literally every Muslim preaches peace, she said, because obviously that has not been the case. What she meant was that a true and deep understanding of the Quran, an understanding that Sheik Ghorab demonstrated in his sermons and lectures and workshops and advice, yielded a peaceful approach to life and its discords. This has been her experience in mosques here in the United States, she said. And it was her experience with Sheik Ghorab, who said simply that the Prophet Mohammed was "a kind and gentle man."

Ghorab came to Philadelphia to preach several times before September 2001. He was well received in the city and eventually invited to help minister to the faithful at Al Aqsa Islamic Society—the city's largest Arab mosque—during Ramadan in 2001. By that time, however, the wounds of 9/11 were fresh in the streets, and fear was growing everywhere. The leaders of Al Aqsa, financially substantial members of the city's Middle Eastern community—businessmen, property owners, players in the political arena—were determined to protect themselves, their community, their mosque, and their interests in an increasingly hostile environment. They were willing to work with federal authorities who had launched interviews with

5,000 Middle Easterners across the nation about ostensibly suspicious behavior and individuals. Philadelphia police, on the other hand, were not happy about being compelled by federal authorities to conduct the interrogations—they understood that the deep resentment and fears engendered by the interviews would not help "community relations," police officials told me, and communication and trust were essential to the flow of timely and useful information. In that light, police acceded to requests from Aqsa leaders and other prominent local Muslims to allow attorneys to sit in on any interviews conducted in Philadelphia. For their part, Aqsa leaders were willing to engage local law enforcement authorities in a dialog to help ease tensions. And why not? There was a palpable fear on the streets. Communication and cooperation made good sense.

Ghorab, who liked the Islamic community in Philadelphia but found the overall post–9/11 situation unlike anything he had ever encountered, was also willing to participate in such activities, his friends say—but apparently only to a point. He was not prepared to modify his deeply held religious beliefs in order to accommodate the well-to-do leaders of Al Aqsa or local law enforcement officials. That may appear suspicious, yet much of the friction seems to have revolved around the Quran's injunctions regarding diet. This had been a historically sensitive area for Al Aqsa, and several imams who argued that it was sinful to sell pork or alcohol—both forbidden by the Quran—had been let go in the past, well before 9/11, well before law enforcement watched every movement at the city's mosques for hints of bad things to come. If Ghorab had been circumspect and more politic, he might simply have stayed off the subject, since mosque leaders owned delis and grocery stores selling forbidden foods, as well as restaurants serving alcohol. But when asked, Ghorab said the Quran forbids alcohol and certain unclean foods. There is no difference, in actuality, between this position and that of observant Jews who must avoid many of the same foods. But in the post–9/11 atmosphere, warnings about bacon and wine could have serious ramifications.

"There has been a series of five imams at Aqsa, and four have fallen on the same issue," said one frequent visitor. "The lay leaders [of the mosque] found the same faults with all of them. These leaders have large grocery businesses. They sell pork and ale and beer in the Spanish community, and the imams criticized them for it. That is not extremism of any sort for a religious leader to pick a bone on these issues. Jewish dietary law resembles this on many points, but here, the worst construction is put on Muslims, and I find that intolerable."

Aqsa is hardly the only mosque in the city that has seen internal controversy arising from the business practices of the lay leaders who administer the mosque. Even well-known song writer and music producer Kenny Gamble, who opened a mosque in the early 1990s on South Fifteenth Street in Philadelphia, has faced similar criticisms from pious Muslims unhappy with his past involvements in the music business, according to a sympathetic local Muslim leader. "This is a frequent type of divisive issue," said one Philadelphia imam. "There is an IHOP near my home, and the owner was able to get IHOP to offer alternative choices on the menu—turkey bacon rather than pork. He did that because of his desire to serve Muslims. IHOPs are attractive investments to Muslims because they don't serve alcohol."

In any event, with the fallout from 9/11 fresh and spreading and with Muslim businesses and citizens suffering, Aqsa leaders decided not to renew Ghorab's short-term contract. Marwan Kreidie, a prominent member of the city's Middle Eastern community who often serves as Aqsa's public face but is not directly involved in the running of the mosque, said he was uncertain why Ghorab's contract was not renewed. Kreidie did not personally know Ghorab but said he had heard talk that the imam was "radical."

"I don't know what 'radical' means," Kreidie allowed, adding that Aqsa leaders said Ghorab was "anti-American," although why they considered him so is unclear. Perhaps, at least in part, radical meant bad for business or off-putting or unconcerned with the opinions of others. Perhaps Ghorab was too unpolished or too willing to criticize policies—whether they were the policies of the U.S. government in Afghanistan or the policies of the mosque leaders in North Philadelphia. None of the Aqsa leaders would discuss Ghorab or his association with the mosque, referring all questions to Kreidie, who finally said, "They didn't like his style."

After Ramadan, however, Ghorab was largely unconcerned with the views of Al Aqsa's lay leaders anyway. By that point, the end of 2001, he had decided he could no longer put off establishing his own mosque, a place where he could minister to lost souls and to the poor, a pure place that would breed good health and family. In late autumn he started to look around and in December stumbled on a filthy and rambling old garage at the corner of Aramingo and Wakeling. "For Rent." Perhaps the sign should have been a warning, but instead it served as a beacon, a siren. It was God's sign.

"This is what Mohamed always wanted," said Alakbar. "He cared so much for people, particularly people who had nothing."

THE DAY AFTER THE Ansaarullah raid, federal agents interviewed people in South Philadelphia in an effort to develop information for the case, and Ghorab's congregants drew together in the mosque. My colleague Tom Ginsberg ran into Atef Idais at Ansaarullah that day—as he might have virtually any day. Many nasty rumors were already circulating on the street by then, often after a boost from repetition in the media—Ghorab was a radical fundamentalist; he supported al Qaeda and the Taliban; he was an anti-Semite and a political extremist. Idais told Ginsberg that such things were not true and that federal agents "watch you and target you when they can" because of religion and ethnicity. Ghorab, Idais said, was a positive force, a man responsible for helping many people determine what was important in their daily lives.

"A lot of guys here were gambling, losing money, clubbing, chasing ladies," Idais told Ginsberg. "Now they're building families."

Ghorab's acquaintance, Ayman Ahmed, said the imam was definitely known "for talking about safeguarding your family from Satan, from the paths toward glory and self-gratification." In Ahmed's view the government had "overreacted" to Ghorab's hardly unusual opposition to the Iraq War. They hit Ansaarullah, he said, "because of what he was saying and the way it was said." Samir Ouldali said Ghorab had criticized the government. "He just criticizes what's happening and Bush—he calls him a crusader," Ouldali said.

Not everyone praised Ghorab by a long shot. One anonymous man said Ansaarullah was known as the "Taliban mosque." Another said Ghorab was rigid in following the Quran. Leaders of Al Aqsa, the city's largest mosque catering to Middle Easterners, were mostly silent, although Marwan Kreidie told Ginsberg that Ghorab had a right to freedom of expression.

Pointed anonymous remarks, the willingness to pass on rumors, the queasy fear seeping everywhere—all in evidence in the wake of the raid—would begin to eat into Ansaarullah over the next several months. Atef Idais—fluent in English, learned in the Quran, available—eventually began to lead prayers. It was at this time, he later said, that suspicions about informers began to fester and spread, and it became very noticeable that the mosque was being watched by law enforcement authorities. They seemed to know whom they were watching. And those who were watched were well aware of it. Interrogations, detentions, arrests, and deportations would soon overwhelm Ansaarullah, splitting families, compelling American citizens to leave their "homeland," depriving children of their parents, obliterating a generous and charitable religious institution from a needy neighborhood, and shoring up fears and energizing rumors throughout the city.

"Every Friday you would see cars in the church parking lot across the street, two or three cars, just watching," Idais told me later. "I was followed a couple of times."

Early one morning, as he prepared to leave home and open the mosque, Idais saw a dark, unfamiliar car on Ormes Street. The street was empty in the half light of dawn. Quiet. As Idais stood on the sidewalk, the driver got out and walked slowly over, pulling back his suit jacket to show a pistol. He asked directions to a nearby street, then returned to his car and slowly drove away. "The only thing that didn't scare me about the guy with the gun is that I knew the guy," said Idais with a shrug. "He was FBI." Following Ghorab's arrest, Idais became keeper of the keys and would open the mosque early in the morning. Meriem was increasingly consumed by money worries, and in the days after the raid, she decided to pull her daughter from the Greenberg School and send her elsewhere—the humiliation of the arrest in front of everyone at her old school proved too much. "You can't imagine what people said to her," Meriem later told me. "'Your father and mother were arrested! Your father is a drug dealer!' She came home in tears. 'Mommy, I can't go back there.'" She blamed the mosque. She blamed her mother and stepfather. She blamed Islam. Why did this happen? she asked over and over again.

Meriem had no answers.

I wondered what the answers could be myself.

ABOUT A HUNDRED DEMONSTRATORS rallied at the federal building in downtown Philadelphia on June 11, 2004, to express their dismay over the Ansaarullah raid. Meriem Moumen spoke to the crowd, and her daughter read an anguished letter she had written to the immigration court, describing the pain of watching her stepfather arrested and pleading for his release. A demonstrator described the letter to me: "'My dad, he takes me to school every morning like every other dad does. He drops me off like every other dad does. My girlfriends come over to the house, and they play with me like in every other dad's house.' You understand, his daughter is writing this to the government and the judges to try and get them to understand, 'Please, whatever perception you have of my dad, it's not that way.'"

Isa Abdul Mateen of Majlis Ash-Shura, a coalition of local mosques, said several area leaders were made extremely uneasy by the raid and arrest. They had never organized a collective demonstration before. But this time, joined by members of the American Friends Service Committee, they felt it was necessary to speak out collectively.

"The disrespect given the *masjid*, the situation with the imam—he was arrested! For what? It was an immigration matter. What was the reason for even arresting him? What we could see was that it was an attempt to intimidate the Muslim community," Isa Mateen said to me many months after the demonstration. Meriem, he said, described offensive behavior during the raid—the presence of dogs and firearms in the mosque, the tearing of the Quran, the walking on sacred texts, name calling. "It was designed to humiliate, and it was an attempt to intimidate," said Isa Mateen, still indignant. (No other source that I spoke to said that JTTF agents ripped pages of the Quran or walked over sacred texts. They did, however, manage to break up a newly constructed stairwell banister.)

"Nobody was a terrorist. It's ridiculous. It's not even good investigative technique. You don't catch any terrorists by intimidating a whole group of people, none of whom are terrorists. The raid seemed aimed to create an example and a display, to humiliate and to frighten."

In the end, that little demonstration, on Market Street in summer of 2004, was the only public support shown for anyone caught up in the Ansaarullah raid and its aftermath. There were lawyers aplenty, for sure. There were court documents, often sealed. Public hearings, often closed to the public and even families. It was all a routine skirmish in the war on terror. But for me, it was a window that opened onto dissonant landscapes. I saw my own past and the country's past. This time it was an Islamic community and a mosque. It could have been a university. A political group. A gathering of women or African Americans in a rural church. This time it was largely informers. It could have been surveillance cameras or phone taps or electronic microphones or monitored computers feeding information. I remembered the 1950s, when federal agents virtually controlled the moribund Communist Party, and the 1960s, when informers spread through Columbia University and many other colleges. And I remembered all the supposed plots, the strange deaths, the trials, and the lengthy imprisonments that grew from antiwar and civil rights activities. Now 9/11 had changed everything.

Why only one small demonstration? Why no broad protest? The bombing of a church in Birmingham and the deaths of four little girls became one of the horrific spurs of the civil rights movement. Clerics were significant leaders of that movement and of opposition to the Vietnam War. They were spied on and prosecuted for their efforts—which in turn galvanized supporters. But what was happening now? Why did a raid on a house of worship cause no more than a ripple of opposition within a sea of hostility?

TWO

A Snake with Its Head Raised

T HE DAY AFTER SEPTEMBER 11, 2001, still sorting through events of the previous twenty-four hours, I was grappling with a story on the law enforcement response to the calamity and what it might signify in the weeks and months ahead. No one I interviewed said precisely that the previous day's events "changed everything," but they came very close. Stephen Gale, a well-known political science professor at the University of Pennsylvania and a longtime student of terrorism, told me that the attacks in New York and Washington marked "a turning point for America."

"We now have got to make a decision on what kind of country we want to be," he said. "It may just be that we have to start thinking about what modern society is about instead of what our eighteenth-century constitution is."

I thought about Gale's comments in late 2008 as I walked along Philadelphia's South Seventh Street, a poor neighborhood deep in clannish South Philadelphia. Before September 11, South Seventh Street and its pinched two-story row houses had been home to a small but very visible Pakistani community. Many of those who lived there—although by no means all—were undocumented immigrants. Now there were no Pakistanis or Bangladeshis on the street. Aslam's Market, once a hub, was closed. Other groceries, once so bursting with aromas of curries and spices that the street became a pungent annex of the delicacies within, were all closed. Pakistani laborers, who once gathered in the mornings looking for transportation to under-the-table day work in New Jersey and elsewhere, were gone. Cambodian and Vietnamese markets now proliferated, and Southeast Asians and Latinos were prominent along the street, offering their own volubility, aromatic delicacies, and difficulties.

The entire area had been cleansed of Muslim South Asians. Deportation, fear, and flight wiped the streets, peeled families from homes, transformed daily life into a dangerous exercise for a vulnerable group of aspiring Americans. Some had been picked up by immigration authorities, jailed, and bounced out of the country. Some had picked themselves up and run off to Canada or anywhere else but here. Some were in prison or in hiding. Some had died. "There's no one left," lamented Victor Gill, a Pakistani who lives in the city's Northeast and had lost all of his own contacts. "They are all gone," he said to me quietly.

MARWAN KREIDIE, A LEBANESE-AMERICAN civic leader and a member of the Philadelphia Civil Service Commission, was running a hearing on the sixteenth floor of the city's Municipal Services Building on the morning of September 11, 2001. His assistant came into the meeting early on, Kreidie recalled one day as I talked with him over coffee at the Reading Terminal Market in Center City Philadelphia, a vast collection of food shops and stalls within a mammoth old train shed. "You're not going to believe this, but a plane just hit the World Trade Center," she reported. Kreidie was instantly alarmed—and not a little fearful. "Knowing what the reaction was to Oklahoma City, I immediately canceled the hearing and called John Timoney," he told me. Timoney was the city's police commissioner at the time.

Kreidie's anxiety, which increased exponentially when the second plane hit the towers, was well founded. In the wake of the 1995 Oklahoma City bombing, numerous terrorism experts took to the national airwaves and speculated with great assurance that Muslim extremists were responsible. It was obvious, they said, that Arab radicals had taken out the federal building in Oklahoma City and murdered countless innocents. Early news reports claimed Middle Easterners were spotted fleeing the scene. Steven Emerson, terror expert and former journalist, was on television the day after the Murrah Federal Building was blown to bits, arguing that Middle Easterners were surely responsible. Why did it seem so clear to him? Because, he said, "to inflict as many casualties as possible—that is a Middle Eastern trait," he told CBS News. "Oklahoma City, I can tell you, is probably considered one of the largest centers of Islamic radical activity outside the Middle East." Former Congressman David McCurdy told CNN on the day of the bombing that "my first reaction when I heard of the explosion was that there could be a very real connection to some of the Islamic fundamentalist groups that have, actually, been operating out of Oklahoma City."

Such widely broadcast assertions spread through the media, inflaming what followed over the next several weeks. On the day of the bombing, Wednesday, April 19, a Jordanian-born American citizen traveling from his home in Oklahoma City to London was stopped and interrogated in Chicago. Ibrahim Ahmad, who had no connection whatsoever with the blast and was clearly stopped because he was a Middle Easterner from Oklahoma, was allowed to continue on his way by federal agents, but when his plane landed in London, he was detained, strip-searched, interrogated, and told by British authorities he was under arrest for the Oklahoma bombing. Back in Oklahoma City, following the quick leaking of Ahmad's name to the news media, his wife was threatened and spit upon, even though her husband was quickly cleared in Britain.

The next day, shots were fired at a mosque and community center in Stillwater, Oklahoma. In Oklahoma City, as Sahar Al-Muwsawi, a twenty-six-year-old Iraqi who was seven-months pregnant, sat in her living room watching news accounts of the bombing, she heard a car slam to a stop outside the house and angry shouts fill the air. Rocks hit her windows. People pounded on her door, screaming obscenities. Terrified, she gathered up her two-year-old and his playmate, ran into the bathroom, and locked the door. Huddled against the toilet, clutching the toddlers, she felt horrible abdominal pains. Blood began flowing across the tile floor. The *Daily Oklahoman* reported that, hours later, a son—named Salaam (Peace) by his grieving parents—was stillborn following a miscarriage.

Sporadic threats and violence against Muslims and dark-skinned people mistaken for Muslims broke out around the country and in Philadelphia—and continued even after authorities arrested Timothy McVeigh, a white, right-wing Christian, and charged him with carrying out the attack. A Muslim woman was pelted with rocks as she left a Wal-Mart in Arkansas. Someone tossed a sack into the day care center of a mosque in Dallas and shouted, "Bomb!" Threats abounded. "I will kill all the children," a caller swore to leaders of another mosque. The Islamic Center of Greater Springfield, in Illinois, was badly damaged by fire on June 6. Traces of gasoline at the source led officials to suspect arson. More than two hundred such incidents were reported to the Council on American-Islamic Relations in the aftermath of Oklahoma City.

In Philadelphia, there were acts of vandalism, threats, and insults aplenty and a few street scuffles, I recall, including some roughing up of Hispanics and non-Muslim dark-skinned taxi drivers. While the Philadelphia violence quickly dissipated, Kreidie and others in the city's Arab and Middle Eastern community were shaken by the threats and attacks and by the fear they engendered. They realized then and there that they needed decent lines of communication to law enforcement agencies, particularly to the Philadelphia police and the local office of the FBI, if they had any hope of quelling future disturbances, God forbid.

"WHEN THE SECOND PLANE hit," Kreidie continued, "I spoke with Timoney and with the Human Relations Commission." By mid-morning, they had set up what Kreidie called "a war room" in the commission's sixth floor offices on Eleventh Street, ordered some pizzas, and hit the phones, working with police brass to craft a strategy to shield the city's Arabs and Muslims from violence that Kreidie was sadly convinced would come.

John Timoney, a sharp, urbane veteran of New York City's police command and Philadelphia Police Commissioner since 1998, when he was appointed by then-mayor Ed Rendell, shared Kreidie's concern. There are "knuckleheads" everywhere, Timoney said. And Muslims and Middle Easterners "are guaranteed protection like everyone else."

On the morning of the attacks, Timoney was leaving his apartment on Rittenhouse Square when his wife called after him, saying that a plane had just crashed into the World Trade Center. Timoney's immediate assumption was a commuter plane accident. He looked back and then kept right on walking out the door, headed for the mayor's regular Tuesday cabinet meeting in City Hall, just a few minutes away.

Shortly after 9:00, before Mayor John F. Street had arrived at the conference room, Timoney's pager went off. It was his home number. What the hell? he thought.

"I called my house," Timoney remembered, as we talked later. "My wife says, 'Listen, a second plane just hit.' I said 'What!', hung up, and I knew right away. And just as I hung up, Street is walking in, apologizing that he's late. I said, 'Listen, put on the TV.' I says, 'We're gonna have to change.' I says, 'Forget this cabinet meeting. We're gonna have to go into an emergency session.'"

Like everyone else who had heard, the top officials of the city were glued to their television sets.

"I'm saying, 'Holy Christ!'" Timoney said. "You gotta remember I was in New York the first time it was hit in 1993."

Calls were coming in to City Hall and police headquarters. Information was at a premium. No one seemed to know what was happening. Not the FAA. Not the FBI.

Call after call: What's going on? Timoney asked—or was asked himself. No answers, certainly not from the feds. "They didn't know. They didn't know. No. No. You're on your own."

When the fourth plane crashed in a field in western Pennsylvania, a weird flashback swept over him. Not to the gaping hole he inspected following the 1993 terrorist explosion at the Trade Center, a blast crater that stretched up four stories into the guts of the building, leaving nothing but jagged emptiness and death and ruin. No, Timoney suddenly remembered his childhood when he had seen a vivid science fiction movie starring Gene Barry.

"I swear to Christ I thought of when I was a kid growing up, that movie where the spaceships start to land, *The War of the Worlds.* I said, 'Shit, that was four planes that hit.' And there was no indication that it was over. The assumption was: 'They'll keep coming. Where's the next one?' So now I have to admit, I wouldn't call it panic, but certainly deep, deep concern. 'What the hell is going on?' I kept standing there thinking, 'How the fuck did this happen?' I knew somebody screwed up. I wasn't sure how, but surely somebody had screwed up. So now we're concerned with Philly."

But what could he do that day? Timoney knew that there was no way to stop a rocketing airplane. Nevertheless, he dispatched police to key points in the city anyway, to iconic buildings in the historic district and along heavily traveled downtown streets.

Everything became a worry. Two trans-Atlantic flights scheduled to land in Philadelphia within hours of the attacks were out of touch with radio operators at Philadelphia International Airport. Was this unusual? What was wrong? After what seemed like forever, one plane, bound from Madrid, finally responded. To this day, Timoney doesn't know about the other.

And what about the flip side of the story—the possibility that the city's estimated 20,000 to 25,000 Arabs and its 100,000 Muslims (most of whom are African American) might be subject to reprisals? Was that a concern?

"Clearly. When you're a police chief or a commissioner, you've got to be thinking about all of those things. And clearly, we were—I was certainly very sensitive to it. And so was Mayor Street."

The city's Arab population is concentrated in three neighborhoods—a largely Maronite Christian area in South Philadelphia; an area around the large Al Aqsa mosque, just north of Center City; and in the Feltonville neighborhood, well north of Aqsa. Those areas needed special attention, in Kreidie's view. Timoney agreed.

"The Philadelphia police had a squad car in front of every mosque in the city by 2 p.m.," Kreidie recalled. "Because we had built up a relationship after Oklahoma City, I could talk to them. They knew who I was. We identified every school with an Arabic population. We identified all Arabic neighborhoods and flooded them with cops and Human Relations Commission members to insure there was no backlash. Timoney was great. He issued a directive that police could not ask people their immigration status and he had that read at every roll call. That was critical. We did not have people dragged out of cars in Philadelphia like happened everywhere else."

Well, not quite. I remember vividly the immediate aftermath of the attacks in Philadelphia. I had spent September 11 reporting from around the city, beginning with the closure of Independence National Historical Park, where weeping tourists were escorted from the Liberty Bell pavilion, sidewalks and streets were blocked off, and bomb-sniffing dogs were loosed on the historic ground to investigate telephoned threats. (By a week later, Philadelphia police had logged eighty-seven bogus bomb threats around town.) I had waited endlessly with other reporters for Mayor Street and Timoney to convene a City Hall news conference amid confusion and swirls of conflicting and false information.

When these officials finally tore themselves away from television and entered the press conference, it was painfully obvious the mayor had few options. Perhaps not knowing what else to do, Street ordered all public buildings closed. In the post–9/11 world, public officials always need to demonstrate the ability to do *something*. The police commissioner, operating on next to no real intelligence, assured citizens of their safety and of police resolve. New York is only ninety miles away, they reminded everyone. Outside, on Center City streets, massive traffic jams developed—in the rush to leave, no one could get anywhere.

"The city, itself, self-evacuated," Timoney told me much later. "It was like one of those Japanese Godzilla movies. Everybody was fleeing town, and of course I was in emergency operation by 9:15. We were bringing in all off-duty officers, putting everybody out on traffic posts, as many cops as you could down to Center City to help with the evacuation."

I finally headed back to the *Inquirer* through the clogged streets, car horns blaring everywhere, to file a story. But by the evening of September 11, as I walked through the center of the city, those same streets were deserted. No cars. No pedestrians. Silence. Suburban Station, hub of regional transport, normally full of people hurrying one way or another, was empty. Not even a homeless person wrapped in a blanket was visible. Only police with dogs wandered the underground concourse. The city seemed depopulated—"a ghost town," Timoney called it—as though an entire urban region had been roped off as a crime scene.

ALMOST IMMEDIATELY, THE RANDOM acts of Philadelphia violence began. People were, in fact, dragged from cars and threatened. There were many different victims—more often than not they were Indian Sikhs in turbans, not Arab Muslims in kufis. Several Sikh cabdrivers were attacked in their taxis and beaten. Not Muslim, not Middle Eastern, but vaguely similar in appearance, they proved tempting targets for a gathering, free-floating anger.

A North African man leaving a bar was roughed up by an angry crowd. Knives were pulled and threats made on city buses. "Let me kill the Pakistani!" one man screamed as police wrestled him off a bus and into a patrol car, the *Inquirer* reported. A half dozen convenience stores, owned or managed by brown-skinned people, either South Asians or Middle Easterners or Hispanics, were attacked—two with two small bombs.

The most infamous local incidents occurred right outside the city limits. On the afternoon of September 11, Nabil Ayesh, a Palestinian, was stopped at a red light near an Upper Darby police station when a suspicious officer noticed an Arabic bumper sticker on the rear of his car.

Ayesh was arrested, charged with a traffic violation, and quickly shipped up to the Metropolitan Detention Center in Brooklyn, where he was detained for more than a year without being charged with any offense. During that time, his wife and children were also seized and deported. After he was finally released, Ayesh was arrested again, this time for being the passenger in a car stopped by New York State police. No more releases for Ayesh. He was held and then deported.

A day after the Ayesh arrest, an off-duty Philadelphia cop brandished a gun at a Pakistani clerk in a convenience store in suburban Bala Cynwyd, just beyond the city limits. The cop let loose with a string of slurs and threatened to kill the man.

"Fucking Arab! Fucking Arab!" echoed down many city streets. I heard it myself—screamed from a passing car at a bewildered and extremely fearful Sikh gas station attendant. In the working-class neighborhood of Kensington, a mob chanting "Fucking Arab!" gathered on the street near a bar and attacked a Tunisian, kicking and punching him to the sidewalk, and when that wasn't good enough, someone pulled a knife and slashed him. The man later said he called for help from passing police. He was ignored.

Such incidents rolled across the country. Beatings, arrests, and detentions proliferated. They seemed to appear from nowhere, as though people were waiting for an excuse to release their anger at any immigrant target. For a decade, since the end of the Cold War, nativist sentiments had been gaining currency. Now their time had come.

In the immediate hours and days following the terror attacks, all of the defining characteristics of the post–9/11 public environment erupted across the country: the anxiety and fear, the confusion, the anti-immigrant and ethnic hostility, the aggressive patriotism, the desire for revenge, and the hunger for strong action—traits that would form the backdrop and support for official policy and practice for years to come.

THE MAGNITUDE OF THE vigilante attacks in the autumn of 2001 obviously dwarfed those that followed the Oklahoma City bombing. Hundreds and hundreds of threats were reported to authorities and civil rights groups. Mosques and Muslim gathering places were attacked by arsonists and thugs hurling Molotov cocktails in Los Altos, Encino, San Jose, Anaheim, Ontario, and San Mateo (where a gasoline bomb failed to explode when it was thrown through a window, hitting a three-year-old Sikh child) in California. Arsonists and fire bombers made their mark in Chicago; in Rockville and Bethesda, Maryland; in Somerset and Weymouth, Massachusetts; in St. Louis; in Matawan, New Jersey; and in Palermo, New York. And of course, reprisal fires erupted in New York City—in Flushing, Queens; in the Bronx; in Brooklyn. In Bedford, outside of Cleveland, and in Youngstown, Ohio, firebombs and arson were reported. Denton, Texas; Salt Lake City, Utah; Tacoma and Seattle and Kenmore, Washington—all saw 9/11 arson attacks. There were no arrests.

Some of these incidents were directed at Muslim organizations, mosques, and homes. Others were aimed at Sikhs. There is something particularly unsettling, something acutely and uncontrollably destructive about such arson. Each of these attacks was a small echo—not only of the 9/11 conflagrations themselves but of urban fires in the 1960s, racial fire-bombings in the 1950s and 1960s, and on back through decades of racial and ethnic conflict to the roots of the American nation. We are haunted by flames.

Half a dozen murders—and possibly several more—around the country drew their inspiration purely from 9/11. Perhaps the most infamous involved the shooting death of Balbir Singh Sodhi, a forty-nine-year-old Sikh father of three, born in the Punjab, who made his way first to Los Angeles in the 1980s and finally to Phoenix, where he was able to purchase a gas station in Mesa. On the night of September 15, Sodhi was shot five times and killed instantly. Earlier in the evening, Frank Roque, forty-four, confided to any and all that he was going to "kill the ragheads." He left the Wild Hare sports bar, drove his pickup to the Chevron station where Sodhi was planting flowers, and shot him.

Roque then drove to another gas station ten miles down the road and blasted away, missing the Lebanese-American clerk. Not satisfied, Roque drove to his old house, then owned by an Afghani family, and fired off several more rounds outside. Police arrested Roque the following day, reporting that he shouted, "I am a patriot! I stand for America all the way!" In 2003 Roque was convicted of first-degree murder and sentenced to death; the Arizona Supreme Court overturned the death sentence in 2006 and imposed life in prison.

In San Francisco, a year after September 11, Balbir's brother, Sukhpul Singh Sodhi, age fifty, was shot to death while driving his cab. Two of six brothers had now been killed in America. Their father had urged all his children to return to India in the wake of 9/11 and Balbir's death. Sukhpul and his younger brother Lakhwinder, age thirty-five, refused.

Lakhwinder told the *San Francisco Chronicle* that his father "wants some safety for his family."

"He's thinking this is a terrible place," Lakhwinder continued. With the gathering in of the Sodhi clan from the United States and elsewhere, their Punjab district lost a vital source of overseas funds. Money sent home helped support not only family but schools and other essentials in the poor region. No more.

Police, with no motives or suspects in Sukhpul's August 3, 2002, death, did not believe it was related to events of September 11. In their view, it was a random act of urban death, a coincidence, a stray bullet. For Lakhwinder, that bullet marked "a terrible, terrible year."

In Texas, on September 15, 2001, the same day that Balbir Singh Sodhi was murdered in Arizona, Mark Stroman gunned down Waquar Hassan, a Pakistani father of four. Hassan was cooking hamburgers in his Dallas store—Mom's Grocery—when Stroman showed up and blasted away—at least that's what Stroman later told a jailhouse informer. On October 4, Stroman shot and killed Vasudev Patel, a forty-nine-year-old Indian, at his Mesquite convenience store. An avowed white separatist with a long criminal record, Stroman justified his actions in a television interview, no less, by declaring, "We're at war. I did what I had to do. I did it to retaliate against those who retaliated against us." The jury deliberated for less than an hour; he was sentenced to death.

Stroman also shot Rais Uddin, a Bangladeshi gas station attendant, leaving him blind in his right eye. Uddin told a Bangladeshi reporter that there was a lot of reaction in Texas to the attacks of September 11. On the afternoon of September 21, Uddin said Stroman came rushing and screaming at him with a shotgun. "I held up my cash box, but he kept coming at me like a snake with its head raised. He said something I did not understand, and I said, 'Sorry.' That's when he shot me in the face."

For the Hassan family, anguished after the gunman's first killing, Stroman's rampage was only the beginning of the nightmare. Deprived of income, the family faced rising debt and foreclosure on their home—despite the fact that Hassan's widow, Durreshawar, worked nights on a Styrofoam-cup assembly line and the three oldest of her four daughters worked after school. They all lived in suburban New Jersey outside of New York City and had planned to move to Texas to join their husband and father when he had firmly established his new business there. His death, however, made the entire family imminently deportable. Only special legislation backed by Representative Rush Holt three years after the murder allowed the family to stay, according to the *Newark Star-Ledger*.

On September 29, 2001, Abdo Ali Ahmed, a Yemini Muslim with eight children, was gunned down while working at his convenience store in Reedley, California. No suspects were ever arrested, and the crime was not classified a hate crime by police—even though no money was taken and two days earlier Ahmed found a threatening note stuck under his car's windshield wiper. "We're going to kill all you fucking Arabs," it said; at least that's what he told his family before tossing it in the trash. Following the shooting, four young men were seen racing away in a white car by witnesses in the Hawg Jaws Bar next to the store. Ahmed made his way into the bar, where his wife, Fatima, rushed to his aid; he died in her arms before medical assistance arrived.

Reedley, a small Central Valley community with a large percentage of Hispanic residents mixed in with Middle Eastern shopkeepers and Anglos, was torn by the crime. Ahmed had lived in this country for thirty-five years, and like many in town, he taped a small American flag on the store wall after the 9/11 attacks. Maybe that was simply cover, some wondered.

"They've been here forever, but then you hear about these other people [involved in the 9/11 attacks] who've been around for years," a worried Liz Gallardo told a *San Francisco Chronicle* reporter shortly after the shooting. "You think everybody's undercover. It's not right, but it's the paranoia."

Some months later, Fatima and her children were still living in fear and prostrated by grief. "When they killed my husband," she told a *Fresno Bee* reporter, "they killed me."

No money was taken from the International Market in San Gabriel, California, owned by Adel Karas, a Coptic Christian from Egypt who was shot to death there the night of September 15. Police declined to classify the killing as a hate crime or a reprisal attack. But Karas's wife believes her husband, like so many others, was mistaken for a Muslim—and murdered in revenge for 9/11.

On October 13, the Minneapolis *Star Tribune* reported that local Somalis—there are more than 40,000 Somali immigrants in the

Minneapolis area, the largest concentration in the country—had do-
nated money to groups with links to Osama bin Laden. On October
15, Ali W. Ali, an elderly Somali, was viciously beaten at a bus stop,
dying nine days later. A witness said a man simply walked up to Ali,
started punching and kicking him, looked down at the crumpled
body on the sidewalk, and walked away. Police first ruled that Ali
died of natural causes but later classified the death as a homicide.
Ali's family and local Somalis believe it was sparked by the *Star Tribune* story, which led to a flood of anti-Somali incidents around town,
they said. "One elder is already dead, beaten by hate-mongers; many
women have been harassed; children were taunted; and rumors of
death threats have spread through the community like wildfire,"
Zabat Awed said in a statement issued on behalf of local Somalis. A
month after Ali's death, U.S. Treasury officials closed down Somali
money-transfer offices in Minneapolis, making it difficult for many
to send funds home to family members. "Things have been very
rough for the community," Omar Jamal, a microbiologist and executive director of the Somali Justice Advocacy Center, said to a *Baltimore Sun* reporter a year later.

Other deaths were quite likely inspired by 9/11 anger. Ali Almansoop, an Arab immigrant from Yemen living in Lincoln Park,
Michigan, was shot and killed by Brent David Seever, who found
Almansoop in bed with an ex-girlfriend. Immediately before opening fire on September 17, Seever declared his fury over the terror attacks. Almansoop protested his innocence. Seever was undeterred
and shot him. According to Human Rights Watch, prosecutors declined to charge Seever with a hate crime, arguing that jealousy mo-
tivated the attack.

On Sunday, September 15, Surjit Singh Samra, a seventy-year-old
Sikh, left his home in Cerces, California, for his daily constitutional.
He never returned. Following two days of searching, Samra's body
was found in five feet of water in the Turlock irrigation canal. His
turban was missing, but wallet and cash were in his pocket. Police

were confounded by the incident. Samra's family was not. An autopsy revealed that a stroke was not the cause of death, as authorities had initially suggested. "I strongly believe somebody pushed him," Samra's son, Davinder, told local reporters. "Somebody did something to him." The Samra family was convinced the death was a 9/11–related killing. Police said there was no evidence to support the family's suspicions.

Similar suspicions surrounded the death of Abdullah Mohammed Nimer, a middle-aged Palestinian American clothing salesman found shot to death October 3 next to his car on a street in south central Los Angeles. The unlocked car contained quantities of untouched merchandise; a large amount of cash was found in Nimer's possession. Police concluded robbery was not a motive. Again, the family is convinced the murder was another revenge killing. The crime remains unsolved.

In a particularly murky September 14 incident, twenty-one-year-old Kimberly Lowe was driving with friends through Tulsa, Oklahoma, when a car full of young white men began following and harassing them. "Go back to your own country!" they screamed, according to a widely disseminated early account from an official of the Cherokee Nation. Lowe, a Native American whose aunt was also a Cherokee official, stopped her car and got out when the men started throwing rocks. At that point, the men rammed Lowe as she stood in the street, pinned her against her car, and then backed over her body, killing her. But Tulsa police investigating the incident said that witnesses changed their story, subsequently attributing the fatal incident to "road rage" mixed with alcohol. The police determined that September 11 was an excuse after the fact, not a motivation in the killing, according to *Native American Digest*.

There are at least six or seven other instances where the circumstances and motives are suggestive but in the end unknowable. Were they 9/11–related deaths? In the absence of suspects, motives, or more information, it is virtually impossible to say—a killing goes into the great hopper of killings, and the nation moves on to a new day.

And then there is the bizarre case of Jawed Wassel, a forty-two-year-old Afghani filmmaker whose dismembered body was discovered in two bloody boxes by police when they stopped Nathan Chandler Powell's speeding van on a Long Island highway the night of October 3. The head was missing. "Where's the friggin' head?" police demanded, according to the *New York Post*. "I have no idea," Powell replied. Wassel's head was later found stuffed in Powell's refrigerator.

Nathan Powell, it turned out, was an investor in Wassel's film *Fire Dancer*, based on the filmmaker's life in Afghanistan and the West, which had just opened in New York City. Powell told police he expected the movie to earn a million dollars, and as an investor he was entitled to 30 percent of the gross. He had a contract. He had paper. Police reported that Powell ignited with rage when Wassel sought to limit his cut to 10 percent. They argued, police reported, and Powell struck Wassel with a pool cue, stabbed him to death, and later cut him apart.

But Powell's story evolved as his 2003 trial approached. Rather than a story of deadly anger fueled by greed, it became one of anger and traumatic stress fueled by 9/11. Wassel, he said, had been taken in by the Taliban. And when the World Trade Center came down, Powell claimed, he began to fear the filmmaker's emerging radical political views. Prosecutors were incensed that the defendant would use 9/11 as excuse for murder. Nevertheless, as Powell's trial approached, they agreed to a guilty plea of manslaughter, dropping charges of second-degree murder. Powell was sentenced to twenty years. At the time of the plea agreement, Powell's lawyer, Thomas Liotti, said that his client wanted "to be very clear that he was not in any way taking advantage of 9/11."

Fires and killings offer only the most dramatic instances of post–9/11 reprisals. In the ten days following 9/11, the Council on

American-Islamic Relations received nearly six hundred reports of retaliatory actions and threats from all over the country; the Sikh Coalition logged over two hundred. These reports included everything from numerous gunshots fired at mosques, people beaten with baseball bats, women stabbed, bomb threats made, children threatened. Virtually every state saw some form of retribution—from Alaska, where vandals attacked an Anchorage print shop owned by an Arab American; to Bridgeview, a suburb of Chicago, where police had to hold back an angry mob of several hundred marching on the Bridgeview Mosque (bearing signs reading "God Bless America" and "Kill All the Arabs"); to Florida, where bullets slammed into the wall of the only mosque in Hernando County, an arrow was shot into a Muslim-owned laundromat, and bomb threats were as common as alligators in a swamp. In the week following 9/11, the South Asian American Leaders of Tomorrow toted up forty-nine assault reports that made it into the local press.

Muslims, Middle Easterners, and South Asians, confronted by suspicious and fearful fellow citizens, were blocked from boarding or were thrown off airplanes, trains, and buses. Women, easily distinguished by Islamic dress, feared leaving their homes. Rumors abounded. Along the Kentucky side of the Ohio River, more than forty Mauritanian Muslims were arrested in a September 14 sweep. Someone told federal authorities that a Mauritanian was taking flying lessons. Someone else said they looked like hijackers. Immigration and law enforcement pulled them all into jail for questioning and interrogated hundreds more in the days to come. American Muslims were reported jumping for joy when the planes hit the towers. They were speaking in coded messages into cell phones. They were simply there.

NOT SURPRISINGLY, THE FEDERAL government's public response to the 9/11 catastrophe was initially confused and chaotic. As Timoney noted, in the immediate hours after the attacks, no one seemed to have a clue. Attorney General John Ashcroft's Justice Department, however, quickly cobbled together a massive investigation, dubbed PENTTBOM, eventually involving over 7,500 FBI agents and support staff. A dragnet was emerging. Within a day, tips began flooding in from the public, authorities began detaining immigrants, and vague, menacing stories filled the newspapers and airwaves. A train from Boston was stopped at Providence. Passengers were ordered out, and a man in handcuffs was seen being led away. What was going on? No answers. Agents flooded several towns in northern New Jersey. Was something about to come down? Was that where the hijackers had lived? Was there some connection with the 1993 Trade Center bombers who lived in the area? Maybe. Maybe not. A dozen people were detained for questioning at New York airports. Knives were found. The airports were closed. Was another attack unfolding? Federal agents warned of terrorist attacks in Richmond, Virginia, and Atlanta, Georgia. What had they heard? What was about to happen? No answers. How big was this conspiracy? The nation, feeding on the mass media, became a fantastic rumor mill, with stories gathering force and currency in the fecund emptiness marked out by government silence.

On Friday, September 14, authorities made what Washington officials labeled their first PENTTBOM arrest (although dozens had already been detained). They picked up a man at a New York City airport, did not charge him, would not identify him, and used, for the first time but hardly the last, a material witness warrant to legitimize imprisonment. Although the unidentified man was not actually charged with any crime, anonymous officials said he had a bogus pilot's license. He was labeled a 9/11 suspect with supposedly relevant information and held in prison for questioning by a grand jury. No grand jury ever heard the testimony of the man, Abdullaziz Al Angari, a pilot for Saudi Arabian Airlines. Al Angari's name on his pilot license simply didn't match the name on other identity papers in his possession. He was held for three weeks because of the purported discrepancy and then quietly released on bond, returning to Saudi Arabia.

Such material witness warrants used to pick up Al Angari and at least seventy others in the burgeoning investigation had previously been used sparingly and were intended only to insure testimony of witnesses in court proceedings. Material witnesses were supposed to be held as briefly as possible—to secure their testimony or to take their depositions—and then released. Now, however, authorities began using the warrants to clear the streets and secure indefinite detention, regardless of actual evidence, possible testimony, or imminent court proceeding. By Wednesday, September 12, at least five people had been detained on immigration charges, too—the first trickle of what would become a flood.

Two of the initial five post–9/11 immigration detainees were portrayed in particularly sinister fashion in the media, an example of the overheated dynamics at work and the enforcement template being established. They were arrested by authorities (supposedly conducting a routine drug investigation) after being found on an Amtrak train bound from St. Louis to San Antonio. The pair had $5,000 in cash and box cutters in their bags. Here is how CNN reporter Eileen O'Connor described the incident during a September 17 television broadcast: "They took them into custody Wednesday, took them off a train. The train was from St. Louis to San Antonio, but the men had tickets [for] and had been onboard a plane that left Newark toward San Antonio on Tuesday. That plane was diverted when the hijackings began. Those men then got on a train [and] started going toward San Antonio. They were taken off the train and—shockingly, according to law enforcement sources—they had box cutters on them. Now, we know from Barbara Olson, who was on the plane that left from Dulles and crashed into the Pentagon, said to her husband [U.S. Solicitor General Theodore Olson] the hijackers had box cutters, were using them as weapons. So that was a pretty chilling discovery for investigators."

The two men, as those same investigators quickly learned, were childhood friends from India, Gul Mohammed Shah, who also used the name Ayub Ali Khan, and Azmath Javed. The men used box cutters to slice the plastic binders girdling newspaper bales delivered to their newsstand, and they were heading to Texas in the hope of establishing a new business there, a fruit market. This was all clear in a matter of days. Nevertheless, the men were detained on immigration charges and shipped to the Metropolitan Detention Center in Brooklyn, where they were held without bond, largely in solitary confinement, for well over a year. Eventually the two were deported after pleading guilty to credit card fraud.

It is a not particularly chilling story about two hapless Indian immigrants, possibly petty thieves, who had overstayed their visas. Nevertheless, because of the secrecy wrapped around these cases, much could be made of them by authorities, and the public had no way to measure their import or the effectiveness of what the government was actually doing—beyond the melodrama of broadcast news. A month after the attacks, with hundreds of uncharged people in custody, an anonymous FBI official told the *Washington Post* that four of those then incarcerated presented particularly ominous problems for authorities. "Nobody is talking," the official complained, citing the two Indian news dealers, a Boston cab driver, and Zacarias Moussaoui, a French Moroccan imprisoned in Minnesota a month before the attacks. "We are known for humanitarian treatment, so basically we are stuck," the FBI official continued. "Usually there is some incentive, some angle to play, what you can do for them. But it could get to that spot where we could go to pressure . . . where we don't have a choice, and we are probably getting there." The official added: "Frustration has begun to appear." Faced with that frustration, officials were considering the use of drugs on the captives or, in the *Post*'s words, "pressure tactics, such as those employed occasionally by Israeli interrogators, to extract information." They also were considering the extradition of suspects to countries where security services are known to employ torture or "pressure tactics."

"In this autumn of anger, even a liberal can find his thoughts turning to . . . torture," liberal columnist Jonathan Alter wrote at the beginning of November in that most mainstream of magazines, *Newsweek.* "OK, not cattle prods or rubber hoses, at least not here in the United States, but something to jump-start the stalled investigation of the greatest crime in American history. Right now, four key hijacking suspects aren't talking at all."

"Some people still argue that we needn't rethink any of our old assumptions about law enforcement," Alter continued, "but they're hopelessly 'Sept. 10'—living in a country that no longer exists." Few readers wrote in taking Alter to task, and he later said he was surprised by "people who might be described as being on the left whispering, 'I agree with you.'" Besides, Alter said, he wasn't advocating torture; he was just putting it out there.

In the 1960s, torture and assassination were certainly part of American policy, as anyone who recalls the Phoenix program in Vietnam or the long list of secret CIA activities that finally began to emerge publicly in the 1970s can attest. But here 9/11 indeed represented a turning point: Americans pondering torture of captives taken on American soil. And it seemed to be a "discussion" launched to justify what was already underway. Better to have court-monitored torture, Harvard law professor Alan Dershowitz argued, than Manhattan saturated with nuclear radiation.

At the Metropolitan Detention Center in New York City, where large numbers of domestic detainees were held in the wake of 9/11, conditions were systematically abusive from the very beginning, as the U.S. Bureau of Prisons and the Justice Department later admitted. Within the first weeks after 9/11, as prisoners poured in, stories of beatings and "pressure tactics" appeared in newspapers, printed on the inside pages, and rights groups sought accountings. In 2003, after Ayub Ali Khan and Azmath Javed, the erstwhile newsdealers plucked from the train to San Antonio, had finally been deported to India, Khan told Indian journalists that he had been denied access to a lawyer and subjected to "torture of the worst kind," including sleep deprivation and constant hammering on his cell door, according to the BBC. He was shackled for long periods of time, thrown against a wall, and, while chained, kicked and punched by guards, he said. Azmath told a similar tale. Thin and weak when he finally returned to India, Azmath said he had been made "to stand in freezing temperatures in the open for four to five hours a day to force me to confess to a crime I had not committed," the BBC reported. He, too, was locked in solitary confinement and, he said, treated "worse than an animal."

"When I was shackled, they would bang my chest against the wall," he said, describing treatment by detention center guards. "They would step on my shackles, and it would hurt my ankles." While he was in prison in America, Azmath's wife, a Pakistani, faced deportation from India, and his son, Bilal, was born—another child immediately facing loss and uncertainty ushered in by 9/11.

Immediately following the Trade Center and Pentagon attacks, few non-Muslims seemed concerned about tales of abuse or rough tactics, and some applauded what was invariably described as getting tough with the terrorists. In Muslim and immigrant communities, though, everyone was interested, everyone was worried, and within weeks, virtually everyone knew someone who had disappeared or had been interrogated. The grapevine in those communities is long, sensitive, and infinitely enduring. If something happens, particularly something bad, it happens on the grapevine as though it were yesterday.

An elderly couple, Indian physicians, traveling to Philadelphia from Libya in the days after 9/11 to visit their daughter, were detained at Philadelphia International Airport and questioned by the FBI. They had visited their daughter, who lives in suburban Philadelphia, several times in the past, but despite that and despite quick FBI clearance, immigration agents denied them entry, labeled them "a threat to national security," and ordered them out of the country.

"They were handcuffed, shackled, and taken to prison in Chester . . . and they were sent back out of the country the next day," Iftekhar Hussain, a computer engineer and a board member of the area Council on American-Islamic Relations, told me some time later. "We got involved trying to find them the next day. They were being deported, and we were trying to get an explanation."

Hussain said authorities repeatedly demanded to know why the couple came to visit their daughter and told them neither their presence nor their money was wanted in the United States. Even after the couple was thrown out, Hussain asked Joe Hoeffel, a Philadelphia-area congressman, to find out what was going on. Immigration officials told the congressman "there were questions" about the two. Not surprisingly, Hoeffel wanted to know what the questions might be. Immigration authorities declined to provide any answers. They didn't respond at all to similar inquiries posed by the U.S. embassy in Malta, which issued the couple's multiple-entry visas in the first place.

Some months later, the couple returned to the United States, this time through New York, without difficulty.

Stories like this—and it is still talked about in Philadelphia several years later—"make the rounds," Hussain said. They become grist for the rumor mill; sometimes they morph and become a different story, often worse. There are all manner of similar stories circulating through the Middle Eastern community, becoming nastier and nastier, more and more threatening with each retelling. Such stories are refreshed, like dying flowers, with a steady beat of new incidents to this day.

"You hear things," said Hussain. The story of the Indian couple "has made so many rounds. People still talk about it. 'Oh my god! That was horrific! They were shackled! They were jailed! No food!' It happened, yes, but now it is urban legend."

More accurately, it's urban actuality, and in some small measure
it encapsulates the arbitrary government power ruling Islamic life
in America over the last several years, a power viewed by American
Muslims as capricious and inescapable as fate itself. That's why the
story persists. The couple and their run-in would probably be considered a fluke if it didn't resonate so loudly. The why of these incidents is unknowable—who can explain the ways of government
to man?

IN THE SUMMER OF 2005, I visited the International Muslim Brotherhood, in West Philadelphia, the oldest mosque in the city (founded
in 1949). It's located in an unpretentious building in an African
American neighborhood, and most of its energetic congregation
consists of black Americans. After Friday prayer, I spoke with Sheik
Anwar Muhaimin, the mosque's president. Sheik Anwar, an African
American with a very measured manner and rich brown skin, casually told me that his brother-in-law, Abdallah Higazy, is an Egyptian
computer engineer who had the misfortune of spending the week
of September 11 at the Millennium Hilton, directly across the street
from the World Trade Center. About three months after fleeing from
his room the morning of the attacks, the sheik said, Higazy returned
to the hotel to fetch his belongings. He was immediately seized as a
material witness by the FBI and accused of possessing an aviation
radio, a transceiver used in communicating with airplanes, supposedly found among his belongings.

"It was planted in his room," the sheik calmly said. "He didn't
know anything about it. But they took him, shackled him, and threw
him into that detention center." No one knew what had happened
to Abdallah Higazy, son of an Egyptian diplomat and a graduate student at Brooklyn Polytechnic University. (It was the university, faced
with a housing problem, that booked Higazy into the Hilton in the
first place.) His then-girlfriend, Nafeesah Muhaimin, the sheik's sister, witnessed the arrest but had no idea what was going on. Agents

appeared everywhere, she later said, and they hustled Higazy away; he wasn't tracked down for days.

"We tried to defend him," said the sheik. "We tried to reason with the FBI, but they wouldn't listen. He was terrified. It was incomprehensible. He couldn't believe such a thing was happening."

But it was. After many days in solitary confinement, days of interrogations and shackles and strip searches, Higazy agreed to a lie detector test, administered by the FBI without his lawyer present. After more than three intense hours, during which Higazy said an agent threatened that "if you don't cooperate with us, the FBI will . . . make sure Egyptian security gives your family hell," Higazy did indeed confess. He was deeply afraid for his family. He was hyperventilating and near collapse, he said later.

Yes, the radio was his. He told the agent that he found the radio under a bridge. Then he said he found it on the subway. Finally he settled on stealing it from the Egyptian air force.

You are a terrorist, Michael Templeton, the agent administering the lie detector examination-interrogation, told him. You were involved with the attacks. No, Higazy repeatedly said. No. His denial was adamant and deemed irrelevant. On January 11, with scores of reporters alerted, federal authorities charged Higazy with perjury—denying ownership of the airplane transceiver. Stories prominently noted he was staying across the street from the Trade Center on the fifty-first floor of the hotel—making communication with low-flying planes a simple matter. The assistant U.S. attorney prosecuting the case said it was "a potentially quite significant part" of the PENTTBOM investigation. The news had terrorism and complicity oozing from every line.

There was only one problem, which came walking through the door of the Millennium Hotel a few days later. An American commercial pilot was in search of the transceiver he had left behind at the hotel in the frenzy of his own September 11 escape. It had apparently been stolen.

The case against Higazy quickly unraveled, and a hotel security guard admitted he had placed the radio with Higazy's Quran and other personal effects. Higazy was released, without notice, the night of January 16, 2002. He was stunned.

"They said, 'You can go,'" Sheik Anwar recalled. "He had nothing. No possessions, no money, no clothes. He asked for some and was told to leave the detention center. He had no money, and some officer took pity on him and gave him subway fare. It was January and bitter cold. He only had a prison jumpsuit, and an old lady felt sorry for him on the subway and gave him her coat." The sheik drove to New York City and gathered up Higazy at a relative's apartment. "He's scared," the sheik said. "He couldn't believe such a thing could happen in this country. It was a devastating experience."

Higazy's story and its aftermath struck a deep chord in the East Coast Muslim community, lending strength to the increasing certainty that Middle Eastern Muslims were indeed "disappearing" in America and that the government was uninterested in investigating, uninterested in truth, and absolutely uninterested in civil rights and liberties. The story, still vividly repeated, retains its potency for Muslims. For authorities, who were so certain of their case that they did little checking, it was just a mistake.

(At the end of September 2009, the FBI paid Higazy $250,000 to settle a law suit and make the mistake go away. The agency admitted no liability as part of the deal. "I don't think there's any amount of money that could return him to the way he was before this happened," Higazy's attorney, Jonathan S. Abady, told the AP following resolution of the lengthy legal action. His client lives in Egypt and works as a school principal. "I think this is still a traumatic memory that will never leave him completely. He still hesitates to return to the United States. I think he still has concerns about being in the FBI database and being potentially the subject of another mistake.")

Such mistakes and arbitrary actions quickly piled one on top of the other in the weeks after the Trade Center and Pentagon attacks.

They happened everywhere, inspired by policy directives, fear, zealousness, racism, simple circumstances, public tips, informers, pressure, anger, and highly publicized government alarms. The alarms seemed relentless and so lacking in detail that they served only to infuse the air with anxiety. That became their legacy; was it their purpose? "Well, I wasn't rattled," President Bush told reporters after a vague alert about bridges at the beginning of November 2001. "What I've been saying all along is we're in a new day here in America."

At the end of September, the State Department issued a worldwide alert, warning Americans of plots uncovered by the CIA, the National Security Agency, and foreign intelligence services. Radical Muslims in Indonesia, Malaysia, Tajikistan, Uzbekistan, Pakistan, the former Soviet republic of Georgia, the Philippines, and Bahrain were planning attacks on Americans, State Department officials said. No details were forthcoming, however, beyond vague references to a surge in threatening rhetoric. "Chatter" entered the public vocabulary. This alarm followed weeks of similarly vague warnings and rumors of wider 9/11–related plots: additional airplane hijackings; possible attacks using crop dusters, tractor trailers, gas, and chemical and biological weapons; and possible attacks on nuclear plants, refineries, amusement parks, the Mall of America, the Sears Tower, stadiums, and the nation's ports. Suspicions of money laundering led to arrests at jewelry kiosks around the country. Suspicions regarding bogus hazmat driver's licenses were tied to the attacks. Waves of arrests followed.

"One objective of these people is to inspire fear and make people change their behavior," an American intelligence official confided to the *Miami Herald*, referring, in this case, to terrorists. "One way to do that is to check out a lot of places and make a lot of threats so nobody feels safe anywhere."

(There was no alarm, however, on September 18, when someone quietly dropped envelopes addressed to various news outlets into a Trenton, New Jersey, mailbox. And on October 5, a photo editor at

American Media in Boca Raton, Florida, who handled one of the Trenton envelopes, became the first American in thirty years to die of inhalation anthrax.)

On October 8, the day after U.S. and British war planes began bombing Afghanistan at the onset of the war there, Attorney General Ashcroft issued a new national alert, warning the nation to be on the lookout for renewed and invigorated terror attacks. He had just warned the country the previous week that a U.S. attack on Afghanistan and al Qaeda's camps there would likely produce retaliatory terrorism on American soil. Now Ashcroft repeated the warning, and his Justice Department followed it up by dispatching a list of close to three hundred names of people wanted for questioning to 18,000 law enforcement agencies and 27,000 private businesses all over the country. (This list, first drawn up with about a hundred names and disseminated within a day or so of 9/11, would grow and mutate and find its way eventually onto the internet, where anyone could read it and copy it and add to it and pass it on. By that point, months later, the *Wall Street Journal* reported that FBI officials knew they had lost control of the list and companies and citizens thought they had their hands on a list of actual wanted terrorists— not simply people wanted for questioning or people added to the list by who knows whom. Such is the nature of government lists. They grow and expand. Bad information metastasizes. One list gives birth to another. A few short months after the initial terror attacks, lists fed in part by the 150,000 tips that poured into the FBI within just two weeks of 9/11 were beginning to dominate certain aspects of public life, most commonly air travel.)

In Ashcroft's October 8 warning, companies were told to keep their eyes on employees and visitors. Immigration officials were told to watch the borders. The coast guard began regular patrols in San Francisco Bay in response. Bridges received particular scrutiny everywhere. The Detroit Metropolitan Airport closed all parking lots save one. Trucks and cars were searched randomly. Reservoirs were monitored, and access to water-treatment plants was severely restricted nationally.

Three days later, on October 11, one month after the 9/11 attacks, the FBI issued yet another warning. The country should be on "highest alert," the agency announced, because "certain information, while not specific as to target, gives the government reason to believe that there may be additional attacks within the United States and against U.S. interests overseas over the next several days." Citizens were urged to report any and all "unusual or suspicious activity." President Bush said he had reviewed the "intelligence," which, he said at a news conference, amounted to "a general threat on America."

"I hope it's the last, but given the nature of the evildoers, it may not be," Bush said. Nevertheless, the president told Americans to "go about their lives: to fly on airplanes, to travel, to go to work." They should take comfort, the president said, because "their government is on full alert." In Philadelphia, Timoney opened up the city's lead-lined emergency operations bunker, and the director of the state's emergency management agency said, "We cannot allow ourselves to be paranoically frightened by the things that are going on."

TAREK ALBASTI, A NATURALIZED American citizen born in Egypt, was cooking pasta in his Crazy Tomato restaurant in Evansville, Indiana, on the evening Bush told Americans to "go about their lives." That's when the FBI showed up with some questions. Albasti called his wife, Carolyn Baugh, and told her federal agents wanted to speak with him. The FBI had already interviewed Albasti a few weeks earlier, curious to know about the flying lessons he had taken. But that had been cleared up when they learned that the lessons had been a surprise gift from his father-in-law, a former American diplomat, a prominent Indianapolis attorney, and an avid flyer.

Several hours later, Albasti called his wife again and told her he would not be home.

In fact, Albasti disappeared. So did seven other Egyptians from the area, largely old friends, many of whom rowed with him on the Egyptian national crew team before coming to America and a new life in the isolated heartland of southern Indiana. Carolyn Baugh, who met Albasti as a graduate student in Cairo and fell in love, grew increasingly worried as the night wore on. Neither she nor her parents—who had wide-ranging legal and political contacts—could get any answers from authorities.

Following his last call, as it happened, Albasti and the others were immediately seized by the FBI and detained on material witness warrants. They were held in the Evansville jail and then bused first to a holding pen in Kentucky and later to the Metropolitan Correctional Center in Chicago. Dark plots were suggested in news accounts at the time, in particular a suspected plan to blow up the Sears Tower (a favorite scenario, it seems, of many supposed plotters over the years and a subject of continuous, media-driven rumors and speculation). A gag order was imposed on everyone involved in the case.

Albasti was terrified. His family had no idea where he was being held, and authorities in Indiana and Kentucky refused to disclose what happened to any of the men. The family retained savvy Chicago attorney Kenneth L. Cunniff to find out.

"I've never been more frightened in my life," Cunniff told me. "I never saw anything like it, and I've been a lawyer for thirty-four years."

Cunniff had actually seen Albasti before becoming involved in the case.

"I always have the news on in the background here at nighttime," he said from his Chicago office. "I happened to look up, and I saw eight guys being pulled from a jail, and they were wearing the James Cagney–type prison suits from the Big House. Shackled together. On national TV. It was the most amazing thing. I couldn't believe they could do that in the modern day and age, that they would do that type of stuff, that the perp walk wasn't just that they got their pictures, but that they had these guys looking like they belonged in the Big House. With no basis! Nothing! They were material witnesses. There was no allegation they had done anything wrong."

Cunniff was certain the eight were being held in Chicago. Authorities, even longtime colleagues, denied it, but Cunniff located the men anyway. According to court papers eventually filed by prosecutors, the eight Evansville detainees were suspected of hatching "an imminent plan to execute a terrorist attack in Chicago related to the terrorist acts on Sept. 11, 2001." The basis for prosecutorial suspicion and allegation? An informant who was "an individual closely related" to one of the eight, the *Chicago Tribune* reported nearly two years after the arrests. The informer claimed that "a particular individual had stated that he would be traveling to Chicago's O'Hare Airport, was going to engage in a suicide crash, and that he would be dead on Oct. 12, 2001."

Cunniff telephoned Albasti's mother and father-in-law in Indiana with some hard news.

"I managed to be reasonably coherent," Mary Francis Baugh, Albasti's mother-in-law, told me. "The night Ken called me up and said, 'Well, you might not believe this, but the prosecuting attorney is going to try for the death penalty for your son-in-law.' I said, 'Well, you'll get him off, won't you? The death penalty for cooking spaghetti?' 'Yeah.' So I cried and cried all night."

Patrick Fitzgerald, the U.S. attorney in Chicago, pressed hard on the investigation, which quickly led nowhere. The informer, as it turned out, was an angry estranged wife of one of the eight, and the "tip" was her imaginary figment. After a week in shackles, interrogations, and solitary confinement—a week of media infamy—the eight were released. Prosecutors said they had no connection to anything related to terrorism or 9/11. How did this happen? I asked Cunniff. How did what amounts to a crank phone call from a vindictive spouse mutate into a potential capital case?

"Because they're Muslims, because they came to our country, because they banded together, because my guy took flying lessons in Florida," he said. "And they would come to Chicago to go to wherever the Egyptian restaurant was, like around Devine and Western, in that area, all those ethnic restaurants. They could get the kind of bread that they couldn't get anywhere else. Because they came together and because they took pictures of the Sears Tower. You weren't here, but there was a rumor that al Qaeda was about to blow up the Sears Tower and that these were the guys that were going to do it."

Following the unraveling of the case, despite complete exoneration, things did not go well back in Evansville. Business plummeted at the Crazy Tomato on Green River Road. Mark Miller, an Evansville attorney who was involved in some parts of the case, told me he had heard that the restaurant had "taken a hit" after Albasti was released. But there was still a small but active Muslim community in the area.

"The Muslims, the Jews, the Christians were all praying for their release, and they came together, in kind of one voice, to say, 'What the hell is going on?'" recalled Mary Frances Baugh. "And they were supportive of the restaurant. It never closed. They even volunteered to be servers. And a judge came to serve as well."

But business declined anyway, and then Albasti and some of his friends discovered another problem—their names started to appear on a variety of government watch lists. Albasti was detained returning from a visit to Cairo. He was stopped and interrogated at airports. So was one of the other eight innocent Evansville men. One of them had his application denied for an apartment. Another was blocked from permanent residency. Despite being cleared of any wrongdoing, let alone a connection to 9/11, their names became associated with terrorism in proliferating government databases. In April 2003, Thomas Fuentes, special agent in charge of the Indiana FBI office, apologized publicly for the problems and promised to correct them. But problems continued. "It's not like flipping a switch" to get the names off various lists, said the FBI official who volunteered for the task, according to the *Evansville Courier and Press*. All databases are interlinked, he said, allowing for easier entry and dissemination of names. But those links are not reversible. Easy in does not mean easy out. Two of the eight Egyptians, fed up, left the country.

"We're glad we got what we got," a resigned Albasti said at the time of the FBI apology. "We got our dignity back, and it cleared our reputation with certain people. But it's kind of like too late. It's kind of like you can't do anything about it anymore."

He and his wife sold their house, sold the Crazy Tomato, and left Evansville. They now live in a large city, and he runs another restaurant. I promised Albasti's mother-in-law I would keep the location to myself.

"They aren't bitter," said Mary Francis Baugh, a thoughtful and protective woman. "They have just moved on. They would rather have people come to [the restaurant] for the good food and not out of sympathy." And then there is the stigma, which adheres regardless of truth. "After 9/11 people still think that if the FBI is involved, well, they've got a reason," said Baugh.

With all the tensions erupting across the country, local political and religious leaders in Philadelphia believed they had to act to calm anxieties. Jewish and Christian leaders quickly volunteered to escort members of the city's largest mosque, Al Aqsa Islamic Society on Germantown Avenue, to and from work and on shopping trips. Muslim women wearing distinctive *hijabs* felt particularly vulnerable faced with the minefields of the streets. Police maintained a protective presence as well. The Friday after September 11, when about three hundred people showed up for prayer at Al Aqsa—about half the usual number—several city officials turned out to soothe frayed nerves and offer support. City Controller Jonathan Seidel told congregants, "You are as much American as all of us standing before you. Today I am not here as an Orthodox Jew. Today all of us are Muslims. All of us are Americans." Timoney urged anyone experiencing harassment of any kind to call police immediately.

"We need your help," he said. "It's one community. We're not looking; we're not blaming you. If you know or saw something, let us know. But if you become the victim of wanton violence, you've also got to let us know. And listen, you almost have to expect that—not excuse it, but expect it. And we need to know."

Not every Al Aqsa congregant was impressed by the official talk at the time, as my colleague Tom Ginsberg reported. "Inside here, they say all the right things," said one disenchanted man. "But we know when you go outside on the street, the situation is the same."

In Washington the following Monday, the president himself sought to dampen the flaring anti-Muslim threats, drawing a distinction between terrorist mass murder and Islam. "These acts of violence against innocents violate the fundamental tenets of the Islamic faith. And it's important for my fellow Americans to understand that," Bush told clerics and citizens gathered at a well-publicized session at Washington's Islamic Center on September 17. "The face of terror is not the true face of Islam. That's not what Islam is all about. Islam is peace. These terrorists don't represent peace. They represent evil and war," he said.

That very day, however, at a press conference across town, the president's attorney general reported that thousands of federal agents were already pursuing 55,000 tips and leads connected with the attacks. Many of the tips simply reflected anti-Muslim and anti-immigrant phobias precipitated out of the ether. Hundreds had already been questioned. Material witness warrants, sealed and secret, had been issued, and an undisclosed number of those suspects were in hand. An undisclosed number of immigration law violators had been rounded up. No names were released. No places of incarceration were revealed. No charges were detailed. Despite all of this, said Ashcroft, federal efforts were hampered by undue legal restraints, and the threat of terrorism loomed, growing larger and more malefic with each minute on the ticking clock.

"In the next few days," Ashcroft said, "we intend to finalize a package of legislative measures that will be comprehensive. Areas covered include criminal justice, immigration, intelligence gathering, and financial infrastructure. While the final details are still being discussed, I can highlight a few of the items that we will address in the proposal. Under intelligence gathering, we want to provide additional tools to collect intelligence on terrorists, including expanded electronic surveillance, search authority, and the ability to identify, [seize,] and forfeit terrorist assets."

Even as Ashcroft spoke, federal agents were already deep into forays onto college campuses. Within days of the Trade Center and Pentagon attacks, agents from the FBI and INS had contacted university officials and campus police all over the United States, seeking information about Muslim and Middle Eastern students. An October 2001 survey by the American Association of Collegiate Registrars and Admissions Officers found that at least 220 colleges had been contacted by law enforcement authorities following September 11. Police or FBI agents made ninety-nine requests for private "nondirectory" information, such as course schedules, that under law could not be released without student consent, a subpoena, or a pending danger. Only eight schools denied the requests. College police from at least a dozen institutions were ultimately given slots on expanding local Joint Terrorism Task Forces, linking federal anti-terror law enforcement directly to the halls of the academy. At the same time, the U.S. Department of Education began sharing student loan application information with the FBI in a program dubbed Project Strikeback. (In 2005, the National Security Higher Education Advisory Board was formed, further tying universities to the FBI. The board is composed of twenty university presidents—including Graham Spanier, president of Pennsylvania State University, chair; University of Pennsylvania president Amy Gutmann; and Susan Hockfield, MIT president—and aims to keep universities in the national security loop as the war on terror grinds on.)

THE COMPREHENSIVE MEASURES Ashcroft announced while Bush was shoeless at the Islamic Center ultimately became the USA PATRIOT

Act, vastly augmenting federal power of surveillance and detention and zeroing in on the foreign-born in America. Following congressional approval of the act, President Bush told Americans that "we cannot let the terrorists achieve the objective of frightening our nation to the point where we don't conduct business or people don't shop," and Ashcroft announced that federal agents planned 5,000 "voluntary" interviews with young Arab and Muslim men, including students, all over the country. The interviews were portrayed publicly as friendly efforts to gather information and leads. Privately, however, agents were told otherwise. A memo from the Justice Department went out directing regional immigration offices to detain any interviewee without bond if federal agents requested it. INS offices were told to detain anyone with immigration irregularities. Eventually, twenty interviewees across the country were detained and three arrested on charges unrelated to terrorism. No links to 9/11 were discovered. Fresh from this success, Ashcroft opted to interview 3,000 more. He noted that "a significant number" of the initial 5,000 did not show up for their voluntary interrogations and could not be located by officials. He vowed to find them.

A little more than a month after announcing the interviews, the Justice Department launched another program, the Alien Absconder Apprehension Initiative, aimed at foreigners who had not responded to or complied with old deportation orders. Over 314,000 names of purported absconders were funneled into the FBI's vast National Crime and Information Center database, which gave local law enforcement agencies across the country access to names of many people who may have even been unaware that immigration violations were alleged against them. Once in that vast database—accessible to police making even a routine traffic stop—the names potentially spread to other databases, local and national, increasing the risk of erroneous detentions and unwarranted interrogations. The Justice Department emphasized that it would initially target the 6,000 names of men from the Middle Eastern and South Asian countries associated with al Qaeda, 1.9 percent of the total. They'd get around to others later.

At the same time, near the beginning of 2002, the federal government began clandestinely monitoring U.S. mosques, homes, and other Muslim sites for radiation levels. When the activity finally became public in 2005, officials said the air sampling was deemed necessary because of fears that a nuclear device or dirty bomb might be used by al Qaeda or its supporters. Officials denied that Muslims were the sole focus of the program, though no other targets were ever publicly identified. (In 2003, FBI agents were also directed to count the number of mosques in jurisdictions nationwide, and the Department of Homeland Security sought data on the location of Arab residents from the U.S. Census Bureau in 2002 and 2003.) Muslim properties in Washington, D.C., and its suburbs, Chicago, Detroit, Las Vegas, New York, and Seattle were monitored under the program, according to *U.S. News and World Report*. In Washington, nearly 120 sites were monitored daily. The secret program was run by the FBI and the Energy Department's Nuclear Emergency Support Team, which sought no warrants to conduct activities on private property. An FBI spokesman said in 2005 that the investigations and monitoring were based on intelligence regarding criminal or terrorist threats. "There is no nuclear- or radiation-monitoring program targeting mosques or other places of gathering by Muslim or any other particular group of citizens," said Mike Mason, head of the FBI field office in Washington. The program, or at least some variation of it, continues.

THE CONTINUOUS FOCUS ON Middle Eastern and South Asian Muslim "suspects" was so intense at the time and received so much media attention that it led many Americans to believe by its very magnitude that such people should be targets of heightened scrutiny and law enforcement action. If so many law enforcement authorities were searching in the same place, something must be there. It just wasn't being seen.

Who could argue such logic? Didn't young men from the Middle East carry out the horrendous September 11 attacks? Yet Richard Reid, the so-called shoe bomber who was caught in the act of trying to ignite a bomb on December 22, 2001 (by alert flight attendants and passengers, not covert surveillance or watch lists), was British. Indeed, all the focus on Middle Easterners may well have eased Reid's passage onto American Airlines Flight 63 bound from Paris to Miami.

But in the aftermath of the attacks, fear focused attention on Middle Eastern and South Asian Muslims, and renewed alerts and alarms kept it there. According to a CNN/*USA Today* poll conducted by Gallup two days after the 9/11 attacks, 58 percent of the public supported special, more intense security checks for Arabs, including U.S. citizens, before the boarding of airplanes; 49 percent said they favored special identification cards for Arabs, again including U.S. citizens; 32 percent believed Arabs should be subjected to "special surveillance"; 33 percent said they supported "making it easier for legal authorities to read mail, e-mail, or tap phones without the person's knowledge"; and 29 percent supported granting authority to police to stop people at random on the street and "search their possessions."

Confirmation of al Qaeda's responsibility for the attacks, the demonization of bin Laden, and the constant alerts and arrests kept those poll figures high in the weeks and months that followed. And poll numbers and potential marketing opportunities never escaped the administration's notice. In August 2006, nearly five years after the original terrorist attacks, a *USA Today*/Gallup poll found 39 percent of respondents felt at least some prejudice against Muslims; 39 percent believed Muslims, including U.S. citizens, should be compelled to carry special identification "as a means of preventing terrorist attacks in the United States"; 34 percent said they believed Muslims in the United States were sympathetic to al Qaeda; and 57 percent said Muslims should receive extra security scrutiny at airports. By July 2007, according to a *Newsweek* poll, 52 percent of

Americans sanctioned wiretapping of U.S. mosques. All of this directed at a Muslim population in the United States estimated to be 5 to 8 million, a third African American. The Census Bureau estimates that perhaps 150,000 Middle Easterners are in the country without adequate papers—out of a total population of at least 11 million so-called illegals.

On October 25, 2001, the day before the president signed the USA PATRIOT Act, Attorney General Ashcroft told about a hundred mayors gathered in Washington for what was billed as an Emergency, Safety and Security Summit that harsh measures were in store: "Robert Kennedy's Justice Department, it is said, would arrest mobsters for 'spitting on the sidewalk' if it would help in the battle against organized crime," Ashcroft told the mayors. "It has been and will be the policy of this Department of Justice to use the same aggressive arrest and detention tactics in the war on terror. Let the terrorists among us be warned: If you overstay your visa—even by one day—we will arrest you."

For a Middle Eastern visitor, a visa violation now effectively translated into a charge of terrorism. But just as important, similar remarks from Ashcroft and others in the administration served to remind the broader population that suspicions were important to maintain. You can't be too suspicious. And particular groups warrant particular scrutiny.

Given the huge numbers of immigrants who are in the United States without proper documentation, the Middle Eastern numbers are tiny. But the post–9/11 focus on that small community has been overwhelming. In April 2002, the Council on American-Islamic Relations (CAIR) estimated that some 60,000 Muslim residents had been subjected to some form of 9/11–related government action—interrogations, raids, arrests, detentions, and other action that "negatively impacted" civil rights, as CAIR put it. Other estimates put the number at three or four times that.

It makes sense, people often said to me. Why waste time investigating Swedes? The problem with the approach developed by Ashcroft, however, would become clear in practice to anyone who took the time to look. It was the same problem that manifested itself during the McCarthy period after World War II: There is a difference between interrogating an actual suspect about a specific crime and rounding up thousands of people simply because they are who they are or know someone who knows someone else and on and on. There is an obvious practical problem in this approach. Focusing so much attention on masses of largely innocent people diverts resources and agents from targeted, more effective investigation. The FBI complained about this very circumstance when they were inundated with mountains of fruitless leads derived from warrantless NSA wiretaps, according to the *New York Times.* Too much information, not enough shoe leather, too many false leads. Then, of course, there is the question of what happens to people erroneously detained, erroneously interrogated, aggressively pursued in error. Whatever the outcome of their particular cases, their lives are permanently swathed in suspicion steeped in ethnicity; careers are destroyed, and personal and professional relations are left in tatters. Suspicion seeps everywhere around the tainted, and their names are flagged in databases as if they carry some abominable virus. In the end, mass arrests or arrests based on former acquaintanceships or arrests for dissenting political views or arrests growing from ethnic targeting are the corrupt acts of a misguided and corrupted power.

By November, more than 1,200 people had been swept from the nation's streets and held, often incommunicado and often in severe conditions that included extended solitary confinement and psychological and physical abuse. The numbers continued to grow, but in November 2001 federal officials simply stopped providing a public count. A Justice Department spokeswoman explained that the numbers were "confusing." Virtually all of these detainees were Muslims from the Middle East or South Asia, although some Israeli tourists were swept up as well. Rights groups estimate the number detained in the initial PENTTBOM dragnet to be over 2,000, though that cannot be verified because the government still refuses to provide information on the sweeps.

Safe to say, people were picked up all over the country, like the Egyptians in Evansville, and shipped from one place to another, often winding up at the federal Metropolitan Detention Center in Brooklyn. That's where the Indian news dealers, harboring box cutters used to slice ties on paper bales, were taken. It is also where Nabil Ayesh, picked up for a traffic violation outside of Philadelphia on the very day of 9/11, wound up, spending over a year in a windowless, continually lit cell. Muslim communities everywhere were riddled with reports of disappearing young men and of horrors inside the nation's detention centers.

The office of Glenn A. Fine, inspector general of the Justice Department, finally mounted an investigation of detainees caught up in the sweeps and verified many allegations of abuse at the federal Metropolitan Detention Center (MDC), among several other holding facilities. The inspector general's 2003 report described detainees housed in isolation units, subjected to round-the-clock lighting, constant shackling, incessant strip searches, indefinite periods of incarceration, and a host of other questionable practices. In several instances, detainees were not charged with any crimes. Fine's office also found sporadic physical and verbal abuse at the MDC, some of it captured on videotape, which the federal Bureau of Prisons fought to withhold from investigators. There are no such tapes, prison officials told the inspector general's agents. But one day, after a year of such denials, agents asked to see a detention center storage room, and there they found the long-sought tapes clearly documenting abuse.

Detainees were slammed into walls and doors, stepped on while chained, and physically attacked by prison guards. At least initially, those held believed they could take some solace in their religion. Their prayers were greeted with hoots and derision from guards, Fine reported: "Shut the fuck up! Don't pray. Fucking Muslim.

You're praying bullshit." And for good measure, these federal officers added: "Welcome to America." Prisoners were slammed into a wall and had their faces shoved up against an American flag T-shirt pinned there. "These colors don't run," it read.

Not that detention in a place like York County prison in Pennsylvania or any other county joint around the country was somehow a blessing or a haven. Muhammed Butt, a fifty-five-year-old Pakistani immigrant who was held at the Hudson County New Jersey prison, never left custody. He died of a heart attack on October 23, 2001, lying dead in his cell for several hours before anyone noticed. On September 19, 2001, Butt had been hauled in by the FBI after a sharp-eyed, suspicious pastor reported that swarthy men piled out of two vans and entered Butt's New York City home. But federal agents determined Butt was nothing more than a visa overstay, and after holding him a day, the FBI turned him over to immigration authorities for deportation. Immigration stored Butt at the Hudson jail where he died, leaving two sons, three daughters, and a wife adrift in Pakistan.

Human Rights Watch sought information about Butt shortly after his death, but the group was rebuffed by the Immigration and Naturalization Service. "In a December 6 response," Human Rights Watch reported, "the INS refused to disclose any information regarding Muhammed Butt, 'due to laws relating to privacy.'" Immigration authorities told rights advocates that, when seeking further information, "please be sure to have written consent from Mr. Butt stating that that office is able to release information concerning his case to you. This statement should contain his name and your name and his alien number along with his written signature." Dead men tell no tales, nor do they sign any statements.

Many early detainees around the country were eventually deported. In fact, more people were deported in the waves of arrests and detentions immediately following 9/11 than during the infamous Palmer Raids at the height of the post–World War I Red Scare, when federal agents swooped down on immigrant and working-class communities nationwide, arresting 10,000 supposed foreign radicals. In the year following the World Trade Center and Pentagon attacks, 3,208 people from thirty-three Middle Eastern and Muslim countries were deported from the United States, compared to the 1,836 deported the previous year, the *Philadelphia Inquirer* reported in 2003. About 750 were deported during the height of the Red Scare in 1920 and 1921. (Immigration authorities have declined to provide any official tally of deportees to date.)

By December 2001, the criticism of government detentions, its eavesdropping on communications between detainees and their attorneys, its secrecy surrounding the detentions and arrests, the allegations of abuse, the reports of disappearances, the alarm over the broad powers granted under the PATRIOT Act, and the government's decision to establish special military tribunals for those captured overseas had all finally coalesced into one enormous, hydra-headed, increasingly malignant issue in the media and in the courts. Civil liberties and civil rights organizations were preparing and filing lawsuits demanding answers. And in Congress, questions were being asked of increasingly testy administration officials.

On December 6, John Ashcroft appeared before the Senate Judiciary Committee to discuss the administration's vague proposal for military tribunals for battlefield detainees. But his message amounted to a broad attack on administration critics beginning to show themselves across the political landscape.

"To those who pit Americans against immigrants, citizens against noncitizens, to those who scare peace-loving people with phantoms of lost liberty, my message is this: Your tactics only aid terrorists, for they erode our national unity and diminish our resolve," Ashcroft said. "They give ammunition to America's enemies and pause to America's friends. They encourage people of good will to remain silent in the face of evil."

Not only were critics serving as terrorist supporters and puppets, the attorney general said, they were doing so in complete ignorance of the plain facts.

"Our efforts have been crafted carefully to avoid infringing on constitutional rights, while saving American lives," he added. "Charges of kangaroo courts and shredding the Constitution give new meaning to the term 'fog of war.'"

Senator Patrick Leahy was more than a little taken aback by having his committee associated with support for al Qaeda. "The need for congressional oversight is not—as some mistakenly describe it—to protect terrorists," he said. "It is to protect Americans and protect our American freedoms that you and everyone in this room cherish so much. And every single American has a stake in protecting our freedoms."

For me, that exchange crystallized a critical aspect of what was happening in the country: It was now clear that an immense power struggle was underway. The administration was not simply fighting a war on terror—whatever that might mean; it was fighting all efforts to check the steady aggrandizement of its own power. As Dick Cheney later said to Leahy on the floor of the Senate, "Go fuck yourself."

Up to this point I had viewed unfolding events as more or less undirected chaos. That's what it looked like at the time—perhaps because I had never seen anything quite like it in this country. I remember, back in the early 1980s, talking with some members of the Chinese foreign service who were studying in Boston and were visiting with my family. Late one night, Mr. Li—I always called him that, even though he was about my own age—sat at our kitchen drinking tea. I listened as he leaned across the table speaking very softly, almost as though he were afraid of being overheard, recounting the bizarre chaos of the Cultural Revolution and his own involvement, first as a Red Guard then as a victim—a jailer jailed. None of it made any sense from where he was sitting in our kitchen in a farmhouse in the Berkshires of northwest Connecticut. "We were so certain," he said, speaking of his Red Guard days twenty years before, "and we knew nothing." Nothing, he said, but the exhortations and alarums of the nation's leaders, the specters they described blossoming around the country, and finally the fear—fear of threats, fear of subversives, fear of pursuers, fear of what was not known and what was thought to be known. He began first as a pursuer and became the pursued as power fragmented.

Is there an analog there? The American experience pales by comparison, although African Americans, immigrants, and leftists have all been targets of ongoing hysteria during the not-distant past. What strikes me now about Mr. Li's painful description of China in the 1960s and 1970s is the importance he placed on government-stoked fear—ultimately it drove everything until Mao's death and the long climb back began. Fear undermined the entire culture.

Looking around after 9/11, however, I didn't quite grasp fear as policy. All the detentions, all the warnings and alerts, all the banked suspicions, all the rational discussion of torture, all of the over-heated reporting had communicated confusion as much as anything else. Cutting through that confusion was what one saw on the streets: thousands of American flags attached to cars on every block in the city, an urban parade of red, white, and blue. Spontaneous chanting of "USA, USA, USA" greeted the president at Ground Zero and broke out at sports events. "Fucking Arab! Fucking Arab!" greeted less eminent people on darker streets.

The administration heard those chants and understood them.

About a week after 9/11, I wrote a story, killed by an editor as "off message" and somehow partisan, that contained what is still for me a rich metaphor for those early days. At that point, Bush had already determined that the nation would mount the war on terror, "a monumental struggle of good versus evil." Pat Robertson and Jerry Falwell, supporting the president, mused that those responsible for the attacks included the ACLU, gays, pro-choice advocates, and "pagans," views shared by many in the president's political base who also applauded Bush's vow to engage in what he called a "crusade" against terrorism. On Sunday, September 16, Bush noted that "this crusade, this war on terrorism, is going to take awhile." Muslims (and Europeans) were hardly pleased with that language.

I asked Alan Guelzo, a Lincoln scholar and now professor of history at Gettysburg College, what he made of the language and confusion. Who was the enemy in a battle mounted against a tactic like terror and an elastic label like "terrorist"? What did he make of the presidential language? What kind of war was this, anyway?

"Indian raids on the frontier are probably the best single analogy," Guelzo said. "In those incidents, the Indians would sweep out of the west, burn down the town, and then disappear. Then everyone would run around saying, 'We've got to do something. We've got to do something. Exterminate the savages. Burn their villages.' That's what it feels like to me. Those Indian tactics in the nineteenth century, the hit-and-run raids, the quick attacks on forts—those were thought to be uncivilized, savage, and senseless in a way that approximates the view of terrorism today. This is not Pearl Harbor. There is no target."

Not quite so. The target lay within. The supposed plots unmasked and the trials of purported terrorists over the next several years, the sweeps of more and more immigrant communities, the color-coded alerts, and the other features of this new war—all amounted to booster shots of fear, periodic revitalization of that initial, overwhelming terror that showered ash on a bright September day. Only a robust presidency, to use Vice President Cheney's terminology, could immunize millions of potential victims against future calamity. Arrests and show trials would demonstrate the government's effectiveness and resolve.

THE HUNDREDS OF MIDDLE Easterners and South Asians I spoke with in the years following 9/11 shared revulsion toward the attacks and the carnage with their fellow American residents. Yet they looked at all the fanciful arrests, the intimidation, the trials, and even the ludicrous names found on watch lists—"Mohammed the Egyptian," "Mohammed the Tall," and simply "Mohammed" actually appear on one important government list—and were overwhelmed by humiliation at the least.

Mohamed Ghorab, born and raised in Egypt and newly arrived in Philadelphia just prior to 9/11, was no different. He was Mohamed the Egyptian. He was Mohamed the Tall. He was Mohamed. He shared such names and descriptions with literally millions of people here and abroad. Such lists and alerts were just silly, he believed, and dangerous. He was his own man, not a generic apparition conjured from a database or haunting a list.

Ghorab was stubborn, and no manner of watch list or interrogation campaign or detention threat would prevent him from pursuing his dreams and speaking what he believed to be the truth—God's truth or man's. That the United States was in the midst of a nativist spasm of gargantuan proportions was utterly irrelevant to this man. Ghorab believed, as virtually all Middle Easterners believed, that they were being watched and targeted by the government. He knew people were being arrested—wrongly in his view. But he also knew, with a certainty, that he could bring many of the lost to Islam and that Islam would transform their lives, animating their souls. They would turn away from self-aggrandizement and embrace God. What issue could be more compelling? This was America, not Egypt. This America was like home—the place that took you in when persecution fell like hail in all other lands. He counseled fellow Muslims to maintain personal dignity and respect for America, no matter what. Never forget that America was a place where Islam could be freely practiced. It is the law.

The only appropriate response to 9/11 was condemnation of the attackers, he said. But they had nothing to do with him. He did not fly planes. He did not advocate violence. He did not urge attacks; he urged an end to attacks. It was God's will that he establish a new mosque, here, on a grey and out-of-the-way street in a grey and out-of-the-way city. Islam would blossom. He could feel it.

THREE

They, Like, Attacked This Neighborhood

S IDDIQUE IS A TALL, bespectacled African American, a man who
says he comes from "a rough, rough, rough background" but
who embraced Islam a quarter century ago and discovered in it a
way of navigating daily affairs and of building a working spiritual
world. It was, he says, like discovering life itself.

One afternoon, during the holy month of Ramadan in November
2002, Siddique found himself running late. Usually he attended
Masjid Jamia, a mosque in West Philadelphia, but he was a long
way from there, driving from work as manager of a drugstore in
Germantown, northwest of Center City; there was not a chance he
could make the service miles away on Walnut Street on the other
side of the Schuylkill River. But a friend, a bus driver who attended
the Taha Mosque, mentioned several days earlier that a new
mosque had opened near Aramingo Avenue somewhere in Frankford. Near Bridge Street, maybe around Wakeling Street, the man
said. If Siddique could find it, he would be in time for prayer and
fulfill his obligation.

He drove down Aramingo, looking, and when he came to the corner of Wakeling, he saw a familiar whitewashed, cinder-block garage where he had taken his own cars for repair several times. But it was no longer a garage.

"There was a couple guys standing outside for the parking lot, making sure people found the way to park," Siddique told me one hot summer evening a few years later. We were sitting in that same garage, now empty, with fading daylight angling through the pulled-up bay door. Out the door, across the street, the huge Baptist Worship Center dominated the street, with the Excitement and Risque video stores off to the side. A jarring and strange landscape in a downtrodden neighborhood. There were no lights on in the old garage-turned-mosque, and the broad ceiling fans were off—testimony to the crushing debt that now suffocated the Ansaarullah Islamic Society. But Siddique wanted me to know what it had been like when the mosque—the *masjid*, as Muslims call it in Arabic—was alive and growing.

"They were dressed in traditional Muslim garb, and I said, 'Ah good!' Drove right up. Came in. 'This the *masjid*?' 'Oh, yeah.' Parked my car. Came inside. Was maybe thirty, forty people observing Ramadan, ready to breakfast. And I came in, and I made the prayer. And they offered me to stay. 'Stay. Here's some food. Sit down.'"

I looked around the dying mosque—soon it would shut down completely—as Siddique spoke, trying in the dimness to conjure up an image of the past vitality of the living space. In the corner across the large room stood an old circular clothing rack with dozens of black and grey athletic jackets—Ansaarullah Islamic Society stitched on the back—displayed for sale, a reflection of imam Mohamed Ghorab's rocky background in the clothing and textile business. The jackets were sold (but more often remained unsold) to defray mosque expenses. Siddique and I sat at a long industrial worktable near the center of the room. A line of text from a prayer praising God, inked in Arabic script across a pale banner, hung from one wall.

Behind us was a counter with dozens of cassette tapes bearing Ghorab's sermons, also for sale and also unsold. Paperback copies of the Quran were stacked in a case below the counter, and next to it was a basket of well-used children's toys and a small basketball game and net. More toys—foam bowling pins, balls, a large bouncy bunny—lay in the corner near the open bay door. A newly constructed wooden staircase led to a loft above the cassette and book sales counter. There had once been a well-crafted railing on the stairs, but that had been broken somehow during the 2004 raid on the mosque. Opposite the stairs was a small kitchen, and beyond that was another large room, which had served as the auto body shop's office area and had been converted to a separate place for women to pray; it was shrouded in darkness. The whoosh and honk of cars on busy Aramingo Avenue filtered into the room, even at this evening hour. The *masjid* seemed an austere vessel ready to absorb and hold the white drone and spectral images from beyond its doors.

"You can't really refuse the hospitality," Siddique continued, drops of perspiration pocking his forehead. "Here every *masjid* belongs to God, and you walk in, and you belong there. And any person who walks inside the mosque, you take care of them. In Islamic culture, you have to be a person who offers good hospitality. You have to be. I said, 'Okay,' and I was sitting down, and I ate some food. And one guy particularly, he was playing with lots of kids—there were three or four children around him—and he was playing and playing, and you *know* he was itching for a conversation. He's, like, inching closer to where I was sitting at the table and sitting there playing with the kids, and I said, 'Hi, *Assalamu Alaikum*. How you doing?'

"'How you doing?'

"Just looking for conversation, and I introduced myself, and he introduced himself to me. And we sat there, and the conversation that started with just a brief hello, hello, lasted for about two hours. Him and I just sat there. After I finished eating, I left, and they said, 'Please come back any time.'

"But the next couple of days I wasn't late, and I was able to make it down to Forty-third Street and Walnut, where I was at. And subsequently about four days later I came by again and was well received. The people was looking forward to me. It was, 'What happened to you? We missing you!'

"They didn't know me!"

"'We didn't see you for days. Where were you?'

"Then you feel bad trying to give an explanation.

"'Well, I went to this other *masjid*.'

"'Oh, well, you're welcome here anytime. You can come here anytime.'

"And I sat down, and the same guy, he came back, and we talked again. We talked for hours! The other people, they thought he was disturbing me. They said, 'He's a guest; you're monopolizing all his time.'

"I said, 'No, it's okay. We having a good friendly conversation.'

"It started that way."

To say that Siddique felt welcomed is understating his feeling about Ansaarullah, which by that point had been in operation for a few months and was still very much in its infancy. When Ghorab agreed to rent the old garage and the ragtag house next door, he had a handful of associates, some from Aqsa, some from other mosques in the city, who helped him raise the money for the hefty $4,000 monthly lease for Ansaarullah—the name means "Helpers of God"— and begin to clean out the garage. It was a mess, said one congregant. Discarded machinery, oil stains thick on the concrete floor, junk in the basement. They worked tirelessly to move out old pumps, motors, oil drums, jacks, compressors, scrap metal, and other car-repair detritus, clearing and cleaning the main room and laying down carpet remnants to make it possible to pray. They asked for God's blessings on the house.

Even with the percolating fear in the aftermath of 9/11, Ghorab had attracted a following for his spiritual venture within a few months. It was all word of mouth. One person from Aqsa told another. People brought friends. Ghorab was an excellent speaker, former congregants say, and he conveyed a sense of knowledge and wisdom that people, particularly immigrants from Arabic countries, wanted to share. "Ghorab was a very charismatic imam," said one man who knew him. "He was a dynamic leader and speaker, so he drew a lot of people to him."

"I heard the sheik speak," said another man. "I was doing *jumah* [Friday prayer], and he was very straight with me. He was very straightforward, and you could tell the truth of what he was saying. He was only encouraging people to learn to pray. Learn the proper way to speak Arabic, learn how to address people. The Muslim neighbor is the best neighbor. These are things in the Quran. Muslim neighbor is the best neighbor. Muslim person is the best person. If you have a sour disposition about yourself, you're not really understanding Islam. If you think that God almighty has chosen you to be a Muslim, and the Prophet, peace and blessings be upon him, is a beautiful man who teaches you how to live, you ought to be happy and satisfied and show gratitude to God and not walk around pent up and reserved. Show pleasantness because you have to invite people to the religion with how you behave and how you act. So if people see that you act and you're satisfied with yourself and you're fearing God and living in a loving way—men can be strong and be loving at the same time—this invites people to the religion. It's an attraction. The people, they become attracted."

This, affirmed Siddique, was Sheik Ghorab's primary message. He was teaching his congregation basic human and social relations: how to comport themselves on a daily basis. How to behave appropriately. How to live in accordance with principles drawn from the sacred texts. Study the Quran, Ghorab said, and a peaceful, harmonious life will emerge. And if bad or unexpected things happen to disrupt the harmony, the Quran offers ways to resolve the impasse, or it offers strength and solace to survive the troubles.

"The primary audience was Arab," Siddique said, recalling his early visits to the mosque. "He was teaching them. He was talking in Arabic, and they had a gentleman sitting down with a microphone translating into English. No—we hadn't had a microphone yet. We got that later on. He had us sitting down next to him, and he was saying, 'This is what the sheik is saying, and this is going on.' I was, 'Good, good.' It was a great thing. A lot of times people don't have the time to translate to you what is being said. From that day on I became a person who came here just to try and help out and because of the good, family, clean environment here. It's a good, good peaceful Islamic environment."

ATEF IDAIS, A YOUNG Palestinian who came to the United States from Hebron on the West Bank in 2000, a few months after Ghorab, used to translate the sheik's sermons for the assembled congregation, which may have been largely Arab but also included Somalis, Pakistanis, Senegalese, North Africans, and a smattering of Hispanics, Anglos, and African Americans. (Such a heterogeneous mix is not all that unusual in urban American mosques, which often exhibit a breakdown in ethnic distinctions that seem far more important overseas.) Idais eventually became ensnared in the collapse of Ansaarullah, his wife and small children traumatized, his finances in ruin, his life completely shattered because of criminal charges arising from student visa violations. But in the early days, he was a man of dreams, dreams of a life and family in America, dreams of a college education, a home of his own, a decent job with decent wages. Unassuming, very American dreams. He had planned to attend the University of Toledo, studying speech pathology, but when he arrived in the United States, violence broke out on the West Bank, his family's toy business was forced to close, banks were closed, chaos ruled, and money did not come from the West Bank to pay for tuition.

When the twenty-four-year-old Idais landed in Detroit (a key entry port for Middle Easterners) in August 2000, he also planned to marry a young woman he met in an internet chat room, Rrahime—an Albanian immigrant and permanent U.S. resident who lived with her mother and father, a staunch anti-Communist, in Philadelphia. Atef and Rrahime had engaged in a virtual romance—the internet serving as electronic chaperone—and by the time Idais stepped onto U.S. soil, the couple had already fallen in love. In fact, he came to the United States at her urging. You can come here, she said. Life is good. You can continue your education here. There are good schools and good jobs. I am going to school, and I'm going to continue, she told him. Where else could that happen?

Later, after it had all come crashing down and Idais was locked up for months on end, he told a federal judge how much he had yearned to come to the United States and how much of a symbol his visa application had been.

"I certainly remember the moments I enjoyed filling the application because I was in love with my wife and I wanted to come to this country and continue my education and meet a happy family, that's all," Idais told U.S. District Judge John Padova in a Philadelphia courtroom in 2005. "I remember even enjoying that moments of filing the application, and I also had another documents [*sic*] filed with the application that the government failed to bring forth too."

By that point, Idais was sitting in an olive brown prison jumpsuit, federal marshals standing all around him, as though he might leap up at any moment and require restraint. Such was never the case, of course. When he was floundering in the court system, Idais was a despairing, deeply disillusioned man who could not even begin to understand the relationship of freedom and law emerging in the United States.

But when Atef Idais first arrived in Philadelphia in the late summer of 2000, he found his love—a small, energetic, smart young woman of nineteen, with large dark eyes and a determined nature—and he was captivated. Their physical meeting confirmed their virtual love a hundred times over, Idais said, and they married in Philadelphia in October, moving in with Rrahime's parents.

Despite the fact that disorder spread on the West Bank following the visit of Ariel Sharon to Jerusalem's Al-Aqsa Mosque in September 2000, Idais says he still hoped to attend college relying on his family resources. His new wife, a diligent and dedicated student herself, was attending Philadelphia Community College and won a scholarship to attend Penn State. Idais, now based in Philadelphia and obviously not attending the University of Toledo, decided to apply to Temple University to study computer science. He loved computers and their technology, and while he believed that his initial plan to become a speech pathologist was an important and humanitarian goal, computers were, well, more fun. He was accepted into Temple at the end of 2000, but family money still did not come, turmoil still reigned on the West Bank, and while he visited and toured Temple, he never enrolled.

Idais was attending Philadelphia's Al Aqsa mosque when Ghorab worked there briefly in 2001, and he liked what he heard, sometimes to the point of tears. That was Ghorab's power.

"When he came to Philadelphia, he was first at Aqsa," Idais recalled. "He deeply took everybody's heart in his hands. Everybody loved this man. I remember his first speech was about parents. It was so unbelievable. After that first speech, I called my father and said, 'Dad, no matter what, I love you. I just love you.'"

Ghorab spoke about tribulations and how to weather troubles, and there were many troubles in those days. At Ramadan in 2001, Idais said, "Aqsa was loaded with people, and most of these people were coming to the mosque to hear this man." But some of the lay leaders of the mosque and school were not pleased with Ghorab, who believed the Quran's dietary and financial rules should not be violated. It is an old story of many, many mosques in America and elsewhere. But in late 2001, some Aqsa members said Ghorab's brand of Islam was conservative and not appropriate. Others whispered he was too political in a fearful time.

"They said, 'There are certain lines you cannot cross. You cannot say that delicatessens and restaurants and gambling are wrong,'"

Idais remembered. "Ghorab said, 'I'm the imam. I should be telling you what to do, not you telling me.'"

Ghorab left the mosque, said Idais, "and some people whose hearts were captured by him said, 'We are ready to help,' and they went with him."

That was in late 2001. A few months later, in early 2002, Idais was working a pizza delivery job—"which I hated"—when he learned that businessman Jabi Khatut was looking for someone who could handle office work. Idais contacted Khatut and agreed to meet him at a new mosque in Frankford Valley for an interview following evening prayer.

"I was shocked to know it was the same imam I knew from Al Aqsa," said Idais, recalling his surprise when he first entered Ansaarullah. "I didn't know him personally at that time, but I knew he was a man of wisdom, a very knowledgeable man."

Idais got the job from Khatut, and he began attending the mosque.

"Ghorab used to make lectures every day," Idais told me as we sat in the visitor's room of the Federal Detention Center in Philadelphia one day a few years after he first walked into Ansaarullah through the open bay door. "I liked the man. Everybody liked him. I know a man who approaches Islam the right way, and I know a man who approaches Islam the wrong way. I'm not fooled. I can't be because this is what makes me a better man. His lectures were about having faith in Islam, and I started attending every day, and I became close to people there. I liked the society."

Ghorab's preaching and advice, he said, had a major impact on many young men who attended the mosque. "I've seen a lot of guys, they never had a goal in life. By the end of the week, their money is gone. They have no goals. They started coming to this mosque and listening to this imam and began learning to respect each other."

The founding constitution for the mosque was simple: "There is none worthy of worship but Allah," it said, "and Muhammed . . . his messenger." The mosque, Ghorab pledged in the founding

principles, would remain independent "from all parties, organization[s] and governments" and would guard against "concepts foreign to Islam . . . which have marred the beauty of Islam and
prevented the advancement of Muslims."

The activities of the mosque were spelled out: Friday preaching
and lessons in the Quran. During Ramadan, daily breakfast and collection of *Zakat* funds—charitable contributions—for distribution
"to poor Muslims and Christians in the U.S." During Muslim Eid
days—holidays—the mosque pledged celebrations, including "toys,
candies and happy activities which bring delight to both children
and adults." Ansaarullah also established itself as a site for "the Islamic wedding ceremony" conducted by the imam.

This was hardly a stern environment. Ghorab has a good sense of
humor, say those who know him, and is mindful that a life completely made up of study is not necessarily a full life. His major supporters, including well-to-do Jabi Khatut, president of the mosque,
encouraged him to reach out to the community in all ways. So the
flyer went up around the Frankford Valley neighborhood: "Ansaarullah announces the beginning of sports activities! Soccer, table tennis, ground tennis and volleyball! Every Sunday after *Fajer* prayer."

"We would all bring our children here and our families here,"
Siddique said. "I was married here. And when my son was born, we
had something called Akika—it's equivalent of a celebration of the
child. I had my wedding party here. My mother, my sisters, my
brother, Christian ladies, they came, and I asked them to put a little
scarf on their head, and they didn't, my sisters and them didn't.
People knew it was my family. Every time we had things here, we always invited children from the neighborhood to come down. It's a
safe haven. If it's raining outside, let your children come and play
here. They come play; you don't have to worry about it. They come
inside and play inside. We always had balloons, games, Ping-Pong.
We were like a neighborhood recreation center."

Red, green, blue, and yellow balloons were tied to the old chain-
link fence around the mosque parking lot. The gate and the bay

door were always open. Children would come inside and play with the inflatable Elmo and the balls, and many people in the neighborhood were thankful that the mosque provided a place other than the street for children. Rasheed, age eleven, loved to come in and play Ping-Pong. Youssef, age ten, whose family lived down the street and had converted to Islam, would bring his friends in for pick-up football games.

"When the mosque was open, you knew your kid could go there and be away from the cars in the street, you know what I'm saying?" said one woman who lived near Wakeling Street. "Oh yeah, they was there a lot."

"We don't have anything anymore," said another neighbor, following the end of Ansaarullah. "They brought a big bag of rice to the door once, those Muslims. They didn't have to; it was just a nice thing to do. Not that we needed it." The woman asked me not to use her name because, like many others, she didn't want "any trouble." Trouble, she believed, follows saying anything decent about Muslims. Trouble from her neighbors who lived in the old, two-story row houses on her block. Maybe trouble from the cops. "You don't know," she said, growing increasingly anxious at having a strange person talking on her stoop. "You don't know what people are like around here. Some people just don't like nothing that they don't already know. Me? I say let a person speak for themselves. But just don't use my name."

Every Thursday, Ghorab arranged for community suppers, nothing fancy—rice, perhaps some chicken, bread. A few Yemenis liked to make a special flavorful chicken dish, which they would fuss over for hours. Moroccans had a taste for couscous. Sometimes simple fruit and salads were offered. Idais began dining at the mosque, too, enjoying the fellowship and watching attendance steadily grow. Not only members of the mosque or even Muslims attended. Non-Muslim visitors were welcome, people from the neighborhood. "Everyone could come," Idais said. "It was a place to congregate, for people to come."

He remembers particularly Ramadan in 2002. "That was beautiful for me," said Idais. "Every night we had breakfast at the mosque. Life was intact." More than a hundred would come for the evening meals, Idais remembered. The food was plentiful, and so were the talk and laughter. Children played with the growing number of toys, throwing balls, laughing. "It was the most amazing thing ever. The most beautiful feast I ever celebrated in my life."

BUT ALL WAS NOT right in the world outside, the world beyond the chain-link fence surrounding the old body shop. And because things were not right it was perhaps inevitable that federal law enforcement authorities became interested in Ansaarullah. Throughout 2002, the PENTTBOM investigation churned across the country, rapidly becoming institutionalized. A permanent state of investigation, with highly publicized raids and arrests, emerged as the post–9/11 world fermented and matured. In New York, many Middle Eastern and South Asian residents of Brooklyn told me that nightly arrests swept across their communities.

"In this neighborhood, maybe fifteen, twenty blocks it is, there were hundreds of people who are disappeared," said Ahsanullah Khan, known universally as Bobby, the director of the Coney Island Avenue Project in the Midwood section of Brooklyn. "The law enforcement agencies were tracking down every building, going door to door, every night, day and night. They, like, attacked this neighborhood. They would be waiting for the shift to change at the restaurant, waiting for the workers to come out. Targeting people in the restaurant. In the night, they would go door to door, and they would take them. It was horrendous. It was collaboration of immigration, FBI, and NYPD intelligence division. They were all working together."

The neighborhood, home to maybe 120,000 Pakistanis, was stunned, Khan said. "It was such a sudden attack. So sudden. People were not expecting anything." The sweeps, he said, created a paralyzing fear. "And that created big chaos in the community. But people wouldn't talk about it. When there was the huge crackdown and they were going door to door, people would not say, even if they have their loved ones, their friends and family members, they would not share what was happening, what happened last night—that their husband or loved one was taken away. They were so harassed." Fear of informers spread.

In Philadelphia, authorities made a number of raids and sweeps through immigrant enclaves. The poor Pakistani community of South Philadelphia, like the Pakistani communities in Brooklyn and elsewhere, was a particular target. One incident describes the whole. In the early morning on July 2, 2002, dozens of federal agents burst through the kitchen door of Nadir Khan's apartment on a shabby row-house block of South Seventh Street.

Khan, a truck driver and legal immigrant from northwest Pakistan, was taken into custody on suspicion, it later turned out, of heroin trafficking. For good measure, authorities rounded up his half dozen roommates, who weren't suspected of anything at all. At the time, an FBI spokeswoman denied that Khan or anyone else had been arrested.

Denial notwithstanding, Khan was in custody and spent the next seven months being shipped around the country from one prison to another, despite the fact that local and federal authorities were aware he was not the suspect they were searching for—Nadar Khan, a younger man with a different name and a different appearance. Nadir Khan was eventually pronounced cleared and released. In the meantime, his apartment, which remained open with a shattered door after the raid, had been stripped by thieves. His car had been towed and impounded. His job was gone. His roommates were deported. His son in Pakistan had been forced to leave school and find work to provide for the family. The whole episode was a personal disaster.

Authorities later admitted the arrest was an error. It appears that Khan's lawyers never argued in court that federal authorities had picked up the wrong Khan. "Those points should have been brought up to the court," Michael Shelby, U.S. attorney in Houston, told my colleague Gaiutra Bahadur. "Obviously the U.S. government has the obligation to arrest the individual who has been charged."

"This is a human process," he continued, "and obviously there are occasions where humans make errors."

The error, however, served to instill and fortify a rampant fear within the South Philadelphia Pakistani community, which includes a substantial proportion of illegal immigrants, like many poorer immigrant neighborhoods around the country. "Our people are in a lot of misery because of this," Sardar Khan, a local Pakistani community leader, told the *Philadelphia City Paper*. "People are scared to go out because of fear of capture." Why not complain to authorities? Khan was asked at the time. "Making a complaint will only make it worse," he replied.

"Any institution, and law enforcement is one of them, is going to go after the path of least resistance," Marwan Kreidie said when I asked him about the Pakistani situation. "Now the Philadelphia FBI and the Philadelphia police knew—I'm not patting myself on the back—but if they had picked up an Arab, I'd be on the phone: 'Tell me about what happened. Is there a reason? What's the reason? And we're going to get him an attorney and blah, blah, blah.' There isn't such an organization that works with the Pakistanis. So what happened there is they wouldn't get any resistance. This is my own interpretation—they're easy game."

Pakistanis and Bangladeshis—often poor, often beset by immigration problems, often overlooked by rights organizations—began fleeing Philadelphia in waves that intensified exponentially when the federal government announced its "special registration" program—the National Security Entry-Exit Registration System, or NSEERS—requiring resident males between the ages of sixteen and thirty-five from two dozen Muslim countries and North Korea to report to immigration authorities for photographing and fingerprinting.

Spreading massive confusion with its conflicting rules and requirements and deadlines, the registration program seemed deviously designed to force people into noncompliance. And noncompliance itself was a deportable offense. From September 11, 2002, when it was introduced—two months before Ramadan—to the fall of 2003, 83,519 immigrant residents registered nationwide under the program. Of those, 13,799 were placed in deportation proceedings, including many in Philadelphia. Immigration officials in the city said they could not determine exact deportation numbers. In other words, for complying with the law, 13,799 residents—nearly 17 percent of the registered total—were ordered out of the country. Slightly under 3,000 people were detained. This program, which has been modified but not eliminated, was supposedly implemented as a tool to fight terror—federal officials said NSEERS would identify terrorists. It is unclear, however, if any terrorists registered with immigration, as they were required to do, although federal officials have reported that eleven registrants were found to have terrorism "links." No explanations of just what those "links" might be have ever been offered. Nor have there been any terrorism-related convictions resulting from the prosecution of anyone swept up in the registration program. Needless to say, this program spread deep fear through Middle Eastern immigrant communities in Philadelphia and around the nation.

Immigration authorities added to the confusion. In Philadelphia, deadlines for filings and appearances were jumbled, and conflicting information was passed out to registrants—who faced the chilling prospect of deportation for doing what immigration authorities mistakenly ordered them to do.

"Some people were turned away," allowed Bill Riley, an official with the Philadelphia Bureau of Immigration and Customs Enforcement, after receiving heated complaints from those who sought to adhere to the law but were actually prevented from doing so by officials. "Something was wrong," Riley told the *Inquirer*.

For Stefan Presser, legal director of the ACLU of Pennsylvania, it was obvious what was wrong with the program: "This is being done in a chaotic, haphazard way," he said. Atef Idais, for instance, sought to do the right thing and was told by an immigration attorney that the NSEERS process "doesn't apply to Palestinians." This was simply not so. For those who navigated the maze and fulfilled their legal obligations, the result was an overwhelming sense of humiliation at the hands of a powerful state authority, a feeling many thought they left behind in their home countries.

"What happened with NSEERS, I think, was it was poorly put together and it was a mess at INS," said Kreidie. "It ruined trust with our community. But more importantly, you ask people to follow the law, and then they put you in deportation proceedings if you did. As I said over and over again, a terrorist isn't going to show up. And that's what it was publicly designed for—to identify terrorists. It compounded the feeling that the Bush administration was doing this anti-Muslim, anti-Arab agenda. What they were doing in LA, where probably the worst was, they were taking sixteen-year-old kids away from their parents and detaining them. It was horrible."

There were mass detentions of Iranians in Los Angeles, with over five hundred people swept up, disappearing into the maws of the immigration holding system. It was so disturbing that volunteer lawyers and others stood outside immigration registration centers wearing yellow shirts with "Human Rights Monitor" printed on the back. They took the names of those who entered the center and checked them off when people emerged. Those names not checked had been detained. Disappeared. The same in New York, several attorneys complained to me.

"We didn't have that here," Kreidie said. "Although some were detained. We had an incident: I got a frantic call over the weekend from this woman whose boyfriend had transferred to a suburban school, had to report to NSEERS, showed up, and because his papers hadn't made it from one school to the other school, they detained him. Now the problem was, this woman, all she heard, he called her up and said, 'I'm going now; I'll call you up in a couple of hours.' And he wasn't allowed to call. So she had no idea for three days what had happened to this person. And he was taken to York. He was detained, and they shipped him out immediately to York."

Hearing these kinds of stories, I couldn't help thinking of places like El Salvador and Chile, Argentina and Guatemala, where citizens in the 1960s, 1970s, and 1980s were at risk of simply vanishing. And many times the American government had criticized countries in Soviet Eastern Europe for similar disappearances. In the old Soviet Union, where my father was a correspondent for many years and where our family had many friends, it was always a possibility that someone would vanish between one visit to Moscow and the next. Now American citizens were putting on the saffron shirts of human rights workers and seeking to keep tabs on vulnerable residents in the United States. I could not recall anything even remotely similar in my experience—not during the 1960s, when government surveillance and undercover police activity sought to smother the antiwar and civil rights movements, and not during the 1950s, when so-called Communists and leftists were blackballed, arrested, and harassed.

A new class of American residents now began to emerge: displaced persons, internal refugees fleeing the American government.

Philadelphia's South Seventh Street enclave of Pakistanis emptied out quickly, largely as a result of what residents say were numerous neighborhood immigration sweeps. First came the vigilante revenge attacks and the FBI interrogations in the immediate wake of 9/11. Immigration authorities quickly got on board. A typical incident, in the spring of 2002, involved federal agents who stood on a street corner and pulled aside anyone who appeared to be South Asian. Pakistanis were questioned; their Southeast Asian neighbors were not. "They asked for everybody's papers," one man told the *Inquirer*. "Everybody but the Cambodians." South Seventh

Street was transmuted from home to no-man's-land. Criminal investigations of jewelry kiosks, supposedly involved in money laundering, netted more suspects ripe for expulsion. The NSEERS special registration program decimated the small community.

The few local leaders who would speak to me didn't beat around the bush. "People are terrified, and they wanted out," said one man. More than half the neighborhood seemed to vanish overnight. Atlantic City, which had perhaps 2,000 Pakistani residents prior to 9/11, saw that number cut in half within two years, community leaders, the *Inquirer* reported.

There were about 500,000 Pakistanis in the United States at the time the twin towers and Pentagon were attacked, a quarter of them concentrated in Brooklyn. But by the end of 2003, as many as 50,000 to 60,000 had been jailed, been deported, or fled New York City, according to community activists and immigration attorneys. By 2004, according to estimates compiled by Pakistani filmmaker Abdul Malik Mujahid, some 90,000 Middle Eastern and South Asian Muslims had been interrogated or investigated by federal authorities in the United States. Officials acknowledged arresting or detaining 6,500 and deporting 3,200, Mujahid maintains; conservative nongovernment estimates put those figures at 15,000 detentions and arrests and 3,200 deportations. At that point, there had been about 13,400 voluntary deportations, and Mujahid says that at least 50,000 have fled the country in fear. There is no way to confirm these staggering figures, but they are plausible. The numbers of those removed from the country were so large that the government chartered passenger jets to carry crowds of deportees. "There were seventeen to Pakistan alone," Bobby Khan, the Brooklyn activist, told me.

The Pakistani embassy estimated that a more modest 15,000 Pakistanis had left the country, including 1,480 deportees, according to a 2004 report published by the Immigration Policy Center, a division of the American Immigration Law Foundation in Washington. Jagajit Singh, director of programs at the Council of Pakistan

Organization in Brooklyn, estimated that "the community has lost about 20,000 people, of a total of about 150,000 to 200,000," according to a survey conducted by his group. In addition, more than 5,000 Bangladeshis fled the country in 2002, according to an estimate supplied by the Bangladesh embassy.

In the waves of post–9/11 crackdowns, people made hasty and frantic efforts to leave Brooklyn. Neighborhood residents reported goods left on store shelves, plates left in cupboards, even clothing left in closets. Families just up and ran, as though Vesuvius had erupted. One account claimed that fifty children had been pulled from the local elementary school during the fall semester of 2002. Workers found that their bosses had been arrested or had fled. Jobs disappeared with them. And, of course, children were separated from parents. "It's dead here," Pervaiz Saleem, owner of a Brooklyn grocery, told *Newsday*. He looked around two years after the Trade Center attacks and saw a skeletal community. "My customers, so many of them did get interrogated, were deported, or just fled. People disappeared."

"This country betrayed us," one man, still in the United States, told a local Brooklyn reporter in 2003. "Why did I leave my country, my relatives, my home? Because over there is no freedom, and over here is much more freedom. But not now. Over here is no more freedom."

The situation seemed little better in the summer of 2005, when Charles E. Frahm, head of the FBI's counterterrorism division in New York, convened a community meeting at the Bukhara Catering hall on Coney Island Avenue. Frahm told those who gathered in the hall that he wanted to air the issues "and hear what you have to say."

According to accounts of the meeting, Frahm kicked off by stating that "a proud cornerstone of the United States Constitution is to ensure civil rights are protected, including freedom of religion." He then added: "But I can say we make no apologies for the actions we must take to protect America. We must be able to obtain information to help you in this room. We service everybody in this room; it doesn't matter if they are a citizen or not. But I also need your help to keep America safe."

Khurrum Wahid, a civil rights attorney, laid out the community's complaints: profiling, capricious "watch lists," and multiplying informers. There is "a serious lack of trust" between the government and Muslim American residents in the aftermath of 9/11, he said. Police and federal agents had undermined that trust by recruiting informants—often informants with deportation orders—to spy on their neighbors and fellow worshippers. In return for cooperation, Wahid said, these informants have been offered the prospect of green cards: looming deportation transformed into legitimate residency as if by magic. Authorities declined to discuss their investigative techniques; suspicion continued on the street.

IN BROOKLYN, I SPOKE with a Pakistani who worked construction and lived in Midwood for many years. We were standing in a sweets shop, cases displaying baklava and a seemingly infinite variety of honeyed pastries. Gourmet Sweets used to be so jammed there was no room to sit, he said. Cars double-parked on the street outside. On the wintry day I talked with people inside, late in 2008, there were no lines and plenty of tables.

"It is much different now," the man, whose name was Mohammed, said of the neighborhood. "It was much better. Now 50 percent of the people are gone from here. Everybody got scared. You see everybody is gone. Business is gone. When you come here to eat any time before, you cannot park here. Now you can come anytime, and you can park anytime. Before there's a line all the time here. People have no jobs, nothing now. I went to Canada six months ago. I went to Toronto; I saw all the people from New York! Same neighborhood. They moved there. Everybody knew me! How many people know me? I go there, everybody. They have shops; some people have business. They think it's better. But, you know, they used to make good money here."

War produces refugees, and we are at war, as law enforcement and government officials said to me repeatedly. The displaced persons and immigrants, from the congregants at Ansaarullah to fearful residents of South Seventh Street, said this is no war: This is the powerful crushing the powerless. For the powerless, sometimes the only answer is to run. Some refugees settled in other, less visible parts of the country. Many sought to immigrate to Canada, as Mohammed told me. During 2001, Canadian authorities reported 44,500 asylum applications, 3,200 from Pakistanis. According to some estimates, 5,000 Pakistanis fled to Canada in 2002. By 2003, border crossings were seeing double and triple the 2002 numbers. Fear trumps cold every time. Fear of the United States even trumps fear of dictatorial and unpredictable Pakistan. Travel agents in Brooklyn's Pakistani neighborhoods reported surges in tickets to South Asia in the aftermath of 9/11. A Sudanese travel clerk told the *New York Times* in 2003 that he had seen a ratcheting up of emigration. "When they come," he said, "they ask for a one-way ticket because they have to go. We don't ask them questions."

I mentioned the emptying out of Pakistani neighborhoods in Philadelphia and Brooklyn to Anser Ahmad, Mohamed Ghorab's Harrisburg attorney, at one point in 2006.

"Wow! I've heard of cities that are pretty much desolate; a lot of the Detroit population has moved," he said. "What I've noticed is an influx into this area, Central Pennsylvania, and also into Maryland. Muslims moving in. Now I've talked to them, and I hear this over and over again: The majority of them are coming from New York and some of these other areas. So it's almost like if you're not leaving the country, then go to some place that's rural where you're not going to have this glaring eye watching every move that you make. But yeah, the number of Muslims in this area has increased— I know in our mosques, I'd say by at least 20 percent, an increase in families living in the area."

At a suburban Philadelphia mosque, I met a man in early 2009 who had fled to Canada in 2002. Canadian authorities told him he could not remain and gave him the option: return to the United States, where he had no visa, or to his home country of Bangladesh. He returned to this country and was arrested in Buffalo and now faces deportation. He has children who were born here. His wife lives here. It is a very typical story.

By late 2008, the nightly sweeps in Brooklyn had passed into history, at least for the time being. But neighborhood activists told me informers were everywhere in the mosques and on the streets—as they had been for over four years. In one instance, documented in a court case, the New York Police Department alone had three paid informants and undercover agents attending services at a single mosque in December 2003. There is no indication that the extensive surveillance has moderated. That said, some Pakistani businesses have revived, but the number still appears down sharply from pre–9/11 levels. Boarded-up stores still lined parts of Coney Island Avenue in Brooklyn's Midwood at the end of 2008. Russian and Jewish businesses were prominent on the street, where once Pakistani shopkeepers and groceries thrived.

With mosques now infiltrated with informers and arrests continuing throughout the past eight years, though at a declining rate, the atmosphere of attack that once defined Midwood in the wake of September 11 has been replaced by a dull sense of siege and a resolve to live, somehow. The fear, though, is still there beneath the surface, Bobby Khan told me. "But when it is too much, it exceeds the limit. People start living with it: 'Fuck. We've got to live.'"

FOUR

We Don't Know If He Was an Informer

A T ANSAARULLAH, SEVERAL CONGREGANTS said that toward the end of 2002 and the beginning of 2003—around the time of Ramadan—federal agents began watching activities at the mosque. At least one informant—possibly several—was in the mosque by early 2003. "Absolutely," said one former member when I asked about the possibility. Looking back, "there's no question in my mind," he said.

Whether those informants were people ensnared by the special registration program and were told they could help themselves by passing along information about their fellow congregation members cannot be known with certainty. Federal officials decline to discuss it. Local authorities suggest, however, that more than one person attending the mosque was passing information back to immigration agents and the FBI. That would hardly be unusual—informants have played a major role in investigations of drugs and organized crime for decades, and informant-driven investigations were emerging as the standard operating tactic in the war on terror. The difference here, however, is that federal agents were not investigating organized mobsters or gangs suspected of specific criminal activity, but members of a community and of a religious group attending regular services—ordinary people who were suspects because they were Muslims and Middle Easterners living in America and practicing their religion. All information, regardless of source and reliability, was apparently now in play. The only remotely similar situation would involve the decades-long infiltration of the Communist Party, labor unions, and "subversive" organizations by the FBI and other law enforcement agencies.

My family was familiar with that history, and as I spoke with Siddique and with others connected to Ansaarullah, I found myself continuously reminded of how easily community is subverted and relationships undermined. It was this shock of personal familiarity that finally awakened me to the cultural continuity represented by the war on terror. Freedom threatened leads defenders to threaten freedom. When has it been otherwise?

In the fall of 1968, in the wake of disruption, turmoil, strike, and arrests, I returned to classes at Columbia University on Morningside Heights in Manhattan. The previous spring had seen the entire university shut down by students angry with the war in Vietnam, angry over racism, angry with the university's complacent and direct involvement in the whole bloody mess. For years Columbia had maintained a quiet leadership role with the Institute for Defense Analyses (IDA), a weapons research organization affiliated with the Department of Defense. When Bob Feldman, a leader of Columbia's chapter of Students for a Democratic Society (SDS)—the key antiwar activist organization on campus—exposed that relationship, the university tried to discipline its way past protests. But the increasing ferocity of the Vietnam War and the intransigent incompetence of university administrators made that impossible. Then at the beginning of April 1968, Martin Luther King was assassinated, and the deadly turn of the civil rights movement was brought home to the nation at large. At Columbia, anger turned to a gymnasium the university was building in Harlem's Morningside Park. A back door of the large facility allowed neighborhood residents access to a small portion of the building, but that was hardly enough in the charged climate—a climate fueled by years of university contempt for the poorer people of color in the surrounding community. "Gym Crow must go," echoed across Morningside Heights.

Opposition to the war and institutional racism fused in these two issues and students, including me, spontaneously began taking over buildings, shutting down the university, demanding a halt to gym construction and a severing of IDA ties. Over a thousand police tried to put an end to the weeklong protest and building occupation, storming the campus in the early morning hours of Tuesday, April 30, beating faculty members and students, and carting hundreds off to the Tombs.

The Columbia demonstrations and subsequent student and faculty strike—dramatic, focused, virtually unprecedented—inflamed colleges across the country, raising the stakes immeasurably in the antiwar struggle. Hundreds of building occupations and strikes followed, and the school year limped to a close.

Late one afternoon the next fall, with the wind cutting hard off the Hudson River, I walked down Broadway to an apartment house on 110th Street to see some friends. Several of them rented a big place there, and as usual, there were lots of people I knew just hanging out talking, as well as one guy I had never seen before. He was tall, blond, and mustachioed and wore a red bandana, blue denim work shirt, and jeans. He said his name was Jason. He didn't go to Columbia; in fact he wasn't in school anywhere. He was just there. The sixties saw a lot of drifting, a lot of people who were just there, and over the next several months, Jason seemed always to be around, listening, blending into the black light.

One day, I asked Bob and David, who rented the place on 110th Street, about this guy. Who is he? Where did he come from? Oh, yeah, they said, don't know where he came from. Where does anyone come from? He's just Jason, Jason the Cop, an informer.

That seemed more than plausible to me—even though Jason hadn't done anything and Bob and David had a tendency toward goofy and melodramatic irony. It was obvious, I thought; of course he's a cop. The university was riddled with spies and snitches. There were plants from everywhere—the FBI, the New York City red squad, army intelligence, probably the CIA, too, we thought. Who knew who was pretending to be a student or a street radical? Who knew what grudges faculty members or even fellow students might bear and act on with stories crafted for the police? The pretenders were everywhere. Or so it seemed.

Even parents had their impersonators, as many arrested students found out when their families received anonymous antiradical letters signed "Father of a 'busted' ex-student." Years later, a memo surfaced revealing that this particular father was employed in the FBI's New York field office. Since the letter went out to the homes of parents of arrested students, it demonstrated that university officials were providing personal information directly to law enforcement authorities—only the university had family addresses of those hundreds of students. Bob Feldman, the former SDS leader and an indefatigable researcher, told me that police agents were watching his parents' home in Brooklyn, interviewing their neighbors, and acting on information they could only have obtained directly from the university registrar's office. Bob's police file, obtained nearly twenty years later, even contained information indirectly confirming that personal information in the possession of law enforcement authorities had been obtained from Columbia officials. Other student FBI files suggest the same. No subpoenas were necessary. The university was simply being helpful—just as many universities freely passed along information on students in the wake of 9/11.

The difference today, of course, is that virtually all of that student information had been protected by the privacy laws enacted in the wake of the Columbia disturbances and the federal surveillance abuses of the 1960s and 1970s. Post–9/11 legislation then undercut the protections. Once an abuse is obviously not always an abuse, just as one man's torture is another man's enhanced interrogation.

IN THAT DUPLICITOUS COLUMBIA environment, Jason easily became a symbol of infiltration and the object of edgy jokes. No one talked about practical politics around him, although I do remember some demonstration planning in his presence—all made up, bogus events for a bogus activist.

Looking back now, it seems to me that nothing is more hostile to and destructive of university life than a culture of surveillance and informing. A college depends on trust and the free exchange of ideas—the first casualties of spying and the suspicion of spying. Columbia, under the pressure of significant political events, cracked open, and into the fractured spaces poured an untold number of grifters on the police payroll. That's what it seemed like at the time, and once that perception prevailed, the mission of the university was subverted.

Infiltrated communities outside the academic environment are subverted in the same way. What can be more destructive of community cohesion—which is, after all, what a larger society is built on—than the undermining of personal trust between individuals? When neighbor suspects neighbor, when friend fears friend, natural social bonds are severed, daily life teeters, and police and government intrusion become of paramount import. Routine, ordinary affairs are then recast in ominous political terms. Why is this man asking questions? Why is this man evading questions? What is he trying to find out? What is he trying to conceal? Why did that woman bring up such a subject? What should I say?

At the Ansaarullah mosque in Philadelphia, congregants came to believe that all activities, all conversations, all associations were at risk. Those connected to the mosque were ultimately unable to live their lives freely, feared gatherings, avoided each other, spent their days afraid of being charged with what they perceived as their ethnic and religious identities recast as immigration transgressions, and finally were unable to practice their religion at all. One person would suspect another—for no reason beyond planted or imagined fears. In Philadelphia; in Lodi, California; in Brooklyn; and in countless Middle Eastern and South Asian communities in America, the certainty of informers in the midst of daily gatherings at coffee shops, bookstores, meetings, and religious services has sown suspicion and mistrust and undercut the essence of the nation's self and identity. Within dissident political communities in Florida, Denver, New York City, and Philadelphia, for that matter—the same.

This is not to say, obviously, that sowing mistrust and making liberal use of informants has no value in specific criminal cases, although every prosecutor and law enforcement investigator well knows that informers present unpredictable dangers. But when government penetrates the independent political and religious realm—not to mention ordinary communities—threats to the social fabric become acute. And that has certainly proven to be the case since 9/11—just as surely as it was during the days of the civil rights and anti–Vietnam War movements. These circumstances mark the most basic corruption of democracy.

No one knew if Jason was really a cop—he was simply perceived to be one. And maybe that was the point. Virtually all political meetings and forums at the college were open and publicized. Attendance and publicity were essential. There was no real need to infiltrate. But fear of spies works for police as well as the reality of spies does, and agents were always happy to have antiwar activists believe that the FBI was "behind every mailbox," as one Bureau memo from those days put it, whether or not informers or covert agents were actually there. For students this was unsettling at best: A bad day and angry words directed at the wrong person might easily translate into a new dossier page in the vast library of Babel maintained in the clandestine law enforcement universe.

My friend Peter, who was very active in radical politics at the time, told me that it was simply assumed that police attended all SDS meetings. That didn't prevent Peter from speaking at meetings and proclaiming "what I believe," he said. But if plans were afoot to disrupt a hearing or some event, "I'd keep that to myself." Informers were not an issue for radicals who subsequently went underground in the 1970s, he went on, for the simple reason that disguised activists were emulating "a normal person living in a normal neighborhood."

"We were all so careful and safe," Peter said. "Nobody ever got close." An underground radical had his or her own completely secret self—a mirror of the cloaked secret selves of informers.

Mark Rudd, SDS leader at Columbia and a key figure in the formation of the radical Weathermen in 1969, had little direct experience with informers. They were, however, in the air. By 1969, he recalled, the "intensity of the repression" against radical groups, particularly the Black Panthers, "increased to the extent that it was assumed that we were being infiltrated and surveilled."

"Later, the full extent of [the FBI's counterintelligence program] COINTELPRO came out, but we certainly suspected it existed at the time," Rudd told me when we spoke well after 9/11. "But it didn't slow us down, possibly because we were young and willing to take risks, and possibly because we were white and middle class and didn't believe there was anything we couldn't survive. In the run-up to the [formation of the] Weather Underground, for example, we said in public meetings exactly what we intended to do. I am quoted as saying, as late as December 1969, at Flint, 'what a wonderful feeling it might be to kill a cop.' Sheesh, that doesn't show much . . . inhibition due to infiltrators."

Whatever the recklessness of Mark's rhetoric at the time—rhetoric that he has come to regret deeply and reject—here he has focused on the critical difference between what we faced at Columbia and what the congregants at Ansaarullah and all Middle Eastern and South Asian immigrants face in the here and now: identity. We were young students of privilege, responsible for ourselves and nothing else. Yes, there were sometimes deadly consequences—students were gunned down at Jackson State University and Kent State University as the country's mood soured and bristled in the wake of Columbia. But those were exceptions. We still saw freedom and power in the streets. Where are the freedom and power for those at Ansaarullah? The streets are to be feared—women are attacked for wearing veils; men are arrested for traffic infractions. A misstep means more than suspension or expulsion from school. It can quickly turn into destruction of a family, deportation, the obliteration of lifelong dreams, the scattering of an entire community. In a sense, this was the aim of the infamous and shadowy COINTELPRO program Rudd referred to.

COINTELPRO—a bland name that cloaks so much disruption, disorder, and pain—is the label the FBI slapped on a series of convulsive secret programs designed to "disrupt" and "neutralize" domestic groups and individuals, according to FBI memos from the time. It went way beyond investigation, way beyond surveillance, and deep into the netherworld. The Senate's historic 1976 Select Committee on Intelligence, chaired by Senator Frank Church, which probed domestic intelligence abuses, eventually published thousands of pages on COINTELPRO operations and provided a succinct description of the whole. "The techniques were adopted wholesale from wartime counterintelligence," the committee reported. Such techniques ranged from "the trivial," such as mailing reprints of *Reader's Digest* articles to college administrators; to "the degrading," like sending anonymous poison-pen letters intended to break up marriages; and on to "the dangerous," such as encouraging gang warfare and falsely labeling members of a violent group as police informers. These often-illegal activities were formalized in the mid-1950s and were first brought to bear on the Communist Party. They were subsequently turned on the Socialist Workers Party, then on what the Bureau called white "hate" groups like the Klan and so-called black "nationalist" groups, such as the Panthers and the Southern Christian Leadership Conference, led by Martin Luther King Jr. The last COINTELPRO, which formally ended in the early 1970s, was directed against the New Left and students. The object, ultimately, was to destroy and render irrelevant. In some instances that led quite directly to suicide and murder.

The self-immolation of SDS in 1969 and the eventual transformation of one faction into the Weather Underground—a group that vanished off the grid and carried out bombings of government and corporate facilities and, most flamboyantly, engineered the 1970 escape of LSD guru Tim Leary from a California prison—was in part triggered by such law enforcement pressure across the country, Rudd said. Blacks, it seemed, were particularly at risk. What should the role of white radicals be when the government itself appeared to be taking dead aim at effective black leaders? What role should students play in the urgent Vietnam drama? These were not abstract questions at the time. Indeed, one of the main purposes of the COINTELPRO operations was, in the words of a March 1968 memo from Hoover's office to agents in the field, to "prevent the rise of a 'messiah' who could unify, and electrify, the militant black nationalist movement." The memo went on to say that "Malcolm X might have been such a 'messiah'; he is the martyr of the movement today. Martin Luther King, Stokely Carmichael and Elijah Muhammed all aspire to this position. Elijah Muhammed is less of a threat because of his age. King could be a very real contender for this position should he abandon his supposed 'obedience' to 'white, liberal doctrines' (nonviolence) and embrace black nationalism. Carmichael has the necessary charisma to be a real threat in this way." Such would-be messiahs needed to be neutralized and the country cleansed, like tainted water.

Informers riddled civil rights groups, most notably the networks around the Southern Christian Leadership Conference and Dr. King, and more militant groups, particularly the Black Panther Party and the Student Nonviolent Coordinating Committee, where Carmichael started his political journey. But informers were employed everywhere possible in the black community. By the mid-1960s, more than 7,000 paid informants were operating within one nationwide FBI program alone, the Ghetto Informant Program. And that number is quite apart from the regular informal contact programs the Bureau maintained with organizations and individuals in the field, a figure that would, at the least, push the number of working informers into the tens of thousands. The number of law enforcement information sources skyrockets when local police are added to the mix. One cop in a community could have scores of casual informants and could run them for just about any purpose imaginable.

At the federal level a single political informant could be very productive. One who worked her way inside the Vietnam Veterans Against the War, for instance, produced enough information for 1,000 separate FBI dossiers. M. Wesley Swearingen, an FBI agent who joined the Chicago field office in 1952, said a quota system was developed there in the 1950s. Every agent had to work five informants for information on subversion. "I mean, the idea sounds great, if you get X pounds of information or a number of documents that you can fill out from two informants, then if you have three hundred agents in Chicago with five informants, then you have fifteen hundred informants, so you're going to have tons and tons of material that you can send back to Washington," Swearingen said, in a 1998 interview.

Beginning in 1967, Hoover ordered the creation of new lists of individual targets—Americans who, in the Bureau's view, were "vociferous rabble-rousers." What was a rabble-rouser? "A person who tries to arouse people to violent action by appealing to their emotions, prejudices, etcetera; a demagogue," according to the director. In practical terms it meant "black nationalists, white supremacists, Puerto Rican nationalists, anti-Vietnam demonstration leaders, and other extremists." The Bureau launched the Rabble Rouser Index of names. It was followed by the Agitator Index, a "Key Activist Program," and a "Key Black Extremist Program." All people on such secret lists were subject to intense and ongoing scrutiny, at the very least. Bank accounts were monitored. Tax returns were evaluated. Informers were sought to report on private lives. "Continuing consideration must be given by each office to develop means to neutralize the effectiveness of each KBE," agents were ordered, referring to black leaders across the political spectrum.

In 1970, the Bureau targeted black student unions at colleges across the country (the Columbia demonstrations were led by SDS and the Student Afro-American Society) and quickly managed to get 4,000 cases up and running—thanks to informer diligence. Informers working in black groups could surely have deadly effects. William O'Neal, an FBI informant who agreed to infiltrate the Black Panthers if federal authorities dropped felony car theft charges against him, provided critical information for the December 1969 Chicago police raid that led to the shooting deaths of Black Panther leaders Fred Hampton and Mark Clark. Those killings, I should say, were the immediate reason for Rudd's remarks in Flint, Michigan, just days later. The killing of Hampton and Clark seemed to him clear evidence—if any more was needed—that police were systematically targeting blacks, killing off the leaders. If that doesn't amount to war, he thought, what does?

In such an atmosphere, for Rudd and many others, the course to take was simple and direct: Only violence could counter violence. A more radical, covert organization, one willing to resort to sometimes explosive force, was deemed necessary to counter the perceived government threat. (There are scattered reports of a law enforcement focus on Muslim student unions across the nation's campuses today. How serious and coordinated this might be remains unclear.)

It seemed to me four decades ago that radical political activity was evolving into a madness. The FBI and radical organizations enwrapped each other in a bizarre embrace. I well remember the national SDS convention at the Coliseum on Chicago's South Side in the summer of 1969. Some friends and I stopped there on our way to San Francisco, knowing that often-byzantine factional infighting was destroying the organization, yet sensing that this was a momentous event in the evolution of dissident politics. The convention climaxed when one group, led by Rudd, Bernardine Dohrn (a graduate of the University of Chicago Law School), and others, walked out—marking the fractious end of SDS and the birth of Weatherman.

What struck me, however, was the sheer number of police atop buildings ringing the convention, all armed with cameras and very long telephoto lenses. Hundreds were watching the splintering movement, recording every face going in and coming out, as though Ho Chi Minh and his entourage had come to town. At the entrance to the convention I looked up, and on rooftops, shoulder to shoulder, men with cameras peered back—documenting a perfectly legal gathering of students from around the country. There were undercover police on the sidewalks, too, trying to chat people up. And, despite efforts to keep undercover police and informers out of the actual SDS meetings, covert operatives dotted the Coliseum floor, probably several keeping tabs on each of the multiplying factions. I remember sloughing it all off—there was nothing illegal about endless arguing and bickering.

Sure enough, many years later, FBI reports—stamped top secret—were made public describing in great detail what went on inside the dilapidated rooms of the Coliseum that June, testimony to Bureau doggedness, if nothing else. While the reports I've seen give a sense of the hostility between SDS factions, they soft-pedal some of the most lurid and controversial comments. I remember a session when a leader from the Black Panther Party likened the women's liberation movement to "pussy power." (In one typically prim FBI informant's report, that was rendered as "P (obscene) power.") Another Panther speaker said the position of women in the movement should be prone. Truly vicious arguments over the relationship between blacks and whites, men and women, action and analysis bounced off the walls. And then the Weatherman faction had had enough of the pointless and debilitating talk. It was time for action.

In the wake of this self-destructive chaos, we left Chicago and headed for San Francisco, spending several months in Berkeley, home of the University of California. Radical street politics dominated life there—whether one was looking for it or not—and the town was infused with high tension. Earlier in the year, police opened fire with shotguns as an unruly crowd demonstrated over the university's decision to transform a community park into a parking lot. One bystander was killed, another was blinded by double-ought buckshot, and over a hundred people were treated at local hospitals for shotgun wounds and other injuries. Governor Ronald Reagan called on the National Guard to impose order and enforce the university's "property rights" over what had come to be called People's Park.

On July 14, several weeks after we arrived, demonstrators managed to cut down the chain-link fence surrounding the park by using wire cutters baked into loaves of bread—a clever and defiant Bastille Day act that quickly escalated into random and nasty street fighting. Police fired tear gas grenades at demonstrators on Telegraph Avenue. Demonstrators hurled them back. Helicopters swooped over the university, Berkeley was smothered in acrid gas, and police made dozens of what appeared to me to be completely random arrests. This was all way beyond political action; police and anarchist street people, flinging tear gas back and forth, were engaged in pure ritual—the rest of the community be damned. In the wake of the SDS convention, it was even more disturbing—violence divorced from any discernible substance. Campus activism in the sixties had been born in Berkeley with the emergence of the free speech movement, led by the brilliant Mario Savio, in 1964. The university had banned political activity on campus; students resisted. But by 1969, the town was awash in hippies and runaways and heads. Telegraph Avenue had become a gauntlet of panhandlers. Undercover agents and informers were everywhere. During the Bastille Day demonstration, I saw a fist fight break out off Telegraph Avenue when one young man was accused by several others of being an agent provocateur employed by the Alameda County Sheriff's Office. He was knocked to the sidewalk by about half a dozen street people. Police moved in and tried to make arrests. It was impossible to escape the suffocating stench of tear gas anywhere in the town.

And then who should show up but Jason the Cop from Columbia. There he was, palling around with kids on the streets of Berkeley. Had he followed us? Had we mentioned this is where we were heading? Was Berkeley simply a sixties mecca? Why was he here? Coincidence? Just checking out the scene? He was not welcome in the little house I rented with several other friends, and he faded away into the paranoid street scene. Perhaps there were richer veins for him to mine elsewhere in that chaotic and unhappy town.

I was troubled by Berkeley's formal chaos and what it represented politically. What did this have to do with Vietnam, or with SDS for that matter? SDS was gone. At a time when violence in Vietnam was escalating, the most astute activists on campus were reacting not to the war or the need to bring it to an end, but to American police and undercover police activity. The delusion that the United States could be brought to its knees was a dangerous one, but was it less dangerous than avoiding confrontation with government forces bent on eliminating all opposition? Who would be left to resist when all resistance was obliterated?

"Overall," Rudd continued, "the decision to destroy SDS and create the underground was a reaction to the repression, that we felt it was war and the only possibility of survival of our movement was clandestinity. That might explain why I wasn't worried about what I or anyone else said at Flint: We were on our way under."

LARRY GRATHWOHL WAS AN infiltrator who went underground—albeit relatively briefly—one of a tiny few, if not the only federal informer who penetrated beneath the surface. Grathwohl was a working-class kid, Vietnam vet, and, in 1969, finally a student at the University of Cincinnati. He spent about nine or ten months with Weatherman and its clandestine successor, the Weather Underground, reporting first to local police and then to the FBI. Grathwohl's undercover work led to a few arrests and, by his own account, a foiled bombing in Detroit. In April 1970, however, police blunders blew his cover, although he worked with the FBI on stakeouts and surveillance for a couple of years after that. At the height of his involvement, the FBI paid him $125 a week for his services. But Grathwohl says money was not what motivated him. He viewed Weatherman as essentially totalitarian, seeking to impose its political views on everyone else and willing to resort to random, even fatal violence to achieve that end.

"The FBI had no people that had actually been prepared to deal with the youth," Grathwohl, now in his early sixties, told me. "Back in 1969, the FBI's experience in dealing with counterespionage was limited to the Soviet threat. Most of those guys walked around in coats and ties. Now all of a sudden they've got long-haired, hippy, degenerate freaks that they've got to deal with. And the FBI still had a code that you still had to wear a white shirt and a tie to work every day. And I happen to know that for a long time they didn't even tell Hoover about the existence of what was commonly referred to as the 'mod squad' [a hipper-looking Bureau unit], which was a play off the TV show. These guys were not prepared. I was prepared."

A lot of people were prepared, I said. A lot of people opposed radical groups like Weatherman. Yet not everyone turned undercover informant. Why did he?

"Vietnam," Grathwohl replied. "You see people die. Innocent people. Women and children. Bombs go off, shrapnel hits. . . . And these people [the Weatherman group] were planning on wreaking that same sort of grief and turmoil, and they made that very clear."

Grathwohl cited the still-unsolved bombing of the San Francisco Golden Gate Park police station in February 1970, in which a police officer was killed; a failed plan to bomb the Detroit Police Officers Association building in early March 1970; and the explosion in a Greenwich Village townhouse, also in March 1970, that left three members of Weatherman dead. All evidence of the organization's malevolent intent, in his view.

"I was in Detroit when the plans were made for the bombing of the Thirteenth Street DPOA building." He worked to foil the plot unobtrusively, he maintained. Weatherman was also responsible for the fatal Golden Gate Park bombing, he said, although no creditable evidence has ever emerged to back this claim and no charges have ever been filed. "I was told what had actually happened at the park police station in San Francisco," he said.

Indeed, during the 2008 presidential election, Grathwohl emerged from obscurity and gained some media notoriety when he charged that Bill Ayers was the source of this information and that Ayers's wife and sixties comrade in arms, Bernardine Dohrn, placed the bomb that killed a police officer. When I spoke to Grathwohl in 2007, however, Barack Obama was only marginally better known than his acquaintance, former Weatherman leader Ayers, now a Chicago educator. Grathwohl made no specific charge about San Francisco in our conversation, although he clearly disliked Ayers. (Ayers and Dohrn have denied any involvement in the Golden Gate bombing. "We killed no one and hurt no one," Ayers said in a November 2008 *New Yorker* interview.)

"The townhouse blown up in New York City, it was allegedly a bomb factory, and I believe that it was," Grathwohl continued, citing the most well-known instance of Weatherman-related violence—a self-immolating disaster that killed three young members of the organization, including my Columbia friend, Ted Gold.

"So they were attempting to do this. Now on what scale it would have ultimately come to—I don't know if they had been successful."

For this undercover federal operative, then, Vietnam was the motivation to do what he was doing—just as Vietnam was a major motivating force behind the rise of the New Left and, ultimately, Weatherman. It is indeed a mirror world. I was losing friends in the jungles of Southeast Asia and on the streets of the United States. Perhaps, then, it isn't surprising that Grathwohl said he liked many of the radicals he dealt with, which caused him a great deal of stress. He still thinks about Diana Oughton, dead in the Greenwich Village townhouse explosion. Could he have said something to steer her away from violence and the dead end of that building? He wonders about it even now.

"In psychology they call it cognitive dissonance," he said, describing the emotional tension of operating undercover. "I spent many sleepless nights. Not over fear over what was going on around me—and there was reason to be fearful at times because of the explosives in the vicinity. But just knowing that certain individuals I had grown to be friends with, fond of, if you will. Fond might be a little too emotional, but you know what I mean. Friendship. And you have to deal with the fact that you're turning around and going to the FBI and telling them about their activities. But keep in mind that the goals of this organization . . . were that of strategic sabotage. That they could put a bomb in the grocery store that my mom or my kids were in, and they could get hurt. And while thirty-eight years later it might seem ludicrous, but then, especially as close to it as I was, it seemed like something they might actually do and be successful at. And of course they did with the park police station."

On the other side, Grathwohl's activities ultimately spawned anger, fear, and contempt after his cover was blown. An account printed in the *Berkeley Barb*, the underground newspaper, in August 1970, captures the riptides of his betrayal:

Larry is working hard to re-establish his identity as a revolutionary in Movement circles around the country; his rage and protests against our charges [of informing] are loud and clear. It's possible that people who don't know the facts will be taken in by him, and will lead him to further chances to destroy work that's going on, and the people who are doing it. . . . Pigs like him are, literally, wired for sound, and anything—ANYTHING—you say to him can be used against you in court, in a new Grand Jury indictment, or whatever. If Grathwohl stays in circulation, Berkeley'll probably get too hot for him soon— he'll move on to a place like Portland or [Isla] Vista, where his pig identity isn't well known, and where kids would be inclined to trust a tough, smooth-talking revolutionary who pulled a knife on the FBI when they were busting Linda Evans. We've got to spread the word about Grathwohl all over the country, and cancel any chance of that happening. Agents like Larry Grathwohl are viciously fucked up.

In contemporary dissident circles, exactly the same sentiments are expressed about a woman named "Anna Davies," an undercover informant—and, in the accounts of many dissidents, a provocateur— involved in government investigations of radical environmentalists and self-styled anarchists. (Her real name has not been publicly disclosed, even though she testified in the 2007 Sacramento trial of environmentalist Eric McDavid. McDavid was convicted of conspiring to bomb federal facilities.) Spread the word. Know your enemy. Keep your mouth shut, even with friends.

W. Mark Felt, the FBI's former associate director—and more recently famous as the unmasked Deep Throat of Watergate, an informer himself—once told Grathwohl that the success of his undercover work could not be seen. It is a comment that prefigures many made about post–9/11 antiterror surveillance and counterintelligence activities. "I suppose the significant thing is something Mark Felt told me," recalled Grathwohl. "You never know the degree to which I had succeeded because it was measured by what didn't happen, not what did."

Grathwohl believes the FBI saw his value, ultimately, as a witness in cases brought against radicals. He testified before a grand jury proceeding in Detroit that led to the indictment of a dozen Weathermen on conspiracy charges related to bombs in four cities. In addition to his old comrades, the indictment named Grathwohl himself—an effort to reestablish his radical credentials, he said. In 1972, he testified in San Francisco before another grand jury exploring more Weatherman conspiracy charges. Nothing came of either case, and the government ultimately abandoned charges. Grathwohl was not pleased. The Weathermen "were more dangerous . . . than when I first met them," he believed. But federal investigators apparently determined that proceeding with the cases endangered "foreign intelligence information deemed essential to the security of the United States," he said, still puzzled by what that actually might have meant thirty-five years ago. Perhaps, he speculated, the decision not to proceed related in some way to other undercover political investigations, part of continuing efforts to link radical American groups to foreign guerrilla movements.

One night in Buffalo in early 1970, Grathwohl met secretly with two FBI agents who took him to a dilapidated shed on the shore of Lake Erie to meet a tall man in suit and tie who, the agents said, was an Arab guerrilla fighter. They introduced him as "Ali Baba." Grathwohl later wrote that Ali Baba questioned him in detail about Weatherman and said he wanted to be the man to establish contact between them and Fatah, Yassir Arafat's Palestinian guerrilla organization. "He suggested I become more aggressive in pushing the Weathermen to make international ties," Grathwohl said in his account of the meeting. "This would enhance my chances of being sent on foreign missions, and I might be able to arrange to meet Ali Baba, thus creating a link with the Arabs." Fatah wanted to show it could "strike anywhere," Ali Baba said. There was talk of terror attacks at the Spokane World's Fair in 1974. There were plans for violence at the 1972 Olympics. He provided no details beyond a warning that Arab guerrillas thought nothing of killing. Grathwohl's FBI handlers whisked him away. Who was this mysterious Arab who spoke English with a British accent? Was he working for the CIA? No answers.

After all the Weather Underground indictments were dropped, Grathwohl found himself wondering if "Ali Baba" and similar provocative covert agents were a factor in that decision. He never found out, not even after eleven Israeli athletes and a German police officer were killed in the attack on Israeli athletes at the 1972 Munich Olympic games. Did the government somehow fear that its foreign covert agents might be put at risk by trials of Weathermen in the United States? How could that be? Or was it fear that the government effort to push domestic groups into foreign terror entanglements might itself be exposed?

Neither, probably. The indictments were dropped for the simple reason that the government had obtained a considerable amount of information from illegal surveillance. Wiretaps; microphone surveillance; opening, photographing, and resealing mail; illegal burglaries and searches—all were employed. In one infamous incident, a suspected radical was confronted in the Chicago SDS office by door-smashing police, threatened with defenestration, and then hung by his ankles out a window several stories above the street. The police wanted information; their target, however, had nothing to say.

In late 2008, William C. Ibershof, chief of the criminal division in the Eastern District of Michigan who became Weatherman prosecutor in 1972, underscored once again that illegalities had riddled investigations of radicals like a disease. Weatherman indictments were dismissed, he wrote in a letter to the *New York Times*, "because of illegal activities, including wiretaps, break-ins and mail interceptions, initiated by John N. Mitchell, attorney general at that time, and W. Mark Felt, an F.B.I. assistant director."

BACK AT COLUMBIA, the belief that police were secretly on campus, a belief first born of caution, grew steadily and, as campus politics radicalized, blossomed into paranoia. Who was on the NYPD or FBI payroll? Who was simply soaking up and passing along information about SDS? Whom could you talk to? Who was wired? Such was college life in New York City, circa 1969. FBI and police documents indicate that informers within the political groups and even in the university administration were passing information to authorities. Identities of those attending meetings on campus, what was said by whom, what occurred at closed disciplinary sessions following various demonstrations—law enforcement agents were privy to all. One FBI memo from 1972 states simply: "By way of information, a number of students and members of Students for a Restructured University, opponents of SDS tactics and the disruption of classes, voluntarily appeared at the [FBI's New York Office] to offer their assistance during the disruptions, but only a handful of faculty members out of 4,900 called the NYO."

Collusion between university officials and police was deep and multifaceted. New York City police, for instance, were allowed access by administrators to a closed 1967 Columbia disciplinary hearing held to determine what to do with eighteen students who staged a sit-in to protest and prevent CIA recruiting on campus. The police memo that detailed the hearing lists not only those charged with the sit in; it helpfully provides the names of over seventy additional students and faculty members who supported those accused of violating a university regulation. Faculty members seemed particularly irksome to the NYPD's Bureau of Special Services. When students occupied buildings in April and May 1968, plainclothes police attacked several faculty members with blackjacks and saps. The first bloodied professor was Richard Greeman, an assistant professor of French. He sympathized with the goals of the students, as I recall, and police were well aware of his political activities and seemed to head right for him. Greeman's name crops up in NYPD files as early as 1965, when he spoke against U.S. involvement in Vietnam at a campus meeting. Seven others spoke at the meeting, which "ended without incident."

"The files of this command," the police memo continues, "have been amended to include the names mentioned in this report" (including "Richard Greeman, French Teacher, Columbia University").

Greeman now lives in France, and I asked him if the police went after him during those demonstrations long ago. No, he said, they went after those who were simply there. He was on the front lines and took the hit. Greeman soon left Columbia for another teaching position, but not, he said, because of blackballing or political pressure applied by higher ups in his department or in the Columbia administration. There is some doubt that the same can be said for younger faculty members in other departments. One now-prominent professor, a brilliant teacher and fine writer, failed to obtain tenure in the English Department, ostensibly because of budget problems that beset the university following 1968. Many suspect that conservative senior department members wanted him out. Others in that department, all markedly more sympathetic to students than senior faculty, met the same fate. Among younger, leftist department members, Edward Said, on sabbatical in 1968 and absent during the demonstrations and strike, seemed to be one of the few to weather the storm. Said would go on to become a leading literary theorist and prominent advocate for Palestinian rights.

At the Columbia law school, Gus Reichbach, now a distinguished member of the New York State Supreme Court, kindled considerable resentment for his participation in the building occupation, strike, and antiwar activities. So much so, he told me, that his entrance to the New York State Bar Association was blocked for two years. In the judge's recollection, Richard N. Gardner, a Columbia law school professor who went on to become President Carter's ambassador to Italy and President Clinton's ambassador to Spain, "wrote a jeremiad against me" to the character committee of the bar association. The professor may have been inflamed, Reichbach said, by Mark Rudd, who called him "some names" during a disciplinary hearing.

In any event, Gardner "testified against my admission before the committee and lined up a few of his law school colleagues against me," said the judge. But Reichbach had his defenders, including Professors Curtis Burger and Telford Taylor, and was eventually admitted to the bar.

(In later years, the judge has been known to quote from his government files during trial. "'The subject'—that is me—'is one of the most dangerous people known [in] the SDS,'" Reichbach recited at the onset of a 2007 trial of an FBI agent accused in the mob murder of informants. Not surprisingly, the judge was quoting his characterization by a 1960s FBI informant. Reichbach "'is an extremely powerful speaker and has a strong charismatic appeal,'" the memo concluded. "I've always appreciated, indeed proudly cherished, that characterization, even though it was not meant by the FBI to be flattering," Reichbach told the courtroom.)

Several professors I spoke with over the last several years believed there may have been informers in their midst but could not name them; others said it was all a constructed fiction of paranoids and romantics. Reichbach has no doubt there were informers. "Certainly after '68 and into '69, people became aware and operated on the assumption that all larger meetings were infiltrated," he said. (Both FBI and New York police memos indicate clearly that informants were active on campus and routinely supplying information and names to law enforcement authorities from the mid-1960s.)

That there were police agents on the campus full-time seems beyond question. In fact the university has a long tradition as hotelier for law enforcement, dating back at least to the early days of the Cold War more than half a century ago.

John Gerassi, a professor of political science at Queens College, vividly remembers a class he took at Columbia in 1951, when no one wanted to debate whether China should be admitted to the United Nations. Many students were happy to take up the case for Taiwan, but when the professor asked for volunteers to argue the case for the Communist mainland, no one stepped forward. Gerassi was hesitant to take the role—at the time, his family was fighting a deportation order—and asked the professor whether "you have to agree with the position, or can you just argue?" Assured he could simply argue in support, Gerassi signed on for the Mainland.

After the class, an older student approached him. "He said, 'Let's talk,'" Gerassi remembered. They walked toward John Jay Hall. "He says, 'You did a good job in there. You better watch yourself. I'm not going to report you, but there are lots of people like me who might.'" The man went on to say that he worked for the FBI. Not only that: The Bureau was covering his tuition. It seems that this student could not afford college on his own, but a helpful employer arranged a meeting with a Bureau agent at a coffee shop.

"We can get you into the college of your choice in the area," the agent boasted at the meeting. Gerassi's confidant said he was excited by the prospect and suggested City College. "No," the agent replied, "we don't need anyone there. We already have a lot." They settled on Columbia, with the Bureau picking up tuition and providing spending money in exchange for regular reports.

"That's how I remember it," said Gerassi, adding that the professor teaching the international politics course had subsequently been fired for refusing to testify before one of the many anti-Communist committees sprouting up across a dank political landscape.

"I was stunned when he told me that he had to report on a student or a faculty member every week," said Gerassi, referring to his informing confidant. "I watched myself very carefully after that."

I am not aware of any operation during my Columbia days as extensive as the one described by Gerassi fifteen years earlier—one that bears a strong resemblance to the covert watching in today's Muslim and immigrant neighborhoods. But you don't know what you don't know.

Mark Rudd, who always projected a kind of amiable bravado, believes that informers and surveillance had a minimal effect at Columbia, serving mostly to stir up paranoid anxiety. Police and federal agents wanted people to believe they were hardwired everywhere, he said. Disinformation. There was, for instance, a story in the *New York Times* published in May 1968, purporting to describe the exploits of a New York Police Department undercover agent at Columbia. Frank Ferrara, a recent police academy graduate, supposedly spent two months on campus as a scruffy faux student. The culmination of his assignment, the paper reported, came when he busted Rudd.

Not true, says Rudd. "I never met or saw Ferrara in my life," he said. The story of Ferrara's campus activities "was entirely made up to make them look better. Pure PR."

That's plausible. But the *Times* also reported that a "Francis Ferrara" was a registered student at the Columbia School of General Studies. A year later, in a May 1969 front page story, the *Times* described Ferrara as Rudd's "trusted bodyguard," which was a laughable unattributed assertion, no doubt ginned up by the police themselves, as Mark suggests. The *Times* did quote one "investigator" on the subject of the national organization: "The S.D.S. can't be a dangerous organization as long as we know what they are up to. So we keep watching it. Nothing the S.D.S. does surprises us." This investigator, speaking with utter assurance, went on to note that SDS was becoming more "conspiratorial," hurting the appeal to "hippies and people like that who think everything should be wide open and who are afraid of political secrets and secret political planning. I think the conspiratorial mood is hurting S.D.S. a lot." That may be, but investigators gave no hint that they had a clue that within a month SDS would suffer a national meltdown in Chicago.

There were other undercover police besides Ferrara who surfaced from time to time at Columbia. Steve Goldfield remembers one at a demonstration on 114th Street. "He was pointed out real early, and he was actually the one who arrested Mark [Rudd] and I," Goldfield recalled. "I was on the steps standing next to Mark, so he came up and handcuffed us together. We were the only ones in handcuffs at that bust. He didn't do anything to us. In fact, when I entered court, he was the one who said to the DA, 'You should drop the charges against him'—because I would have been acquitted if I showed up at trial—'but in the interest of justice we're going to proceed against the other 141' [arrested]."

Goldfield doubts informers penetrated the leadership of SDS on campus, and none have ever been identified (although I have seen an FBI memo that claims an informant was close to radical leaders inside Low Library, occupied by students in 1968). "It's possible they had an informer in" SDS leadership, Goldfield said. "But I don't remember any nonstudents around. The people that in my year were active, people like Ted Gold, Ted Kaptchuk—we'd all known each other for years. So somebody suddenly showing up would have stood out. I doubt that they saw anything threatening at Columbia."

Someone must have seen something at Columbia because FBI and police documents show that close surveillance of SDS political activity on campus goes back at least to 1965—information gathering clearly designed to scoop up names that could be transformed into separate dossiers. FBI and police documents tied to the Columbia disturbances and related political activities are full of hundreds of pages of meeting sign-in sheets—names, addresses, and phone numbers, largely redacted from the federal documents, all representing people tagged like deer by government watchers. And the 1968 demonstrations at Columbia certainly provoked Hoover and contributed directly to the launch of the Bureau's disruptive COINTELPRO efforts aimed at the New Left on campuses across the country.

A memo went out from headquarters to FBI field offices in May 1968, as Columbia still roiled and the contagion was spreading to other colleges:

The most recent outbreak of violence on college campuses represents a direct challenge to law and order and a substantial threat to the stability of society in general. The Bureau has an urgent and pressing responsibility to keep the intelligence community informed of plans of new left groups and student activists to engage in acts of lawlessness on the campus. We can only fulfill this responsibility through the development of high quality informants who are in a position to report on the plans of student activists to engage in disruptive activities on the campus. In view of the increased agitational activity taking place on college campuses, each office is instructed to immediately expand both its coverage and investigation of campus-based new left groups and black nationalist organizations with the objective of determining in advance the plans of these elements to engage in violence or disruptive activities on the campus.

The Bureau couldn't actually define something as amorphous as the New Left, and I don't know that I could or would even want to undertake the effort. One Bureau memo described it as a "loosely bound, free-wheeling, college oriented movement." Another said it was "more or less an attitude." The special agent in charge of the New York field office mused that "the New Left embraces philosophic dicta from every point in the left spectrum—communists, socialists, nihilists, Castroites, Maoites—all mixed together with political screwballs of every description." This colorful definition, far hipper, if not more accurate, than most of those coming from Bureau headquarters at the time (Hoover, caught in language from an earlier era, wrote that the New Left was a "subversive force" bent on destroying "traditional values"), also opened up a virtually limitless field for informants to plow—right at the time Washington was pressing agents for more information on campus disturbances. The agent who supervised the Bureau's New Left activities likened the Washington attitude to hysteria:

During that particular time, there was considerable public Administration—I mean governmental Administration [and] news media interest in the protest movement to the extent that some groups, I don't recall any specifics, but some groups were calling for something to be done to blunt or reduce the protest movements that were disrupting campuses. I can't classify it as exactly an hysteria, but there was considerable interest [and concern]. That was the framework that we were working with. . . . It would be my impression that as a result of this hysteria, some governmental leaders were looking to the Bureau.

I ASKED MY FRIEND Jim, a student at Columbia in the late 1960s, about Jason the Cop.

"We don't know he was an informer," Jim said. "I remember the guy, but there was never any testimony, never any busts."

That didn't matter. In those days, virtually everything could be seen through a political filter. Did you drink at the West End, with writers, radicals, heads, and pukes? Or did you eat a Special Steak at the Gold Rail with straights and jocks and the war-hawk crowd? Suspicion lay right below the surface, and if someone just wandered into a scene and became inordinately friendly—even in complete innocence—a label could be slapped on as quick as a pair of cuffs. Jason had a label, warranted or not.

It was ultimately debilitating, Jim said. In 1971, tired of New York, he headed up to Boston, a city with a large group of radical activists clustered around the colleges.

"I remember going to a [political] meeting and listening to people, and then I said something—I don't even remember what it was," Jim recalled. "Five minutes later the guy running the meeting said, 'This guy's a cop.' He was pointing at me. People looked at me and said, 'This guy's a cop. What are you doing here?'

I looked around and said to myself, 'What *am* I doing here?'"

That was the essence—and the dubious success—of the informing culture. People came to question each other; they suspected anyone and everyone. Normal bonds of trust and accord were shredded. And then people began questioning themselves. Jim saw the change sweep over the landscape. He walked away.

"People started being afraid of everyone," he said. "I never went back, and I left Boston after two weeks."

As I remember Jim, he never seemed particularly suspicious or circumspect, despite the increasingly claustrophobic environment, though that may be a trick of memory. He was not any kind of ringleader. The threat he posed for the government was the threat of ideas, not physical violence. Jim was a kid who believed the war was wrong and that racism was embedded in American institutions. He articulated his beliefs and acted on them. That seemed to me then and it seems to me now—in an increasingly passive culture—a quintessential American attitude.

Sometime later, long after the war was over and SDS radicals had resurfaced from underground, Jim filed a Freedom of Information Act request with the government.

"I got my FOIA file," he told me. "It was pretty thick, and everything was blacked out but my name. There were bits here and there. They were convinced that I was an aboveground conduit for the Weather Underground. I wasn't. But they were convinced I was."

With informers come files. And files take on a life of their own—as Jim learned with some dismay. Bad information—obtained from who knows where by unnamed informants with who knows what agenda—become codified and permanently stored, an alternate identity salted away. Such files are really shadow constructs, looking-glass portraits that lampoon and ultimately undermine the living world. The sixties saw a massive increase in files and in the armies of informers needed to feed them; obscure government storage rooms became repositories of caricatures, all squirreled away, waiting for the day, any day, when character might usefully be transmuted into caricature by the reductive alchemy of surveillance. Computers were also just coming into use for storage, a faint prefiguring of the powerfully computerized and networked surveillance environment today. But use of computers hardly guarantees the accuracy of data stored—only its bulk and the speed with which it can be disseminated.

Steve Goldfield, who graduated from Columbia in 1968, cites a number of typically wrongheaded items from his own government file. In the early 1970s, agents interviewed his parents' former neighbors in New Jersey (just as Bob Feldman said his parents' neighbors had been interviewed).

"So they were doing this one investigation to see, I guess, if I was safe to work in the post office," said Goldfield. At the same time, another set of agents was investigating Weatherman, and one day Goldfield received a phone call: "Bob from the FBI and I want to talk with you."

"I said, 'What do you want to talk to me about?'" said Goldfield, who was never involved with Weatherman at all. "He said, 'The Columbia riots.' I said, 'I have nothing to say about it.'"

That was the end of it—or at least that's what Goldfield thought until he saw his FBI file. "It relates a long conversation, that never happened, in which I say my political activities were part of my youthful days and I've given all of that up," said Goldfield. "I think he was just trying to close the file. But they made up this whole conversation, and it's in my file." Absent from the files, however, was any mention of Goldfield's subsequent work as a printing jobber for the Panthers, he told me.

Jim was not any kind of conduit for the Weather Underground, whatever that may mean. Yet that became his identity on the informer landscape, carefully preserved by government clerks and, eventually, information technicians. He was not part of the Weather Underground. He was not a violent radical. But he opposed the war and supported others who felt similarly. For this, his name entered the law enforcement data universe. It is a typical story. In the effort to capture self-appointed revolutionaries who eventually fell off the map into the underground world, the government scooped up, parsed, and saved information on literally tens of thousands of others—who decidedly had not fallen off any maps and were living in a supposedly open society. By far the bulk of arrests by local police and the FBI relating to antiwar activity in the 1960s and 1970s involved people like Jim, not anyone engaged in actual illegal activity, not anyone moving with "clandestinity," as Rudd called it. Just people.

My FATHER HAD SEVERAL secret files stashed away in the bowels of the FBI, the National Security Agency, and the CIA—and used the Freedom of Information Act to go after them in the late 1970s. Thousands of pages of largely pointless information were eventually released to him (press clippings comprised a substantial portion of the material). But the NSA refused to divulge any information whatsoever, citing national security concerns, a position upheld by federal district court following a lawsuit. My father was deeply concerned about such surveillance—it undermined his credibility as a reporter, particularly in the totalitarian states he had covered for much of his life. He had assured so many cynical and doubtful sources in the Soviet bloc of complete confidentiality. He had repeated over and over to friends in Moscow and Budapest and Ulan Bator that the United States government kept its fingers out of news gathering. Now he encountered disturbing suggestions hidden away in his files—almost-graspable shadows cast by government watchers and listeners. "I am now in a position of a fool, openly shown to have been gulled by my own government," he wrote his attorney, Mark Lynch, in November 1980. "The shock is frankly clear and profound. . . . If, as they say, they are recording secretly everything you transmit, what else are they recording?"

And it is worse than that, he told Lynch. "On the private side we suddenly discover that in the hands of the government via the NSA are or can be the entire content[s] of my private and personal communications by electronic means over the years with members of my family and my most intimate friends. To what use this information may be put or may have been put for purposes of influence or blackmail I have simply no way of ascertaining. But I can only proceed on the assumption that I have no privacy."

Within the piles of paper he did obtain, all of it redacted to a greater or lesser degree, there was a striking absence of information generated by his many years in the Soviet Union at the height of the Cold War and of anything related to his reporting on the U.S. bombing of Hanoi during the Vietnam War. No doubt, he believed, this information was being withheld, if for no other reason than it indicated the vast inclusiveness of the monitoring. What can be said is that, in 1954, following his return from years in the Soviet Union, the Eisenhower administration ordered a sweep of data and information on Harrison Salisbury, and the Johnson administration did the same in 1966, following his reports from Hanoi documenting American bombing of civilian targets. What the sweeps turned up the NSA kept to itself. The FBI, privy to the information, declined to provide any, in deference to its sister agency. But reading the files that have been released one sees the Bureau scooping up information from virtually any source that walks in the door, drops an anonymous letter into a mailbox, or makes a provocative phone call. All was taken in and squirreled away—to be selectively parceled out when convenient.

The redacted report following the Hanoi trip, for instance, notes that the Pulitzer Prize–winning articles written by my father when he returned from the Soviet Union in 1954 "reportedly presented the Soviet Union in a favorable light." It also cited a 1954 *New Leader* article that said Salisbury "sees everything in rosy hues." A 1955 memo, regarding an investigation of someone else, reports that the Bureau contacted my father early one morning and he made no secret of his annoyance. Nor would he agree to cooperate. "He gave the distinct impression he has the right to know the identity of the source of derogatory information," the memo notes. Not only that: "He at no time expressed or indicated a willingness to cooperate and suggested by his statements he is not in sympathy with the program of security investigations of individuals."

But an informant at the *New York Times* had no problem passing along my father's private personnel records to the Bureau, which is noted in a heavily redacted memo.

Certainly one of the most interesting and hair-raising stories that emerged from the documents concerned a series of events set in motion in 1940. That summer, unbeknownst to my parents, a neighbor informed the Mamaroneck police that my father was a German code expert working for the United Press (UP) and that his house was filled with radio and electronic equipment. The police, dubious, nonetheless broke in and found nothing. My parents were away at the time, and the woman watching the house for them wrote with the news that there had been a burglary but nothing apparently had been taken. Some papers seemed scattered, and an old trunk in the basement had been opened.

That was it. The police dismissed the case but informed the FBI, de rigueur practice on the eve of war. An FBI agent made a report, and the Bureau's New York office placed the matter aside, clearly believing it was nonsense. The informer, local police determined, was a gossip whose family was made up of "nefarious prevaricators." But another Bureau agent in the New York office nevertheless forwarded my father's name to Washington for inclusion on J. Edgar Hoover's list of "Persons for Custodial Detention: Internal Security"—a Hoover-inspired compilation of those who would be summarily arrested in a time of emergency. This was the dark list, based, it would seem, on rumor and caprice, certainly not fact.

When my father was about to leave for London to head the UP's bureau there in 1943, he found his passport was mysteriously blocked; only after great effort involving numerous agencies and the UP was it released. All of this was the result of the unfounded story from the nefarious prevaricator—which remained secret until he received his FBI files thirty-five years later. Those same files showed the same story appearing in numerous summary memos, at least into the 1970s. A 1963 memo, for instance, reports that Salisbury had been identified as "in the employ of the German government" during the war, although the information came from a source reported to be "totally unreliable." My father found memos with the same information still being written in 1974.

Not only did the story persist, migrating from file to file, but the secret Custodial Index, ordered destroyed in 1943 by Francis Biddle, attorney general, was simply renamed by Hoover, continuing on, a simulacrum of the undead. The successor list, the Security Index, was ordered destroyed by Congress in 1971. But it simply morphed into the Administrative Index and the Reserve Index. Lists never die. Nor do the stories and names they contain.

My father described the whole affair in a memoir as "a trivial matter" but "for two chilling facts: The placing of my name on a list for 'Custodial Detention' and the possibility that to this day, so far as I have been able to ascertain, it may still be carried on one of the secret FBI lists."

I NEVER SOUGHT OUT any files on myself, a reflection of my withdrawal from the political edge, I suppose. The New York City red squad files were supposedly destroyed in the 1980s as part of the settlement of litigation over the department's disruptive surveillance tactics. Many COINTELPRO files were also supposedly destroyed. A friend of mine said I popped up on a number of meeting lists in some federal files he obtained in the 1970s. Perhaps. Despite the supposed destruction of masses of files, I have managed to get hold of some SDS dossiers compiled by the New York police (thanks to the diligence of Bob Feldman and the pack-rat habits of Mark Rudd), as well as the FBI files on Ted Gold, a friend and Columbia SDS leader who was killed in Weatherman's accidental March 1970 bomb blast. (A cache of FBI files and documents, including Ted Gold's dossier, has found its way into the Bryn Mawr College archives, thanks to author Susan Braudy.)

Ted's files, stacked on a table, stand at least a foot high. Even Larry Grathwohl contributed to the Bureau's clandestine shadow biography. Intellectual and essentially mild-mannered, Ted seemed ill-suited for a role as radical firebrand, let alone murderous bomber. But opposition to the rising horror of Vietnam pushed him to take stronger and stronger positions against the government and the war, until misguided efforts led to tragic death in the Greenwich Village townhouse explosion. Ted's heavily redacted file is full of descriptions of meetings, speeches, names of friends, telephone numbers, organizations—all meticulously detailed by Bureau agents, informers, and memos derived from electronic surveillance.

One typical memo describes a meeting at Columbia's Fayerweather Hall in 1967, attended by 150 people, to discuss the upcoming antiwar march on the Pentagon. Everyone at the meeting was a student, the memo says, "all dirty beatnik, semi-hippie type." Not only that but "all white except for 6 negroes." Blackboards in the classroom were "covered with anti-US, anti-war slogans and meeting notices (mostly outdated). All rather violent and many obscene in phraseology."

Gold was threatened with suspension from Columbia for his role in the 1968 disturbances. But the FBI began gathering information on him in earnest in 1967—his whereabouts, the whereabouts of his parents, the names of his friends—all in preparation for placing his name on the illicit and supposedly destroyed Security Index, which at this point represented a list of those deemed by the untethered Hoover to be so dangerous to America that they would be incarcerated if politically necessary. At that time, Ted Gold had been arrested once, for protesting a speech by Secretary of State Dean Rusk in New York City.

Yet none of this cascade of information, when I read through the hundreds and hundreds of pages, provided any meaningful insight into who Ted Gold was and why his journey took him from intellectual organizer (in 1967) to maker of bombs (in 1970). Here was a kid who loved basketball and baseball, made up funny satirical songs, thought deeply about racism and American ideals—now making bombs planned to obliterate other human beings at a dance at Fort Dix. The key insight into Gold's evolution—and the comparable, if less dramatic, evolution of millions of others opposed to the war— eluded government spies and is glaringly absent from the thousands of pages in his file. What had pushed Ted so far? The dossier is silent on that key question. In fact, such fundamental insights are absent from virtually all files and dossiers built up on students, radicals, and African Americans in the 1960s and 1970s. All that paper, all those reports and lists of names, are really flags of a different purpose, as Rudd suggested: the desire to sow suspicion and mistrust at Columbia and other institutions, to subvert political activity in Harlem and in other black communities, to disrupt opposition to government policy, to build up other dossiers, and to keep tabs on those who would be arrested if necessary. Ultimately, it all amounts to information gathered for its own sake, pieces of a puzzle impossible to complete, a dark foreshadowing of what is currently happening in communities around the United States, including Philadelphia—the shadow world of computerized databases in their infancy.

FIVE

Brothers

AT THE FBI's PHILADELPHIA headquarters, Assistant Special Agent in Charge Brian Lynch sat down in his office one day in the late fall of 2005 and told me that all information was potentially important information, all leads were potentially important leads, and virtually any activity could be considered suspicious and worthy of investigation.

"Every lead that comes in from the public gets addressed, and that is done through the JTTF," Lynch said, referring to the Joint Terrorism Task Force. Jerri Williams, the Bureau's public affairs officer, sat on a small couch opposite Lynch. She nodded her agreement. No off-the-record discussion here. Information is gathered in by the Bureau; rarely does anything come out without careful orchestration. That, of course, has been a hallmark of all federal investigations growing out of PENTTBOM and subsequent 9/11–related probes. Initially, in the immediate wake of the attacks, many suspects and potential suspects were rounded up and shipped to jails with no charges and no notice. Families had no idea where husbands, fathers, brothers, sons could be. Lawyers in some cases were prevented from speaking with clients, and some were told that clients were not in custody—or if they were in custody, their whereabouts were unknown. Hearings were sealed, preventing press and family members from observing proceedings, and then evidence was withheld, routinely it seems, from defendants—all justified by the all-encompassing needs of national security. In the name of security, how many have been rendered insecure? Not one of those cases—and they number in the thousands—has resulted in a substantive terror conviction.

On this day, the FBI's Philadelphia office was opened a crack for me; every response to every question was slow and measured; nevertheless, more information was withheld than given out, and specific questions about specific cases were dismissed without comment, or the responses were swathed in generalization. After only a few interviews with officials at both the FBI and the Bureau of Immigration and Customs Enforcement—universally known as ICE—it became glaringly clear to me that there is a generic script used to give the appearance of providing information; in actuality the script serves to deflect inquiry and cloak actions of investigators. No meaningful information is disclosed. An arrest is its own justification, it seems. Officials make much reference to the "toolbox" of laws and investigatory techniques that they have at their disposal, as though the country itself is a broken-down old house and law enforcement, arriving with its now bulging box, is capable of diagnosing the problem and selecting the right chisel or drill or hammer to shore up the roof or stop the incessant seepage in the basement.

What tools are in use, and what malfunctions are being addressed? The fixers keep that information largely to themselves. Trust us, they maintain, if you only knew what we know. And we never find out, nor do the suspects who are shipped out of the country in almost every instance on administrative visa violations.

That said, Lynch is a dedicated, earnest, and soft-spoken agent who came to Philadelphia in 2003 from the FBI office in Columbus,

Ohio. He was not on the scene in the city when 9/11 hit and local police provided a modicum of protection to local Muslims, but he has sought to maintain open lines of communication to Philadelphia's Middle Eastern community, visiting Al Aqsa mosque on several occasions and speaking there publicly.

The Joint Terrorism Task Force, a cross-agency investigative and field group, was radically expanded in the wake of 9/11, Lynch said. Revenue agents, immigration and customs officials, and agents from such widely scattered organizations as the federal air marshal service, the Pennsylvania State Police, and the Philadelphia Police Department are involved—over a hundred members based in Philadelphia alone. Many of the FBI's agents were pulled from their traditional crime areas and thrown into the antiterror campaign. Lynch calls it an "all-star team." And they go after, as he said, every lead.

"So let's say there's a suspicious person at Seventh and Market," Lynch continued. "It comes in to the FBI, it goes up to one of the squads, and those squads are managed by a supervisor. That lead then gets assigned to a person, and that person can be an IRS agent, a Secret Service agent; it can be a Coast Guard Investigative Service agent—we have the Coast Guard on the task force—it can be an FBI agent. They go out and address that lead. That lead gets addressed until it's resolved. Every lead that comes in, and this is for the entire division—it goes out to Centre County, Pennsylvania, and three counties in South Jersey, that's my division—this division is responsible that it gets covered in a timely fashion. Then we have investigations that are ongoing every day. Task force members are assigned investigations, . . . and those cases get addressed."

What, I wondered, constitutes "suspicious"? Anyone who doesn't look "right" can be the target of investigation, actually, if a citizen chooses to complain to the FBI or some other JTTF agency. While most such dubious leads are no doubt eventually dismissed, the waste of time and effort seems obvious, perhaps more glaringly obvious than the flood of pointless "tips" swamping the FBI courtesy of the Bush administration's secret warrantless wiretap program at the National Security Agency. And once an investigation is opened on someone, their name is associated with a JTTF counterterrorism probe, their name is in the system, and systems are sticky—they rarely give anything up for good. Names gravitate from list to list throughout the terror bureaucracy, as the Egyptians in Evansville learned. Lynch says such concerns are baseless.

"Again, any complaint that comes in to the FBI and to the JTTF has to get resolved," Lynch said. "Many of them are resolved—there's no conviction, no prosecution. There's nothing other than there's an allegation and it proved not to be the case. And during the course of that we have to go out and talk to people. We have to assess the credibility and viability of information we receive. And we do that with the culture in mind of the groups that we deal with. We've had a lot of training on that, where we are aware of the niceties of the different cultures that we are now engaged in. We do it with respect, and we do it with awareness of those cultural differences. Nonetheless, we have to do our job. If there are complaints that come in that we have to go out and talk to people, we do that. We do that to resolve that which has been provided to us. And I think the public would expect that of us. In fact, I think they'd demand that of us, actually. And we do that in a very respectful manner."

Respectful is in the eye of the beholder, it would seem. The manner in which Ghorab's mosque was raided in May 2004 outraged many, many people in the Muslim community, embittering not only Middle Easterners but African American Muslims. Dogs in the mosque. Automatic weapons in the mosque. Armed arrests in front of hundreds of small children at an elementary school in the early morning—all for a visa violation. JTTF officials may have had training in cultural sensitivity—and there's no question that they have—but at that moment of truth, when the busts come, when the knock on the door is made, when the foot stomps against wooden panels, when the interrogations begin—the operations can be something out of the old Robert Stack show, *The Untouchables*.

CHIEF INSPECTOR JOSEPH O'CONNOR, a Philadelphia cop for thirty-five years, a veteran of army intelligence, a speaker of Russian, and a competitive weight lifter in his younger days, presided over local counterterrorism efforts for several years following 9/11. At the time of the Ghorab raid, he was the top local police official involved on the Joint Terrorism Task Force. O'Connor is a quirky, interesting man who does not hide his frustration with a lot of the antiterrorism efforts and procedures that filter down from the federal level. All of it, however, is essential, he maintains.

I talked to O'Connor in 2006 at his office in the old Frankford Arsenal complex not too far from where Ghorab had his mosque. If the FBI office, located in the heart of downtown Philadelphia in the sleek federal building near the Liberty Bell, is an homage to the neutral professional image of the Bureau and its obsessive sense of security—lots of escorts and metal detectors and bulletproof glass—the police offices in Frankford are pure gritty Philadelphia—lots of old file cabinets, linoleum, and bad fluorescent lighting.

"We get hundreds of leads, and when I say 'we,' I mean the Joint Terrorism Task Force, the Philadelphia Police Department," O'Connor said to me. "And to be quite frank, most of the things we get in, many of the things we get in, many of the things would be things that pre–9/11 we wouldn't even pay any attention to. But we follow up now on anything that could have a possible nexus of terrorism. We follow up on these things. It could be something as simple as somebody seeing what appeared to be Middle Eastern males in front of a hotel discussing something. Something that simple. Nothing that's significant. Pre–9/11 that didn't mean anything. And many times you find it's not even Middle Eastern males. It could be males of Hispanic descent or just maybe from India, the Sikhs, and they're a completely different group with different religious philosophy and everything else."

The phone rings, and out go the investigators. In the initial months after 9/11, the calls were a flood, amounting to hundreds a week; they are still substantial, though their number has dropped off, and those calls still prompt action.

"We have to do these things," O'Connor said. "As mundane and as bullshit as some of these stories that come in. Let's say you have someone that calls you—maybe they sound a little funny on the phone. Maybe they sound like they're out of it, but they're talking about something that has a nexus with terrorism. You couldn't—at least I would hope that no one under me, I wouldn't—brush it off, because you never know what type of information people are going to be exposed to—whether they're out to lunch or not. You never know what they're going to be exposed to. So our mandate is that's what we do. Is a lot of it bullshit? Yeah. Is it frustrating? Sure."

In O'Connor's take, law enforcement authorities recognized their ignorance of Middle Eastern cultures—and their lack of good street-based intelligence—in the months following 9/11 and addressed those issues. The FBI in Philadelphia, he says, has made a serious effort to inform its agents about Islam and about the countries where it is the predominant faith. In the end, though, a suspect is a suspect, and a bust is a bust, and you're not going to spend a lot of time infiltrating the local Episcopal Church looking for terrorists.

Implicit in both Lynch's and O'Connor's comments, and in the observations of other enforcement officials, is the idea that terrorism investigations are structured largely the way traditional criminal investigations are structured, particularly investigations of drugs and organized crime. There is a heavy reliance on informants—in some cases paid informants and in other cases informants with something to gain from cooperation. But in dealing with organized crime, authorities are seeking evidence of specific crimes from those suspected of engaging in specific criminal acts and usually belonging to a specific gang. In the case of terror investigations of the Muslim community, more often than not, informants serve as hooks in classic fishing expeditions. But they are not infiltrating an organization or a gang. They are involved in spying on their neighbors and fellow worshippers. That's the way it has to be, O'Connor suggested. Philadelphia is a threatened city, he argued, a city being watched by innumerable, unknown bad guys—the man taking pictures of City Hall or the Ben Franklin Bridge, the man carrying a map with rail overpasses marked, the man asking too many questions about the shipyard.

"I never realized how many Middle Eastern males who had heritage from Iraq and Pakistan like to take pictures of bridges and like to take pictures of the oil refinery and like to take videotapes of our highways and playgrounds and shopping malls," O'Connor said. "There's a tremendous amount of them that like to do that."

As O'Connor said this, I thought of all the artists I know who are fascinated by the lights around the old Sun Oil storage facilities in southwest Philadelphia, the angles of the pipes, the flickering of the lights seen from the Platt Memorial Bridge. In the early days after 9/11, police detained at least two people who were taking pictures of that scene—students. To O'Connor and law enforcement authorities, however, the normal has become suspicious. Anyone looking at something can be dangerous.

"There are stages with regard to an attack," O'Connor said. "First stage is surveillance. If you disrupt a stage with regard to a terrorist plan to attack, they will put it on the back burner. That's not to say they'll eliminate it, but they'll put it on the back burner. I believe we've disrupted surveillances with people that did not have our interests at heart. Can I concretely say that? No. But I just find it amazing the amount of people from the Middle East that are interested in all our bridges from the Ben Franklin to Betsy Ross, the Walt Whitman, to include a map of Philadelphia which includes overpasses, those little rail overpasses at Frankford and Lehigh and places like that. We've encountered that, and we've taken it as far as they can be taken, and no arrests have come about."

Someone taking a photograph of a Philadelphia bridge, someone with a city street map. These activities, apparently, are early warning signs of danger—in a city desperately seeking to promote itself as a tourist destination.

"It was a young officer on the street, the one incident I speak of, where he stopped a person underneath the Betsy Ross Bridge, taking photographs. Now I understand how you might want to see the silhouette of the bridge in the background at dusk, but what I don't understand is people taking pictures of the underside of the bridge. And this officer disrupted that and, along with it, found a map—not on his person, but lying in close proximity—of Philadelphia, and it had seven different bridges within Philadelphia, or overpasses, including Fern Rock station and a number of other things. That's kind of suspicious. And it turns out this fellow, while born in this country, his parents are from the Middle East, both of them, and he had just come back from Texas supposedly to further his education, but there was no listing of him having attended any universities in Texas. Now it was taken as far as it could be taken. But I think that's one incidence that I speak of that we disrupted."

There were, he said, no arrests.

"There's a lot of things that we'd just chalk up to be bullshit, we wouldn't pay attention to it: 'Ah, that's bullshit.' It can't be bullshit anymore. Because you never know where it's going to come from. But we know, and when I say, 'we,' I mean the law enforcement community, that if we disrupt a stage, whether it be surveillance, preparation or practice run, if we can disrupt a stage, we've disrupted and put that incident back for whatever period of time. We know that."

A man, a U.S. citizen born and raised, taking pictures of the Betsy Ross Bridge. A man with a map with rail overpasses noted on it. A man questioned, background explored, released. This is an operation in the war on terror? I thought of those student artists photographing the oil refineries, and I thought of the maps in my own car, all with overpasses clearly marked. I thought of the day some months before when I spent several hours examining a rail crossing in southwest Philadelphia—a prime route for loaded rail tankers—mostly pondering garbage on the right of way and the city's lackadaisical willingness to let Conrail close off local streets and turn them into trash dumps. No doubt I seemed very suspicious.

"The bottom line is that what's taken place, and not just in Philadelphia but throughout the United States, there was a heavy immigration—and this isn't to paint anybody with a broad brush—but there were people who did not have our best interests at heart who came to this country with the idea of almost being a fifth column, and they're here. They are here.

"To be specific, I can't be specific, but the fanaticism, the militancy, the anti-Western hatred is here. Whether it's justified or not, mostly having to do with our foreign policy, a lot of it having to do with our relationship with Israel. These are things that are real, and they're here. But now of course anything that happens over there can have a ripple effect over here.

"The probability? We don't know the probability," O'Connor continued, lighting up a Pall Mall and linking the geopolitical to local law enforcement, "but information is taken; it's vetted; it's disseminated; in some cases it's sanitized."

The information is scooped up by federal agencies for the most part. But what happens then? I wondered. Where does it go? Who does the vetting? Where is it distributed? To the police? To the loyal partners engaged in the InfraGard network, a secretive FBI-corporate collaboration, where executives sometimes hear of threats before local officials? To the press? To the public? To families? O'Connor can't answer those questions. He is sure only that, eventually, local police will be informed by their federal colleagues if necessary—even if the information is, in some cases, "sanitized."

"One thing I'm confident in is the relationship we have with our federal partners, specifically relating to our area, Philadelphia and the five counties surrounding it, and now it's even more, eleven counties. Anything that's significant, we're going to be made aware of in due time to respond and mitigate what might take place."

The Philadelphia police, said Brian Lynch, are "like our brothers."

Siddique thinks three members of Ansaarullah were detained in late 2002 and early 2003, and one of them was deported. Officials are silent on the question. No information is available regarding "on-going cases," I heard from immigration and criminal officials. Atef Idais thinks one person was detained. Meriem Moumen, Ghorab's wife, thinks one, maybe two were arrested. All agree on one point: By the spring of 2003, there was at least one informant inside the congregation of the mosque. Neither Lynch nor O'Connor would comment on informants.

Another local police official said he never heard of any problems with the mosque, certainly nothing to warrant any particular watchfulness. But what did he know? It's all held very closely, he said.

"I don't want to go spooky on you," said O'Connor, "but what you have to understand is that many of these cases, the sources that were availed to us were sensitive sources, so we protect them. And the reason is that one case can lead to another, and I'm not saying it's this particular case, but one case can lead to another, and your sources are always out there, and you want to make sure they're protected because once a source is given up they're dead forever, and it could literally be dead in some of these cases. You could literally have somebody who was supplying the information done away with. That's the reality of it."

"Has that ever happened here?" I asked him.

"Not to my knowledge, no," he replied.

INFORMANTS, AS LARRY GRATHWOHL makes clear reflecting on his experience spying on Weatherman in 1969 into 1970, have complex motives. Maybe money drives them. Maybe ego. Maybe politics. Maybe morality. Some element of these fueled Grathwohl, just as some variation of that mix fuels informants within the Muslim community today, particularly the informants used in major criminal cases arising in the war on terror. Osama Eldawoody, born in Egypt and trained as a nuclear engineer, is a case in point. A paid undercover informant for the New York City police, he was the star witness in the trial of Matin Siraj, a young Pakistani immigrant convicted of planning to bomb the Thirty-fourth Street Herald Square subway station in New York City. In 2007, Siraj was sentenced to thirty years for conspiracy.

The trial and conviction engendered deep anxiety in New York's Middle Eastern and Pakistani communities, particularly in Brooklyn. Siraj had been arrested just days before the opening of the 2004 Republican convention in the city, maximizing the publicity and providing a jolt of fear to the public at large, and his conviction has since been touted by local and federal authorities as a major victory in the war on terror. For Siraj's family and for the broader Muslim community, the case has induced nightmares of almost unimaginable proportions. The day after his sentencing, Siraj's mother, father, and sister were swept up by immigration authorities in a surprise raid, accused of visa irregularities and incarcerated. A wave of protests followed, and the family was eventually released pending appeal of deportation orders.

"How does a supposedly democratic country that claims to fight for human rights around the world create this unjust tragedy for an entire family?" Siraj's mother, Shahina Parveen, lamented following her release. "The government has broken my family into pieces. We are an innocent family. Seeing my whole family in jail, I recall that my son was promised by NYPD-paid informants that his family would suffer the consequences of his noncooperation. That prophecy was realized, and now our life is a nightmare in the land of liberty."

Eldawoody, a naturalized citizen, was fifty years old and scraping by selling goods acquired over the internet when the New York City Police Department recruited him as an informant in the summer of 2002. Police had come to Eldawoody's home to check out reports— provided by a neighborhood informant—that he had received suspicious boxes in the mail.

"I asked them why this discrimination," Eldawoody recalled in a conversation with me in 2007. He was incensed, he said, that Muslims were automatically suspect for the most innocent of daily transactions. Detective Stephen Andrews, who eventually became Eldawoody's handler, was surprised at the comment. "Andrews told me, 'These days are very strange days.' Then I told them, 'Okay. If there is anything I can do about this, I'd be more than happy to do it.'"

That's how it began.

Over the next two years, Eldawoody visited al Noor mosque in Staten Island and al Farooq mosque and the Bay Ridge Islamic Society in Brooklyn over five hundred times, reporting on everything he saw, writing down license plate numbers of cars in mosque parking lots, reporting on the plans of an imam to move to New Jersey and on deals another man was contemplating involving foreclosed properties. He supplied name after name for the proliferating databases.

In 2003 Eldawoody met Matin Siraj, a twenty-two-year-old Pakistani immigrant who worked in his uncle's bookstore next to the Bay Ridge mosque. Eldawoody cultivated the young man, universally described by all who know him as slow-witted, and within a few months a "plot" emerged. James Elshafay, a friend of Siraj who suffers from schizophrenia, was also entangled in the affair.

Some months after the sentencing, I tracked Eldawoody down. He was now living secretly outside of New York, provided by the NYPD with a stipend of $3,200 a month, plus rent, and was deeply unhappy with his portrayal in the media, unhappy with how he was perceived in the Muslim community, unhappy with his handling by the New York police, who paid him about $100,000 for services prior to trial.

Why had he turned to informing? I asked. He said he did it because it was necessary. Other Arabs would not stick with a case until the conclusion. Why? Because they were afraid their fellow Muslims would turn on them. He said this, even though neighborhood activists estimated as many as 1,000 police informants are working the city's Muslim communities, and on at least one occasion in 2004, the NYPD had three separate undercover operatives attending the Bay Ridge mosque at the same time. One, a young police officer identified anonymously at Siraj's trial as Kamil Pasha, had been planted in the community and described himself as a "walking camera."

There is even a standing joke, a former counterterror official told *Newsday*, "that when Friday prayers at the Al Farooq mosque in Brooklyn ends, the NYPD's informants and the FBI's informants are bumping into each other as they leave." Nevertheless, Eldawoody is bitter that his identity was revealed, so much so that he fired off a complaining letter about it to former Senator Hillary Clinton, and he once told the Associated Press that Muslims in Jersey City wanted to "butcher" him.

Has anything like that happened?

No, Eldawoody allowed. But the idea is out there.

"I took that risk," he said. "I did totally for patriotism. I do love America. I am very, very, very much into principle, and no matter what, I am standing with my principles. My principles, I'd do anything for my principles."

No personal attacks came, but many broken promises rained on his life, he lamented. The police blocked a job, he said. They followed him and wired his car and tapped his phone, watching the watcher. He couldn't leave the country. "I was choked. No money. Nothing, nothing, nothing. Some time we were suffering a lot. We spent a lot of money from my wife's savings and from my savings. I spent—we spent all the money we had. I lost my car because of the case, my wife's car."

And still he kept reporting the development of the Siraj plot, and he pleaded with police to postpone the bust. Siraj, who has an IQ of 78 (about 93 percent of the U.S. population scores higher on IQ tests), wanted information on building nuclear bombs, Eldawoody said. He had plans.

"The point here is he criminal before he came," Eldawoody said. "He shot two Pakistani people before he came to the States. And this is, it's recorded with his voice, also, in court. He is criminal. . . . He spoke to me about people he knows in London and if he doesn't find life the way he likes in the States, he will go to England with his friends there. There are some other people in Canada also. Lots of things—I could not come up with any evidence that he told me, but these were not recorded. But I told the [NYPD] Intelligence Division about them. I was very worried when he said, once he said, 'I have twenty-five guys following me.' So. Yes. And I know one of the mafia, Pakistani mafia, that other guys, his real followers, are there in that mosque. But I didn't have the chance to continue to find out more. This is, that was a serious case, not like some people believe it's nonsense case. . . . No, this guy is real, real terrorist, real terrorist. Danger terrorist. I don't know. He came up with plan to explode bridges. I'm sure you know that. To bomb the bridges, Verrazano, Bayonne, yeah. Outerbridge Crossing. All of these. Lots of things."

When the deal went down to bomb the Herald Square subway station, Eldawoody was pretending to act on behalf of a shadowy group known variously as the Brothers or the Brotherhood. Police tapes give the flavor:

"Brother Nazeem upstate is very, very happy, very impressed," Eldawoody says to Siraj as the two discuss plans in the summer of 2004. "He says about the Verrazano: 'It's a little bit complicated. We are not that big, that strong; it's too heavy for us,' things like that. He says, 'in time.' The plan is perfect, but it needs a nuclear bomb, not a regular bomb. So he says that will be later. Thirty-fourth Street is on."

Siraj responds: "Hmm? Tell him that we are very careful about people's lives. Have you told him this?"

"We've spoken of many things," Eldawoody says.

"I don't want to be the one who drops it and have people die," says Siraj.

"No, no. He agrees, he agrees about lots of things. Because that's the principle, you know? No suiciding, no killing."

Siraj wants no part of death.

"No killing. Only economy problems," he tells Eldawoody. "I'm going to work as a planner."

"Are you okay with it?" Eldawoody wants to know.

"I have to, you know, ask my mother's permission," Siraj says, finally.

What can one make of this? A dangerous man, a criminal, a real, real terrorist who must seek his mother's permission to be dangerous.

Martin Stolar, Siraj's attorney, argued in court that his client was entrapped. But that is a notoriously difficult defense, and Elda-woody and the police countered: No, Siraj is an instigator and a dangerous terrorist. And now he has been convicted.

"From my perspective Eldawoody created the crime as an NYPD agent," said Stolar when I spoke with him in 2008 after Siraj was sentenced. "In other words, he took Matin from somebody who would not do something of that nature and convinced him that it was his duty to do so. Remember, there's this other guy who came in who was a friend of Matin's, Elshafay, who was totally nuts."

James Elshafay pleaded guilty and testified against Siraj at the trial. At the time he told jurors that he was taking psychotropic medication for schizophrenia and severe depression. Elshafay was mesmerized by wild schemes, said Stolar. "He originally approached Matin with this idea to blow up the bridges on Staten Island and take over the precinct. Right. This is early on. And Matin said, 'You're crazy. I don't want to have anything to do with this.'

"But Elshafay kept talking like that, so when Eldawoody started talking like that, Matin said, 'Hey, the two of you should meet each other. You say the same things.'

"There's one recorded conversation. Eldawoody is driving Elshafay someplace, and he's talking to him, and it's the kind of stuff that's whipping him up: 'It's your duty as a Muslim. You've gotta kill—you have to do jihad, violent jihad.' And it's the kind of thing I tried to suggest was exactly the kind of conversations he had with Matin before the recordings took place. It was pretty outstanding. Eldawoody was a very active participant in suggesting things had to be done that were violent."

Following the trial, jurors said they considered entrapment very seriously but ultimately concluded there was not overt evidence to support the defense. By the time the tape recordings began, the foundation of a "plot" had already been laid, Stolar said. Absent recordings, an entrapment defense proved too difficult, and the jury couldn't buy it, he said.

To this day, however, Eldawoody claims Siraj was far more dangerous than authorities realized—just the way Larry Grathwohl claims Weatherman was far more dangerous than the FBI understood at the time. Siraj "had other people with him," Eldawoody told me—an assertion not backed up on any police tapes. "He was talking to me about guys and using his eyes for talking, worried about any recording around him, his eyes, his face of pointing into something," Eldawoody said, acknowledging the lack of recorded support for his charge. "He used to do a lot of things like that, all of which was not recorded, of course."

In other words, the New York police closed down the investigation when their star informant was reporting two dozen terrorists embedded in the Bay Ridge mosque. Why would they do that?

"That was a conversation between myself and my handlers about this particular point, and I guess they had orders to stop at this particular time, at this particular point," said Eldawoody. "I believe so. Because I told them let me continue. . . . That's not the time to stop. It's the time to continue at least six more months or a year to find out more about these other guys he had. But I guess, the Republican convention was around that time, and they were worried and stuff like that. I don't know. They stopped. I'm nothing. I'm just a tool. A tool—but I had my own opinion, and my opinion wasn't counted around that time."

Martin Stolar said he had not heard of any such group of people, and no testimony at the Siraj trial suggested that two dozen terrorists were nestled inside of any mosque.

"It's bullshit," said a police official.

Maybe so, but the informers are still trolling for information out at Bay Ridge, and the mosque has suffered severe financial problems because of the climate of suspicion and scrutiny.

"They used to take trucks and vans and park them next to the mosque and spy on us," Zein Rimawi, a Palestinian American and a founder of Bay Ridge, said in a conversation we had in 2008. "This is in every mosque. There is a spy in every mosque. There is a spy. What has happened since 9/11? Nothing has happened. Who is the enemy? There is no more Russia now. No more blacks. You want to make Muslims the enemy. It is nonsense. They are drying up the sources of money. They shut down the Holy Land Foundation and the other charities. If you look after 9/11, you'll find that we didn't open up any mosque, any school, any center. There is no money."

Relations between the Middle Eastern neighborhoods and other ethnic groups in the immediate area have been lacerated by the intense police focus, Linda Sarsour, who runs the Arab American Association in Bay Ridge, told me in 2008—four years after the Siraj arrest. The problems are not merely that money flows have been squeezed and capital and charitable contributions have been scared away. As news of informants spreads, fear and unease spread with it. Community fractures. Sarsour has been angered by New York police officials acknowledging extensive infiltration.

"Our neighbors—we have a lot of Norwegians and Greeks and Italians in this community, some is a very Christian community—that we've been reaching out to, doing joint projects together, inviting them into our mosque, and we've been going to their churches, and we've really been building this trust together and working local issues, like affordable housing, things that affect all our communities, on traffic, on youth issues," Sarsour said, clearly upset. "And now our friends are picking up the newspaper and reading how our mosque, that they've been trusting and working with, has these informants and issues.

"We were angry because we felt that it might in some way affect our relationships with our friends, our neighbors, people who live next door to here in the community."

JOHN KELLEGHAN, ACTING SPECIAL agent in charge at the Philadelphia office of ICE, would not comment on informants or on any investigations. I spoke with him and Linda Valentine, ICE group supervisor, toward the end of 2005. Kelleghan declined to elaborate on any part of ICE's involvement with Ansaarullah—not informants, not probable cause, not even suspicions. He would not allow his interview to be tape-recorded.

"It gives a more complete record," I argued. But Kelleghan was not persuaded.

He did say ICE had not sought to bring down the mosque.

Did federal authorities specifically target Ansaarullah? I asked.

"No," Kelleghan replied.

When immigration violations are found, he said, it is the responsibility of the agency to pursue them. He declined to comment on the uncanny ability of ICE agents to find all those Ansaarullah congregants who had even the slightest immigration difficulty.

"It's amazing how they were able to find everyone," said one lawyer involved in some cases. "If there was a visa problem, an overstay, a technical difficulty of any kind, ICE was on it."

Kelleghan also vetoed any interviews with Mark Olexa, the ICE agent involved in many Ansaarullah-related investigations.

"I've got concerns about who reads the paper," Kelleghan said. "We all live in the same community." Any information "that's already public," Kelleghan said, was available for all to see. "I'm not going to be able to share anything more."

Linda Valentine, sitting on the other side of a broad table in Kelleghan's office, said ICE had formed a good relationship with Muslim leaders in the city who are as concerned about the country's safety as any other Americans. "If they think somebody is bad, I'll check it," Valentine said, a result of the improved communication between ICE and Muslim leaders. The communication appears to be somewhat of a one-way street to many in the Islamic community, however. If a Muslim leader says, for example, that someone is a bad guy, immigration will be on the case, and if the leader says to ignore someone else, he's okay, immigration will still be on the case, community members complain. Nevertheless, neither Muslims nor

Middle Easterners are targets or subjects of profiling, Valentine maintained.

"We're not out there banging on doors and ruffling feathers," said Kelleghan. "We're not looking—today's Thursday, we're going to go and hit the Spanish community or the Muslim community. It doesn't work like that."

"There are many who are here illegally, and the majority of them go to work, put food on the table, and make a life," he continued. "We're interested in those that can hurt America, hurt our country. We're here to insure that our folks are protected. Will we make mistakes? Sure, we'll make mistakes. We're here to cover our bases to the best of our ability. We're here to close those loopholes exploited by criminal elements."

I wondered if the ICE approach, when it came right down to it, was to detain first and sort out later—a kind of "better safe than sorry" approach.

"Absolutely," Kelleghan said. "Absolutely. You never know. You never know what this guy or girl you've got in custody is about to do that you don't know about."

That opens a pretty wide door for law enforcement. A minor infraction, what normally would be considered a civil matter—and most immigration violations are civil, not criminal infractions—could lead swiftly to detention and criminalization. Guilt was assumed; innocence needed to be proven.

Despite the "good communications" between federal authorities and Muslim leaders, anxiety levels among the poorer and more marginal congregants who made up the membership of Ansaarullah began to rise in 2003. The NSEERS registration program was leading to sweeps of the streets in South Philadelphia; members of the congregation were being questioned individually by law enforcement and immigration officials.

Then, on March 25, 2003, Mohamed Ghorab was arrested after he was "identified by JTTF during an investigation," according to papers filed during Ghorab's immigration court case. The records are mute on any circumstances leading up to his identification. He was held as a visa violator.

That an outspoken imam with visa issues should come under federal scrutiny at that particular point is not surprising. Less than a week earlier, the United States had begun its attack on Iraq, and Ghorab spoke out against the war. Thousands of Iraqis in the United States, including U.S. citizens, were being interrogated by federal authorities, reinforcing the notion that a fifth column was present in America—despite assurances from the government that the interrogations were informational and not based on specific suspicions. Ghorab had also been critical of the U.S. invasion of Afghanistan. He was hardly alone in his opposition to either war. But he was an Egyptian, and as authorities quickly determined once his name came up, he had overstayed his visa, and his application for permanent residency had been terminated.

In the atmosphere of suspicion coursing through Philadelphia and other cities with large Muslim populations, Ghorab was ripe for the taking. He was picked up on Wakeling Street and immediately shipped to York County Prison. Once there, he was interviewed by Mark Olexa, the ICE agent, who learned Ghorab had never been arrested or charged with any crimes and had never met Sheik Omar Abdel Rahman, the blind Egyptian cleric suspected of inciting the 1993 World Trade Center bombing and convicted of plotting to blow up the United Nations, New York's Hudson River tunnels, the George Washington Bridge, and a federal building. Ghorab did not "believe in what Rahman has done and is doing," Olexa learned, nor had Ghorab ever trained "to fire a firearm," indeed had "never fired a firearm," according to Olexa's written account of the interview.

Authorities argued for no bail whatsoever. But an immigration judge, usually compliant at the mere mention of the word "terrorism," set bond at $50,000 in Ghorab's case. While not happy about it, federal authorities apparently believed that an imam from a poor mosque in a poor neighborhood would most likely not be able to raise the money at all. Such proved not to be the case. Members of Ansaarullah, including well-to-do Jabi Khatut, raised the bail in donations, and within ten days Ghorab was back at Wakeling Street, startling federal officials.

"They were amazed," said one source. "They didn't think there was any way he could raise that kind of money."

If authorities were surprised by the release, the congregation of Ansaarullah had been equally stunned by the arrest in the first place. "It was a shock," said one former member.

It is true that Ghorab had spoken angrily about U.S. military actions in Muslim countries, but that hardly differentiated him from other Muslim religious leaders in Philadelphia and the United States (not to mention a wide array of Christian and Jewish leaders who were dismayed by American military actions in the Middle East). Even Ghorab's opposition to the Afghan war was hardly unusual in the Muslim community, said one imam, who vigorously disputed the notion that there are "any radical imams in the city."

"That's simply untrue," he said.

This imam said there had been much support among Philadelphia Muslims for the initial fight of the Afghan people to push the Red Army out after the 1979 Soviet invasion of the country. "When the Taliban came along, that was not as popular as the Afghans' own struggle had been," the imam said. "It was viewed as one Afghan faction fighting another Afghan faction." But with people now being deported and arrested in the United States after 9/11, he said, there was a deep sense here that Muslims were "under siege" in a growing number of areas around the world. That fueled opposition to the U.S. Afghan expedition—even among those who were deeply opposed to Taliban policies and al Qaeda atrocities.

"ONE OF THE BIGGEST things was with the INS," said a former Ansaarullah congregant, who said it was obvious that immigration agents became interested in the mosque after the start of the Iraq War. This congregant was uncertain why, however, and said Ghorab was hardly incendiary.

"Mohamed Ghorab would speak about what's wrong with the government because anybody can say that," this congregant said. "You have the right to say, 'This is not right, this is not right, this is not right.' At the same time, his primary premise that he taught was when you came to America, you signed a contract with the government that you would live under the laws and the rules and regulations and abide by the laws like a common citizen of the United States of America. You signed a contract. And a contract to a Muslim is binding unless somebody withholds you from practicing religion, and in America you have the freedom to practice religion. So this is what he taught: 'You can't walk around like you're mad against the government because the government is allowing you to live here and allowing you to practice your religion.' He taught this. Clear. Clear. So clear to the brothers."

What was clear to the brothers was not clear to federal law enforcement officials. When seemingly undocumented foreign nationals became entangled in post–9/11 immigration issues, law enforcement officials believed they could overlook no infraction, as Attorney General Ashcroft made abundantly clear himself.

Ghorab's political views on the Iraq War may have been protected by the Constitution's First Amendment, but they also brought the attention of authorities, who received reports from their source or sources inside the mosque. Ghorab's immigration status naturally came into play.

"The buzzword after 9/11 was 'zero tolerance,'" said Matthew Baxter, an immigration attorney and former head of the Philadelphia chapter of the American Immigration Lawyers Association. Baxter said the common attitude among federal officials after September 11 was simple: "Their view is 'We're not going to make a single mistake.' No one wants to be the one who lets the next terrorist in."

On the street, that means arrest first, figure it all out later—or sometimes don't even bother with that. The stories are endless: the man who went into immigration to straighten out his records only to be immediately put into deportation proceedings; the early morning raid at a relative's house that ended with a trip for all to York County Prison and deportation proceedings; the sweeps on the street of Pakistanis.

And these are cases drawn from the Philadelphia area in recent years—long after officials implied that such blanket or summary actions were no longer common.

"It's illustrative of the enforcement mentality, going after people of Arab and Muslim background, not being careful about whether they have a case," said Baxter. "It's a horrific thing to be dragged out in the morning and handcuffed before the whole family. I'd hoped my government would not go down that road."

Another immigration attorney noted that the early arrests, the initial PENTTBOM arrests and the NSEERS cases, amounted to "picking off low-hanging fruit."

"They got what they could there without much effort. Then the arrests started slowing down a bit, but when an informer tagged somebody, or someone got caught out on a paperwork error, they hauled them in and shipped them out. If anybody else was in the vicinity, they'd take them too. So it slowed a little bit after 2002, 2003, but it continued steadily in 2004, 2005, 2006. The fear thing was important too. Every time you have a big arrest, a well-publicized arrest, it sends a reminder to everyone. Really insidious."

SIDDIQUE WAS SHOCKED BY Ghorab's arrest, but his surprise was tempered by what had already begun to happen at Ansaarullah.

"The first time the sheik got arrested, maybe one or two people got arrested before him," Siddique told me. "The sheik was not the first. There was a guy named Iyman; he was sent back to Egypt. There was Iyman and maybe one or two other guys who got arrested before. Then the sheik got arrested. We got the sheik out of jail. The sheik was mad at some of the people because they didn't try and get Iyman out of jail. Iyman's bail was nowhere near the sheik's, and by the time we tried to get Iyman out of jail, they had already put through procedures to get him deported. Understand? And the sheik said they could have did anything for him. They could have sent him some money or tried to help out, you know. But he said Iyman was a common man, and that's why we left him there.

"Iyman was the guy who would just open up the *masjid*, clean up every day, and he was a humble person here. He was a person who worked at the *masjid* for free. All he would do was come to the *masjid*, do his stuff, do his laundry, do whatever. Just trying to please God. God will make a way for you. You'll get your wife later on, five years from now, a day from now. You'll get your home you supposed to get. You'll get your apartment. You'll get whatever the case may be. You'll get some new clothes. This guy had no interest in stuff like that. He knew he was the one getting a reward just for opening up the *masjid* for people. He was a nice kid, a nice guy as far as I seen.

"Once the sheik was arrested, Iyman was in prison, and the sheik came home, and Iyman stayed. Actually Iyman got arrested at another guy's home. It was another Muslim guy's home, a member of this *masjid*; they raided his home in Chester, somewhere near Chester. They arrested him and Iyman; they arrested four people out of his home, took his computers or whatever the case, and they let him go, the guy whose home it was, he came back home, and Iyman stayed in prison, and they deported him back to Egypt. After that, we had guy number one, guy number two, and guy number three here get arrested. The sheik, he went and raised the bail and got them out on bail; then we got the three guys arrested together who lived in the apartment not far from here, a house apartment; they got arrested as members of the *masjid*. But they had just stopped coming. They used to be guys that come here all the time.

They used to live in the *masjid*, you understand. They would live here, for free, you know—do all that stuff. But they lived inside the mosque, helping out. Then they got theyself an apartment and moved over there wherever, and they came and arrested those guys, and these guys are in prison."

Money was raised in the mosque to help those who found themselves picked up by ICE. Congregants would donate whatever they could, sometimes everything they had. Homes were even mortgaged to help detainees make bond. Atef Idais, who had bought a small row house for $5,000 at a sheriff's sale so that he could move his family out of his in-laws' house, mortgaged his home and put the money up as bond for a friend arrested on immigration charges. Others in Ansaarullah were equally generous—or reckless, depending on your perspective.

Ghorab was adamant that if a member of the congregation was in difficulty, his brothers and sisters in faith needed to come together and help as much as possible. He was deeply wounded when Iyman was left in jail, and he was determined, say associates, to insure no one else at Ansaarullah remained in federal custody.

As Siddique's description makes clear, though, the arrests were snowballing. Yet Ghorab, by all accounts, sought to maintain the continuity of the mosque and its rituals. It was important that daily affairs continue in the face of hardship. He was now entering a protracted legal fight with immigration authorities over the validity of his marriage—at a time when that marriage was breaking up and a new one was forming.

In April 2003, federal agents interviewed the teenage sons of his first American wife, Hajrah Alakbar, who told them that Ghorab was only "a friend" of their mother and had never lived with her. The agents also interviewed the manager of Hajrah's New Jersey apartment building, who said Ghorab was never around. (Hajrah suffered from some health problems and maintained the apartment because it was near a favored medical facility.)

That was enough. Despite the fact that several letters from the couple's friends testifying to the legitimacy of the marriage were submitted to immigration authorities, and despite the fact that Hajrah herself maintained it was a legitimate marriage and that her teenage sons simply disliked the sometimes-strict Ghorab and were trying to get rid of him, immigration authorities ruled the marriage a fraud designed to circumvent immigration law. Hajrah bitterly disputed this finding—even as she and Ghorab divorced and went their separate ways.

She is still deeply upset by the government's handling of this case. Alakbar told me her sons were troubled and resented Ghorab's efforts to impose discipline and order in their lives. Beyond that, she said, government agents interviewed both boys—ages fifteen and seventeen at the time—without her permission or knowledge or presence.

"They were really trying to get him on the marriage thing," Alakbar said. "It was really ugly. They went and talked to my sons without my permission, and they lied, and everything they said, they took all out of proportion."

Her sons, she said, were "acting out," smoking marijuana and involved in gang activities. Ghorab was seeking to stop that. The boys were tired of the Egyptian imam lecturing them, constantly criticizing their activities on the street, angry that he wanted them to focus on school and on religious studies.

"My son was smoking weed, my youngest son was all Crip, and I sent him to his father in Ohio because he was acting out. I had to," Alakbar said.

At the same time, she said federal authorities were uninterested in what she had to say about Ghorab and her marriage.

"They never allowed me to testify for Mohamed. They never allowed me to say nothing. When I came to court, they wouldn't allow me to say 'boo.'" It was, Alakbar said, intensely frustrating and humiliating.

"They didn't care what was the truth," she said. "They wanted to do what they wanted to do."

At the time all this was happening, tensions were mounting between Alakbar and Ghorab. She couldn't understand why the federal government was so interested in the imam and felt somehow she was being misled. Those thoughts, in turn, brought on intense feelings of guilt. Her husband was under attack, he said he did not know why, and the uncertainty and pressure led her to withdraw.

As 2003 deepened, Ghorab had also become interested in another woman—Meriem Moumen—which put additional pressure on his relationship with Alakbar. Moumen had heard "good things" about the imam and came to Ansaarullah at the end of Ramadan for Eid celebrations. She was captivated by a man who struck her as gentle, charismatic, and deeply knowledgeable. He was taken by her intelligence and passion for their faith. She began volunteering, helping out with translation, meals, decoration for special events—anything that might be needed. She stayed at the Wakeling Street house while Ghorab and Alakbar were still together. But, Moumen maintained, she slept downstairs and was not intimately involved with Ghorab at the time. Polygamy is not encouraged in Islam, but it is hardly unknown, even in the United States. Ghorab could provide a complete family by becoming involved with two single mothers—a circumstance in Islamic culture where it could be acceptable for a man to take more than one wife. Alakbar said she accepted the legitimacy of this practice as sanctioned by the Quran. But as a practical matter, it was extremely difficult. She could see Ghorab and Moumen were becoming very close.

"Meriem and I did not get along," Hajrah said. "She was feisty, and she almost got knocked out—I almost belted her one time."

On another occasion in 2003, Hajrah, Meriem, Ghorab, and their children went for an outing at Six Flags amusement park in New Jersey, Alakbar said, describing Meriem's combustible temper. An argument developed, which Alakbar believes was fueled by jealousy, and it ended with Moumen banging on Ghorab with her fists as he drove the car and with children crying in the back seat.

"I couldn't deal with it, and I withdrew from Mohamed," Hajrah said, still upset with her own actions. The tension with Moumen and the ongoing federal investigation were too much for her. Alakbar could not understand why government agents were so interested in Ghorab.

"I said to him, 'What aren't you telling me? Why is this happening?'"

"He was like, 'I don't know.' He said, 'Be patient.'"

"I felt I betrayed him by withdrawing, but I couldn't deal with it. I know the feds were watching me. I felt I had to be careful. I felt I had to be careful what I said on the phone. I don't have to fear anything. I lead a simple life, but I thought, 'Wow. What did I get involved in?' But I felt I betrayed him because I should have been there more."

Meriem Moumen, an American citizen born in Morocco, also unwaveringly criticized the finding of marriage fraud. She told me that federal authorities did not care what the truth was. Alakbar often stayed at the house on Wakeling Street, although she also kept her New Jersey residence, Moumen said. There were even photographs to prove it, she added, almost offhandedly. But federal authorities were uninterested in any of that.

"They didn't care," she said.

IN THE WAKE OF the immigration ruling of marriage fraud, the government maintained that Ghorab now had no other avenue to achieve permanent U.S. residency. And because Ghorab's marriage residency application had been ruled fraudulent, all subsequent applications were dismissible under the theory that once a liar, always a liar. Ghorab's first attorney had also failed to leave open the possibility of attaining legal status as a religious worker, and, according to Ghorab and other lawyers, the sheik was not told he might seek asylum under terms of the Geneva Convention Against Torture if political conditions in Egypt became substantially dangerous. These matters were all subjects of Ghorab's increasingly labyrinthine—and expensive—legal appeals until the time of his deportation at the end of 2005. Credit card debt began to mount.

Nevertheless, the imam was not about to let any of this get in the way of his mosque. He wanted to establish a school. Expansion was necessary, he said, to serve all the poor people in the neighborhood. Out on bail, Ghorab threw himself into his religious work and into improvements to Ansaarullah's building. Members helped install fans in the ceiling. They built a new staircase to a storage loft. The basement, filled with piles of stored belongings and old machinery, was too much; they left it. And ceremonies! Ceremonies became a hallmark. Wedding celebrations were held on Wakeling Street—one for Siddique; another for Sheik Ghorab himself, who wed Meriem Moumen in a religious service in 2003. She was soon pregnant with their first child, Abia.

"There were marriage parties, and we brought in imams from other mosques, one from New Jersey, and kids to sing songs," Atef Idais remembered. "There was a New Jersey Muslim personality who gave a small speech. There were jokes, funny poems, food— roast lamb, baklava, sweet cakes. Arabs love lamb. We made signs. There were balloons and sparkly banners. Great celebrations."

I SPENT MANY HOURS seeking to speak with Moumen after the sheik had been arrested for the second and final time. At thirty-three, she was an accomplished woman with a daughter from a previous marriage and a secular past spent in the American workplace. She had arrived in the United States from Morocco in the late 1980s, married an American and became a citizen, had a baby girl, worked in a variety of jobs around Philadelphia, and basked in the freedom of the place. She speaks English, French, Arabic, and some Berber dialects fluently, but in the period around 9/11, she began questioning the meaning of her life, and the questions led her to Islam.

"I was living in West Chester," Moumen told me one day, much later, long after the disaster of arrest and deportation, long after the mosque was gone and with it family, home, and country. "Most of my friends were American. I was working, and I was living in my house, and I was very happy, really happy. I had a mother; she was watching my baby. And I had a lot of good times. If I want to go out with my friends, my daughter was in very good hands, a safe place. My mom, for God's sake—she was watching my daughter. One summer—I think I was having too much fun, really—one day I got a little depressed, and I was sitting by myself, and I said, 'I'm in my late twenties. Where is this going? Where are you going?' I was think-ing about going back to school. A lot of other questions just popped up in my head. Religion. God. Is there really such a thing as hell and heaven? It was a dream I saw. And the next day I picked up the Quran and started reading it seriously. I was going to a lot of other mosques, and I bought a few books, and I was really convinced that this was it. It made me feel really, really good. But I understand why I did this. I wasn't slapped with an order: 'Cover up—you have to cover up.' When you give somebody something to do and they don't understand why, they will never be good at it. If I give you an order, just do that. No. They have to understand that. They have to under-stand why they're doing it. Why. So that's what I did."

When I first met her in 2005, Moumen was always dressed in a traditional dark *abaya*, a cell phone constantly in her hand. She would furrow her brow as she talked, and her voice would rise and fall in pitch with the quicksilver of her emotions. A Muslim acquain-tance of mine, meeting Meriem for the first time, said simply, "She is strong." Others felt she had a quick tongue and temper made all the quicker by increasing pressure.

In mid-2005, her husband in jail, Meriem was running the mosque, seeking funds to pay the rent, trying to light fires under lawyers, fetching substitute imams from as far away as central New Jersey, caring for her children, fending off creditors, trying to visit her husband.

She would say to me, "There is no time. I have nothing left I can say." And then she would tell me how tired she was. "I am so, so tired, I can only leave it all to God," she said repeatedly.

During the year or so Ghorab was out on bail, and despite the overriding anxiety on Wakeling Street, more congregants were attracted to the mosque; that, in turn, seemed to attract more attention from federal authorities. The Frankford Valley neighborhood, a small enclave several miles north of Center City Philadelphia, is an insular, working-class neighborhood, mostly Polish, mostly Catholic, mostly inimical to change. People worked at the Allied Chemical Plant or in small stores. But there were fewer and fewer businesses and stores after Home Depot opened a mile or two south. That killed all the hardware stores up and down the river.

But still, people who lived in that part of the city—Port Richmond, Frankford Valley, Bridesburg—tended to stay there. When children moved out of the nest, they often bought their own row houses within a few blocks of where they grew up. Older residents often stayed put and maintained deep reserve with those considered outsiders. In other words, Frankford Valley and its surrounding neighborhoods tended to resemble other ethnic areas in other old industrial cities in the Northeast and Middle West: eccentric in its own way, provincial, suspicious, formal, self-sufficient.

While many of the mosque's immediate neighbors, particularly those in chastened circumstances, were happy to see an enlivened and welcoming presence on the busy corner of Aramingo and Wakeling, happy to see a place where children could play on a rainy day, happy to accept bags of rice and flour freely distributed during Ramadan in 2002 and 2003, some in the neighborhood were deeply suspicious. What was this mosque doing here?

One elderly couple alerted the office of John J. Taylor, the neighborhood's Republican state representative. Something strange is going on at the corner, Tessie told Taylor aide Kathleen Zoladek, a lifelong neighborhood resident herself.

"Tessie kept calling me," Zoladek told me one night as we stood out on the street near the mosque, chatting. "Tessie and Henry lived there for probably over fifty years. She says, 'Something's going on down on that corner.'"

"I said, 'What is it, Tess?'"

"She said, 'I don't know.' She said, 'It was like a lot of Muslims and all.'"

"And I went, 'Oh, okay.' What they would do there? We don't know if it meant something: They would hang, every week, different color balloons out on this fence. All the time. I don't know.

"She said, 'What do you think it means?'"

"I said, 'I don't know.'"

"But she was like staying on it. She called me, 'Different color balloons are up there again.'"

"I'm like, 'Tess, I don't know.'"

"'What do you think they're doing in there?'"

"Didn't know."

Then there was Joan, whom I ran into one day on the street. Joan was quite sure the mosque was cooking up something that would be bad news for Frankford Valley and America.

"I used to come home at ten o'clock at night and say to my husband, 'There's something going on down there,'" Joan confided in me. "'Evening prayer,' he said. 'At ten at night?' I go. I was nervous about them being there. There was something weird going on."

I asked her why she was nervous, and she quickly replied—Allied Chemical.

What does that have to do with the mosque? I asked. The vast Allied complex was on the other side of I-95, quite a ways from Ansaarullah, but you could see its pipes and stacks jutting up over the highway.

"Oh," said Joan, "It blew in the '70s. They could blow it up. Some kind of funny business going on there. There's something going on there for sure."

When I talked to Joan, it was after the big Ansaarullah bust, and she was disappointed that the raid turned up absolutely nothing. "It's too bad," she said, "because it makes it look like an innocent place of worship."

Well now.

"There were lots of questions," Joan said. "It terrified me. I'd come home and tell my husband: 'It scares the hell out of me.' He'd say, 'Why?' 'Allied Chemical. They could take out the neighborhood.'"

ONE NIGHT IN MAY 2002, before the arrests, before the troubles, when everything, indeed, seemed to be going well, a police officer noticed a car slowly trolling down Wakeling, lights out. Stopping the car, the cop saw that the driver held a shotgun pointing out the window, aimed at Ansaarullah. A search of the car led to the discovery of several photographs of the mosque and its parking lot, forty rounds of ammunition, and a list of license plate numbers of cars in the lot. The man was promptly arrested.

"We don't know what this guy was up to, but he wasn't out there to hunt ducks," the commander of the police department's Northeast Division told the local community newspaper.

Ghorab was upset about the incident, he told his wife and others, but he did not believe the stalker reflected the sentiment of the community or that there was a broader plot to attack the mosque.

"I think," said Ghorab, "this guy is sick."

SIX

Nothing to Hide

ATEF IDAIS, A TWENTY-SIX-YEAR-OLD Palestinian from Hebron on the West Bank, was arrested early in the morning on October 30, 2003.

He was suffering from a fractured ankle, barely able to walk, and so when federal agents banged on his door near dawn, he had to drag himself, sitting, down the stairs. "I couldn't use the crutches," he said. The day before, Idais had been at Ansaarullah, where he was spending a lot of time, playing football with the neighborhood children. He tried to escape a tag, tripped, and twisted his ankle.

He told me this story, nearly two years later, while sitting in the cold and empty visiting room at the Federal Detention Facility in downtown Philadelphia, a block away from the FBI headquarters and the office of Brian Lynch. Idais was dressed in a standard-issue brown prison jumpsuit and blue slippers. We were instructed to sit immediately in front of the guards' station, a high, wide counter at the head of the room, despite the fact that the rest of the large visiting area was completely empty.

"That's the rule," said Ken Arnold, the bearded, round, deputy warden. In prisons, rules are often momentary conveniences, reminders of control, gratuitous indignities. When the shift changed, new guards told us we could sit anywhere we wanted. Idais smiled, which he does often, and said rules often appeared to be made up on the fly and discarded just as easily. He had a neatly trimmed beard, and though he said he felt under enormous pressure and was deeply unhappy, his manner was engaging, tinged with a kind of delicacy that sometimes slipped into plaintiveness. He described his first arrest with an astonishment that still seemed fresh.

After the ankle injury, Jabi Khatut, Idais's friend and employer and president of Ansaarullah, drove him to Frankford Hospital. X-rays were taken, a soft cast was put on the ankle, and Idais was released. It was very late at night, and as Khatut drove beneath the Frankford elevated tracks on his way to Idais's house on Ormes Street, a police car pulled up behind them, followed for awhile, and then flashed its lights and siren. Khatut stopped and was presented with a ticket for driving without lights. In retrospect, Idais said, this incident seemed eerie. Were they being watched? Even at the hospital? At all hours? And who was watching? Was it the police? Or were the police alerted? Who would alert them? And why?

Following a fitful night, Idais returned to the mosque the next day, prayed, ate a meal there with fellow congregants, and returned home, where he again had trouble going to sleep; his ankle ached badly.

Some time in the dim hours near dawn, Idais was startled from sleep by "banging everywhere, screaming," he remembered. "I thought I'm in a nightmare, a dream! I looked through the blind, and I see uncountable officers and agents. They were all outside with guns, and I thought something has happened in the neighborhood. It's a tough neighborhood. There had been drugs and arrests down the block before."

Idais, his wife, Rrahime, and their infant daughter, Tazkia, lived in a small two-story row house, and on numerous occasions local and federal law enforcement authorities had engineered substantial drug busts in their poor, out-of-the-way Frankford neighborhood, cut off from much of the city by deep railroad canyons and large, street-blocking factory shells.

Peeking from behind the window shade, looking down at the narrow street swarming with agents in police jackets, Idais thought another drug bust must be in progress. Rrahime thought the same. Tazkia, Idais recalled, was thankfully asleep for the first few moments. No one else could be seen foolishly looking out of their windows.

When Idais reached the bottom of the stairs and managed to get the front door open, "ten people were all talking at me at once, and then all at once they're in my home," he said.

"You're under arrest," an agent said to him. "Student visa violation."

Idais was stupefied. Looking at all the agents filling his tiny living room, seeing them poking around the kitchen, rifling through papers, thumbing through books, it seemed as though he were suspected of being a major drug runner, an international thief, a terrorist. But a student visa violator?

"I don't know what you're talking about," Idais finally replied. "Three weeks ago I updated my address with INS. I updated my application for a green card."

The agents were uninterested in that, and by this time, a very alarmed Rrahime was downstairs, and Tazkia was awake and crying. Idais wanted to hold and comfort both.

"They wouldn't even let me hold my daughter," he said to me. "What am I, a murderer?"

Idais was hustled into a van and taken on a three-hour drive to York County Prison. It was like a terrible storm, Rrahime said later, followed by a dead stillness as the sun rose over the dirty street. Now Rrahime, like every other Muslim woman whose husband has been scooped up in similar situations, was left to figure out what to do. She had to locate Atef—no one would tell her where he had been taken—find a lawyer, try to pry as much information as possible from the federal bureaucracy, find some money, speak to her parents, reassure Tazkia.

That was only the beginning.

IT IS LIKELY THAT IDAIS was named by an informer within the mosque, someone who was toting up names of congregants who might have visa problems and passing them to federal agents. The records suggest this, although it is difficult to know for sure. In the weeks before his arrest, ICE agents received letters from both Temple University and the University of Toledo stating that Idais had been accepted at both institutions but had not attended classes. The letters were confirmations of ICE inquiries. John Kelleghan of ICE told me that his agency now has a computerized system that alerts authorities when foreign students fail to materialize at their academic institutions. He would not discuss Idais's case, and it is unclear if this system—a massive database known as SEVIS, the Student and Exchange Visitor Information System—was effectively operational at the time agents swept through Ormes Street.

Fueled by funding authorized in the PATRIOT Act, SEVIS is certainly operational now, tracking and gathering information on hundreds of thousands of foreign students in the United States and retaining the data. According to the July 2007 quarterly report issued by ICE, there were 996,263 active nonimmigrant international students, exchange visitors, and their dependents in the SEVIS system as of July 3, 2007. Beyond that, "data on greater than 4.5 million nonimmigrant . . . international students and their dependents, schools and [exchange visitor] programs can be found in SEVIS," the report says. The information has been accumulating since July 2003.

The PATRIOT Act, it should be noted, provides federal law enforcement agencies with access to other troves of data gathered in supposed confidence for statistical purposes. Student information compiled under the National Education Statistics Act, previously held in confidence, can now be accessed by agents who certify to a court that the data is pertinent to an investigation. Once agents certify, courts must grant the request. The question for statisticians, not to mention students, their families, and educators is this: How accurate can such data be, now that respondents know it is no longer strictly private? Beyond that, of course, is the alarming question of what personally identifiable information is being passed along and for what purpose?

FOR THREE MONTHS FOLLOWING his arrest, Idais remained imprisoned at York. Rrahime and his fellow congregants at Ansaarullah, urged on by Ghorab, tried to raise his bond, set first at $10,000. According to Idais, ICE agents interrogated him in prison, and he told them he had been arrested in Israel in 1999, accused of throwing stones at a bus when he was fourteen or fifteen years old in the early 1990s. The Israeli authorities released him after about a hundred days of imprisonment. It was all a muddle that was blown out of proportion by Israeli police, Idais said. But the ICE agents told him he was in big trouble. Arrested in Israel? He would never fly on an airplane again. He was a terrorist. He was Hamas. He was a stalker, a sleeper, a lone wolf. He was going to be locked up forever. Talk, the agents said; it's your only hope.

"I told them I was arrested in Israel," Idais said, indignant. "They never knew! But I was not going to lie to them. I have nothing to hide. This honesty of mine—I will be honest all my life. I have done nothing wrong. I threw rocks at the Israelis? I am a Palestinian."

Federal authorities told immigration judge Grace Sease that they needed more time to investigate Idais's background.

When Idais finally was able to speak with Rrahime on the telephone, she was weeping and afraid.

"I said, 'Sweetie, calm down.' I thought somebody had died," said Idais.

"You're not coming home," she sobbed.

"It's alright, it's alright. We'll work it out."

But it didn't get worked out for some time. In December, federal authorities opposed any bond for Idais, but Sease, apparently unimpressed by the evidence at the time, kept bail, although she boosted it to $20,000. The New Year came and went, and Idais remained at York. Congregants at Ansaarullah, where he was very well liked—and respected for his knowledge of the Quran—worked to pull together donations for his bond. He seemed, said one congregant, a quiet and unassuming young man, very friendly, raising a family, working for awhile as a pizza delivery man and then as an office worker for Jabi Khatut in South Philadelphia.

Khatut also ran a substantial business selling collectible crystals, and as he got to know Idais, he put him to work as a salesman on eBay. Hour after hour, Idais would sit in Ansaarullah, chatting with children who wandered in, watching over his baby daughter, and selling crystals and crystal objects on the internet—intricate roses, birds, figures, miniature landscapes—using the tag My Crystal Collection. His customers knew him as Arthur, because "it sounds more American," he said.

Both Idais and Rrahime felt very close to the people at Ansaarullah, including Sheik Ghorab. Authorities were very interested in that connection, Idais told me. Who was this sheik, immigration agents wanted to know. What was going on in the mosque? What were they hiding? Idais said he told them Ghorab was a good man trying to teach his congregation how to live in a spiritual manner.

Where did the money come from for Ghorab's bond? agents wondered. From the brothers, Idais said he told them.

Early in January, as the weeks wore on, two FBI agents, both women, visited Idais at York one morning. He was relieved, he told them, because he was getting nowhere explaining his situation to immigration investigators. In the report filed subsequently by the agents, Idais's frustration was characterized as anger.

"He was angry because he had been asking to speak with the FBI for some time," the agents noted.

"I never told them I was angry," Idais said to me later. "I said, 'I'm upset. I'm upset: me being honest with you and you using it against me.' I'm not angry with anybody. I am upset."

After unproductive questioning about some Iranians, the agents zeroed in on Idais's own situation.

"The arrest is causing problems with his current immigration status in the United States," the report dryly notes. "IDAIS told INS about his arrest in Israel, and Homeland Security is using it against him to show that he is a bad person and a threat to airline flights. Idais said he was arrested but said he is a good person and would not hurt anyone. IDAIS supports the ideology of HAMAS because they are only focused on the Jewish people because they are not giving the Palestinians what they deserve. He does not agree with Hezbollah or related groups that hurt tourists or others that have not harmed them."

The agents noted that Idais grew up on the West Bank and that his family operates a produce stand "repeatedly displaced by the Israeli Jews." Much later, in court, Idais said the family also owned land and ran a toy business. In the wake of the most recent Palestinian uprising, the toy business simply fell apart. "The Israelis used tanks and airplanes," Idais said at a courtroom hearing. (In my experience, Idais always alluded to Israelis, not Jews.) "Things had never been like this before." Downtown Hebron, he said, "was shut down" by the fighting and chaos. "In a war situation, no one buys toys."

At York, Idais told the FBI agents he had been arrested in 1999, when he was returning to Israel from speech pathology school in India. He was caught up in the arrests of several others, he said, men he did not even know. After a few months in custody, he was released. The Bureau agents wrote that Idais told them that "it would not be a problem for him to return to Israel"—a boilerplate sentiment that is found in many summary reports of interviews with immigration detainees from a variety of countries. Presumably it can be used against those seeking to remain in the United States. But in

December, Idais had filed for asylum and a stay of removal from the United States under the Convention Against Torture.

His asylum application—which ultimately went nowhere—states that Israelis "jailed, tortured and investigated [him] for a possible threat to Israel." Idais elaborated on this claim in court and during a long interview. His wife also described essentially the same events. Idais told me Israelis shackled him to a chair during questioning. "It was martial law," he said. "They didn't care. I was Palestinian." At the time of his arrest, he said, "I pissed in my pants, I was so scared." A bag was placed over his head; loud music blared in the interrogation room. He was not allowed to sleep. "I cried. I was going crazy." Yes, he said, he threw rocks. So what? It would be difficult to find a Palestinian kid who had not thrown rocks. Based on this experience and on the continuing high level of violence on the West Bank, Idais's asylum application noted that "respondant [*sic*] fears that he will be tortured if he returns home due to past experience."

Federal prosecutors completely dismiss the torture claim, arguing that the admission Idais gave to Israeli authorities "reeks of truth."

"The internal integrity of the statement makes it very credible," said Nancy Beam Winter, the assistant U.S. attorney who handled the case. "It's the kind of statement a real person makes."

In mid-January, Idais placed a routine call to Rrahime. "I have good news," she said excitedly. The bond money was now in hand. "You're coming home!" He was deeply grateful to Ansaarullah. "They helped me with everything," he said.

Idais returned to Ormes Street; the Ansaarullah arrests continued.

EARLY ON THE MORNING of March 25, 2004, Faycal Saghour, an Algerian who arrived in the United States in 2000 as a stowaway aboard a ship, was stopped by ICE and FBI agents on South Tenth Street as he was leaving the apartment he shared with his brother, Nassim, and sister-in-law, Caterina. Nassim was a green-card holder and twenty-year U.S. resident married to a U.S.-born citizen. Both brothers attended Ansaarullah, although Faycal was less observant, showing up only on holidays for the most part. After he was stopped, Faycal returned to the apartment with the agents, and it became quickly apparent he had a problem.

Nassim, it turned out, also had a problem, despite the fact that he was a well-established, hardworking member of the neighborhood, a legal permanent resident with an American wife. Faycal's situation was relatively straightforward: He had entered the country illegally without a visa. Agents took him into custody immediately, and off he went to York County Prison.

How did it happen that agents zeroed in on the Saghours? Government officials contend that there had been rumors that an "Algerian terrorist" was wandering around South Philadelphia. Where these rumors were circulating is impossible to determine at this point, although it is more than likely that an informant at Ansaarullah was aware that Faycal Saghour was unlawfully in the United States. (One federal official said there was a rumor of an Algerian unlawfully living in South Philadelphia and that agents took "quite awhile" to link the rumor to the Saghours.)

For federal agents, the Algerian connection had great resonance, they said, because Nassim Saghour had allowed a purported Algerian terrorist to stay in his apartment during the summer of 1998. It was only natural, federal authorities said, that agents would want to discuss the most recent round of rumors with him. That those recent terrorist rumors ultimately referred to a stowaway who for years had worked in a Jersey Shore burger joint during the summers was beside the point: He was an illegal immigrant, if not a terrorist.

Criminal charges were filed; Faycal Saghour pleaded guilty to illegal entry and was deported from the United States within a matter of months in 2004.

Nassim Saghour presented a different difficulty for authorities, who now wanted more information from him. He was a legal resident, lived in South Philadelphia, and worked as a general contractor.

He owned a house on South Mole Street, which he was renovating and planned to sell in the booming real estate market.

But Nassim had a past. He initially entered the country illegally in the early 1990s. Saghour said he was fleeing political persecution in Algeria, which was veering toward civil war. Saghour told authorities that as a member of FIS—the Front Islamique du Salut—he faced torture and imprisonment by the Algerian government. FIS had won the national legislative elections in 1991 and promptly found its leaders arrested and its operations banned after the military took control of the Algerian government. A bitter civil war ensued.

Despite this deadly situation, Saghour's asylum petition was denied. In the meantime, however, he married an American citizen and filed for permanent resident status. That marriage did not work out, Saghour divorced, and married Caterina, an American-born woman living in South Philadelphia. He was eventually granted his green card on the basis of this second marriage.

In 1997, a supposed member of GIA visited Philadelphia and stayed at Saghour's apartment, according to assertions in federal court documents. GIA—the Groupe Islamique Armé—is a brutal Algerian organization and was a central combatant in that country's byzantine civil war during the 1990s; it is on the State Department list of foreign terrorist organizations. The purported GIA member left Philadelphia after a few days and went to Canada. Some four years later, in 2001, federal agents interviewed Saghour about that visit and contended that he was somehow in cahoots with his visitor and had been harboring a terrorist. Saghour dismissed that idea. The man had left Philadelphia without incident, went to Canada, and eventually returned to Algeria. (Where, Saghour told his attorney in 2005, the man ominously referred to in government court documents as "Terrorist B," was running a used car business. "Some terrorist," Saghour said. Government officials refused to name Terrorist B and insisted he had been deported from Canada.)

All of this backstory came into play when agents picked up Faycal Saghour in 2004. Agents said a "source" told them an Algerian with a false passport was in South Philadelphia. Naturally they came to check out Nassim Saghour, hitting the jackpot with his brother, an illegal alien.

After Faycal was imprisoned in York, FBI agents retuned to question Nassim several times. They wanted to know about Ansaarullah. They wanted to know about Sheik Ghorab. Who else did Nassim know? How long had he lived with his brother? There was no end to the questions, Nassim complained.

Saghour was afraid to speak with me about any aspect of his situation.

"They talked freely to Nassim for months like you and I are sitting talking," said a man who knew Saghour and his story quite well. By the time I had this conversation in 2005, Nassim had been arrested and charged with a federal felony: harboring an illegal alien. I was startled to learn that such a crime even existed, considering all the high-profile illegal nanny cases in recent years. I had certainly never heard of any prosecutions of government officials who had harbored illegal immigrant nannies.

"The FBI would meet in these little coffee houses for I think almost up to a year where Nassim would talk," my source continued. "It was only at a point where they said, 'We want you to help, going into the mosques and giving us information.'

"He said, 'Look, I don't mind doing this, but I don't want to become false to my beliefs. Going to the mosque and telling people I'm there to worship, but really I'm there to report to you guys'— that's where Nassim had a real problem. That's when the FBI said, 'Well, if that's the approach you're going to take, you realize you've committed a crime with your brother, and we can prosecute you.' And Nassim said, 'Well, go talk to my lawyer.' And the next thing Nassim knew they came into his house and arrested him. And the rest is pretty much history."

The man told me this story as we sat in a coffee shop ourselves.

"Oh, they met with him for almost a year after his brother had been arrested, knowing very well that he had been harboring his brother, and really just talking casually," the man said to me, stir-ring his coffee. "'Do you know so and so? Do you know so and so?' And he'd say yes or no. 'What do you know about?' To that extent he was a source. But when they asked him to go an extra step and actu-ally go into mosques that he didn't normally frequent, go to this mosque in Jersey, go to this mosque over here, and 'do some work for us.' He said, 'Look, I've got a life here, and I don't want to go in the name of being Muslim and saying prayers, and really I'm there to snitch on people who I may or may not know have done anything wrong.' But he did say if he'd seen anything wrong or anything sus-picious even, he'd let them know."

Nassim Saghour was arrested by federal agents in November 2004. In March 2005 he pled guilty to harboring his brother. He sub-sequently sought to change his plea, but that effort was denied. He was convicted and deported. Caterina, his wife, was torn about what to do, Saghour's attorney told me. Both her mother and her father were frail and ill, and she was their primary support. But her husband was being forced out of the country. Caterina was asked by a federal judge what she would do if her husband were deported. "My marriage comes first," she said. "I married him through tough times and good times: 'You're leaving, and I'm going to stay?' It just doesn't work that way." An awful choice. In the end, Caterina could not abandon her marriage vows or her parental obligations. She has been back and forth since her husband's exile in 2005, and the cou-ple is struggling to find some way and some place to be together.

THE SAGHOUR EXPERIENCE WAS very similar to the experience of Atef Idais. After his release from York on bail in January 2004, he re-turned to a joyous Rrahime and resumed his attendance at Ansaa-rullah, where he was greeted warmly.

"He's a beautiful man," said Siddique, chuckling to himself. "I laugh because he's my friend, he's my friend." Atef spent many hours with Siddique at the mosque, even after a second daughter was born in the spring of 2004. And throughout this time Idais received visits from the FBI. They came to his home in February 2004, and they interrogated him with IRS agents at the home of Jabi Khatut a few months later—telling Idais that he could help them in their "real" investigation of Khatut for tax fraud.

Idais said he was always willing to answer questions because "I have nothing to hide." Agents wanted more. They wanted to hear what Idais had to say about everyone. They wanted him to go out trolling for information.

Rrahime, who was present at one such session, remains upset by what she says is the disparity between what was actually said and what ended up in official reports written by federal agents and used by the U.S. attorney's office in prosecuting her husband.

"A lot of it wasn't true," Rrahime told me one day. We were standing outside the federal court house on Market Street in Philadelphia following a criminal hearing in Idais's case. Several television camera crews were stationed at the entrance to the courthouse waiting—for what? Something important. Rrahime, Tazkia in tow, and I talked on the side. No one paid any attention to us. It reminded me somehow of Brueghel's famous painting of Icarus falling into the sea. No one paid the slightest attention as he disappeared beneath the waves.

"She twisted things," Rrahime said, complaining about Nancy Winter, the assistant U.S. attorney prosecuting Idais. "She turned good things around and made them seem bad, like our marriage. She made it seem like a bad thing: He came over here to go to school and instead got married. And she was taking right out of those reports the agents wrote. Those agents came to our house and talked, and I was there, and what Atef said wasn't what they wrote down. It just wasn't true."

In particular, she said Atef told the agents that his arrest in Israel was the result of confusion and that the U.S. visa application they showed him was not the visa application he filled out in Jerusalem. It was not signed, Idais pointed out when agents showed him a copy.

It was not his. In their report, agents noted that "IDAIS did not recognize the form."

DURING THE INTERROGATION AT Khatut's home on June 16, 2004, Idais told agents that he paid no income tax on money made from eBay sales—Isn't the internet tax-free? he asked them—and that he made a $14,000 cash deposit of Little Sicily Pizza receipts for Khatut in November 2002. Agents also learned that Idais's father-in-law borrowed $12,000 to buy a house in August 2001.

Having quickly elicited probable cause for a charge of income tax evasion, the agents turned their attention to Ansaarullah and Sheik Ghorab, according to their written report of the interview. Idais told them he collected funds for the mosque, standing with a collection basket near the door, following Friday services. This money would be passed to Ghorab or Abdul Hamid, the mosque's only employee. None of the money goes to other charities, said Idais, "because it is not enough to pay the bills" of the mosque. Nor have there been any collections for Hamas or Hezbollah, he said, although he believed foreign groups came to Al Aqsa to raise money.

"IDAIS stated he has never heard any anti-American statements in the mosque or from Ghorab," the agents reported.

The agents turned their attention to Dawaa Salafia, the Muslim group that Ghorab was involved in while in Egypt, one of dozens of similarly named, unrelated groups all across the Muslim world.

IDAIS stated he believed that Dawaa Salifiya were followers of Mohamed. IDAIS stated that he was not aware of GHORAB claiming membership in this group and he did not know that the U.S. recognized this group as a Foreign Terrorist Organization. IDAIS stated that if GHORAB is a member of this group he should be dealt with and that if he was a "bad" person then he (IDAIS) wouldn't associate with him. IDAIS states he loves America and wants to help finding anyone who wants to hurt it. He stated he would be the first person to step in if someone wanted to hurt America. . . . IDAIS stated he doesn't know anyone who is currently a member of an organization that would want to hurt the United States.

At the time agents took this statement, June 2004, the State Department had recently placed Dhamat Houmet Daawa Salafia, an Algerian sect, on the terrorist exclusion list. The group was completely unrelated to Ghorab's former imam or mosque in Egypt, which shared a name. Ghorab had no connection whatsoever with the group.

"I could easily give you names of other guys, and all of them were people who would go to the mosque, that Imam Ghorab led, they were all questioned about Imam Ghorab with the implication, 'if you help us put something on him, then maybe we can look the other way on what we have against you,'" said attorney Anser Ahmad. "And that was the impression they were given. Atef didn't, and some of the other guys, they've managed to survive."

Another man put it more directly. "Atef would talk about himself. He would talk about bad things he saw, but he wouldn't inform. They went after him."

Federal authorities said no. Here was a guy who lied on his visa application, a member of Hamas convicted in Israel. Were they supposed to ignore him? That Idais's supposed affiliation with Hamas took place when he was a young teenager in the early 1990s—well before the United States labeled Hamas a terrorist organization—was deemed irrelevant. And his denial of "membership" was viewed as a flat-out lie.

SEVEN

Literally and Figuratively a Cesspool

I N A DIFFICULT TIME, keep to yourself.

"For our community in particular it just became so obvious after 9/11—the informants, getting people from within our own community or people who speak our language and look like us, sit in our mosques and in our churches or sit with us in a coffee shop, and you think they're your friend, and they just came from Egypt, when in fact they're working for the government," an indignant Linda Sarsour, director of the Arab American Association in Bay Ridge, said to me one day in 2008. We sat in her small office on Fifth Avenue in Brooklyn, just a few blocks from the Islamic Society of Bay Ridge, where Matin Siraj once attended services. His 2004 arrest and its aftermath brought much into sharp focus for Muslims in the neighborhood. What is safe? Who is safe? Daily worries now in a slippery new world.

"It just isolates people. You can't trust your own," Sarsour continued. "When someone's talking to you about politics, you're like, 'Wait, do I know this guy from somewhere? Have I seen him around before? Do I know if he has a family?' And that's how it is. It's sad that we have to live like that. So it's not a very trusting community."

Her free-fall descriptions were echoed over and over again by Muslims in New York, Philadelphia, California, Ohio, everywhere I contacted Middle Easterners and South Asians. (In New York, activists estimated the number of police informants working the city's Middle Eastern community at 1,000. That seems high to me, although casual street informants could boost numbers well into the hundreds. The FBI's 2008 budget noted that the Bureau needed funding for an expanded force of 15,000 paid informants nationwide.)

But if Bay Ridge felt under siege, laced with informants, losing fearful congregants, and scrambling for funding, the mosque still continued on, and several hundred attended prayer. The mosque remained an anchor for the community.

The few who once attended the Dar Ehya Essunnah mosque, several blocks away, were not so fortunate. Dar Ehya Essunnah was much smaller, more isolated than Bay Ridge, and the imam, Muhammad Khalil, a naturalized U.S. citizen born in Pakistan, preached a variation of Islam with few followers in this country. Members of the community contacted after the mosque closed said they believed Khalil preached a form of Deobandi, a now-conservative branch of Islam that originated in India in the nineteenth century in reaction to British imperial power. The basement mosque on Ditmas Avenue usually attracted followers—generally poor—in the dozens, not the hundreds, to prayer, according to neighborhood residents. (Khalil himself said he ministered to as many as four hundred families.) Beginning in 2002, among those who gathered there was a confidential informant working with immigration authorities, according to news accounts and the indictment in the criminal case brought against Khalil. The informant also happened to have a pending permanent resident visa request under review.

In February 2003, Khalil was arrested and charged with what news accounts and federal authorities characterized as "massive" visa fraud. The indictment stated that over a period of ten years, Khalil had helped about two hundred immigrants fraudulently obtain resident status in the United States as religious workers. When the arrest was made, prosecutors also claimed that Khalil was a devout admirer of Osama bin Laden, the Taliban, and attacks on the United States, the Associated Press reported. We have it on tape, they told the judge at Khalil's bail hearing. This man has called on Muslims to arm themselves. The judge set bail at $300,000.

Authorities closed the mosque, dismissing the congregation as irrelevant, a sham, and a ruse.

Bobby Khan, of the Coney Island Avenue Project, said Khalil was a man who would speak his mind as informants and law enforcement authorities peppered the area. He would even prod his neighbors, who didn't want to be involved, didn't want to attract attention, didn't want to hear the knock on the door at dawn.

"The imam was often having arguments with people in the neighborhood," said Khan. "The mosque was in the basement, and he had a small store for his living on the first floor. In the same building his family was also living. He was like under radar, and he was the one who would often speak out to people in the neighborhood."

Khalil was outraged by the immigration sweeps and the assumption behind them that Muslims, by definition, were anti-American and terror-prone.

"He would speak out, saying, 'This is injustice; this should not happen. Islam is not that kind of religion that people are portraying,'" Khan continued. "He said all of that was coming totally from the U.S. government and it's wrong. So then he started getting city inspectors coming in. There were a few raids conducted in that mosque and about four people who were arrested from the mosque. He had some kind of arrangement where those who don't have any place to live, those who came here recently or whatever and therefore are like homeless, he would have kind of shelter, he would charge very little, and he would charge a very nominal money for that place. . . . And all of them were arrested."

At Khalil's trial, Assistant U.S. Attorney David Burns characterized Khalil's ministry and mosque as "figuratively and literally a
cesspool of fraud." Conviction for fraud quickly followed, and in
January 2005, Khalil was sentenced to fifty-one months in prison.
Congregants of Dar Ehya Essunnah scattered like chaff. There was
no mention at the trial of Osama bin Laden. Nothing about attacks.
Such comments had been floated early on and then faded away. At
trial the only charge was fraud and the linking of Khalil and his
mosque with disease. A cesspool—as though the mosque in Brooklyn were a source of cholera diligently tracked down by investigators. Wiping it out would help sterilize the community and return it
to health.

AT ANSAARULLAH, IN THE wake of the massive May 2004 raid, attendance also began to fall off rapidly. Like Dar Ehya Essunnah, Ansaarullah was much smaller than Bay Ridge, with fewer resources;
moreover, it was isolated in a non-Muslim neighborhood, an island,
another source of infection in the eyes of authorities, it would seem.

Why did attendance decline? With Sheik Ghorab now imprisoned, some congregants were concerned about the lack of a genuine imam to lead prayers and conduct classes. Others argued with
the volatile Meriem Moumen, who was trying to hold the mosque
together according to her husband's wishes—but without his authority or gender. Hamid, who looked after the mosque, fell into a
bitter quarrel with her and left in a huff.

Siddique and several others attribute the flood of rumors and the
difficulties of Sheik Ghorab, at least in part, to the inability of some
members of the mosque to understand his teachings and the hostility sparked by that inability.

Many congregants at Al Aqsa followed Ghorab after he left there in
late 2001 and founded Ansaarullah. Some congregants worked for
lay leaders of Aqsa who owned markets that sold pork products or
restaurants that served alcohol. In his sermons, Ghorab stated that

the Quran forbids association with such food and drink, which did not please some who attended the mosque. At the same time, Ghorab also said it is more sinful to put a family in harm's way by leaving a job and an income than it is to be associated with bacon or beer. Keep the job and support the family, he said. This displeased those who took a more rigid approach to the sacred texts. There were similar issues with the sheik's injunctions against debt and credit. The Quran forbids interest, but how stay in business without loans? How buy a house without a mortgage? Ghorab focused on the lesser evils. Better to have a home for your family than live on the street. He also had little patience with those who sought to cut off women from life in the world. It was an impossibility. Adjust to the world.

Siddique described for me how these disputes played out in the mosque. Every day, Ghorab would seek to teach an important lesson about Islam, an explication of the Quran or some other text and what it actually might mean. For instance, the Quran forbids the consumption of alcohol; therefore a Muslim with a clear understanding of his responsibilities should not associate with any activity involving alcohol and drinking. Ghorab's comments in these lessons were not meant, Siddique said, to be taken personally. For help in understanding how the general rule might apply in a particular circumstance, congregants needed to sit down with the imam, ask the specific question, and receive a specific answer. That's what is required.

"The sheik, he's talking in general, and he's saying you shouldn't do this," Siddique said. "He's not talking to this guy over here or to this guy. He's talking in general. But these guys are taking it like a personal attack: 'He's talking about us! He's talking about the cigarette places, the gas stations, the pizza parlors, the beer gardens!' This is what they did. They would get together with their paranoia and start up their paranoia."

The sheik, they believed, was telling them they were living in sin if they worked in a bar. But the other side was just as obtuse, in Siddique's view.

"If you quit the job and put your family in difficulty and you can't take care of them, it's a bigger turn on you. So he say, 'Keep the job.' And the people have a disagreement with that: 'He said you got to keep delivering it! That's not right!' And these are the people who already have problems because they're trying to justify some of the stuff they're doing. 'He said this guy can keep his job driving this beer truck! He said this guy can be in this store.'"

But that is not what Ghorab was saying at all. "He's not telling them to stay there. He's telling them don't quit under these circumstances. You can look for another job. If this is bothering you that much, and God says to the Muslim and the Prophet, peace and blessings be upon him, say if you doubt a thing, stay away from it. If you ever doubt something, stay away. If there's a doubt in your mind whether it's clean or clear to be in there, you should stay away; you should avoid it. So these people should gradually change. But the circumstances that a lot of us came under, that we have business here in this society, we went to the bank, and we got loans, and we opened up a business. Those business loans were taken out under interest. Interest is *reba*, something that's forbidden in Islam. So these people, it's always behind them; this stuff is all the way inside them already."

Women were another flashpoint at Ansaarullah.

Congregants complained among themselves about the exposure of women in American society. They wanted their women covered, and they wanted them separated in the mosque, which, eventually, they were. Ghorab, Siddique said, was somewhat exasperated on this score.

"A lot of people would say, 'Well, we don't want our wives out, exposed like this,'" Siddique said. "In Islam, the women should be separate, in some circumstances by a screen, to separate the men from the women. For the most part they should be separated. There has to be a screen between them. The screen is for your modesty. So the sheik went on to tell them, 'Y'all making a big issue out of this.' You understand what I'm saying? They're saying, 'I need a wall or a door that separates the ladies from the men,' and he made a statement, 'When you take your wife to Red Lobster or Denny's to eat, doesn't the waiter come serve her? It's a male or a female waiter. Doesn't the person sitting at the table right next to him, isn't he right next to your family? Isn't your family exposed to this? Why are you so extreme about it now?' And again, these people took offense to it. They taking it like, 'He's browbeating us.' They took it the wrong way. Believe me, it's incredible, their perception. And I tried to analyze it. Why is it some of these guys don't really get it? Some of them do, and some of them don't. Do they want to get it? Are they problematic? Are they pragmatic? And it shows now in their character. A lot of people is not here, showing their character. They have a lot of growing and learning and understanding to do in Islam. Islam is a pure religion, pure and clean. We are not, Muslim people, we are not perfect; our religion is. The religion is perfect. We should try to strive to be perfect. But we're not. And it shows in a lot of circumstances— any inconsistencies and inequities, it shows."

It was strange, Siddique said, because what Ghorab said was very clear. And the congregants did not go to Ghorab for clarification of the teaching. Instead, "they wasn't saying anything about this thing that was troubling them, this troubling stuff. It stayed inside them, and they'd brood till the rumors got out that, okay, this guy is talking extremism. He's talking whatever. You understand what I'm saying. I never heard him talking extremism."

As Atef Idais took over the leading of prayer and keeping of keys, Meriem began to ring up charges for lawyers on her credit cards. *Reba*. The fact is, she didn't know what bills to pay or even what bills were due because agents had taken everything as part of their investigation. Meriem called the JTTF and pleaded to get copies of bills so they could be paid. Electricity, water, telephone. They had everything. IRS agents agreed to let her come downtown to pick up what was needed.

"They have my life," Meriem told me one day months later. "They had all our documents in piles on a table."

What kinds of documents?

"Letters, all of my husband's sermon notebooks, business records, notes, letters. When they searched the home, they poked through mattresses, pillows, cushions. What were they looking for? What did they expect to find?"

Whatever was expected—evidence of tax fraud, evidence of "material support for terrorism," evidence of nebulous "terrorist links"— led nowhere. But Ghorab remained jailed without bail on the old marriage fraud immigration charge.

Jabi Khatut, president of the mosque and businessman, told Meriem Moumen that he intended to sell his house and leave the country. She knew agents had been questioning him for some time. He told her he was being harassed because of his association with Ansaarullah.

"People were shocked when they heard this," she said. "The FBI or immigration would go into his pizza parlor asking him questions about the mosque and then said if he didn't start talking, they would go after him too. He was president of the mosque! They wanted Jabi to inform and work for them."

The investigation into Atef Idais intensified too. Immigration authorities received copies of Idais's visa application, which showed, they said, that he had lied to gain entry to the United States. When Idais visited the U.S. embassy in Jerusalem to fill out his visa application in July 2000, he had claimed he had never been arrested and that he did not belong to any terrorist group, immigration agents contended. During the summer of 2004, they received copies of his 1999 arrest records from Israel, which showed he had indeed been arrested and jailed for more than three months for throwing stones and belonging to an illegal organization, Hamas.

By the end of the long summer, after Homeland Security Secretary Tom Ridge raised the alert level in New York, Newark, New Jersey, and Washington, D.C., to orange—based on information that in

some instances was four years old—as a maze of investigations continued on a local level and daily life became an almost unbearable
chore and threat, Khatut sold his house in Bustleton and left the
United States for Dubai, where his extended family had a business.
He had never been arrested, charged, or detained for anything. Yet
his life in the United States, he said, had become untenable.

ON SEPTEMBER 9, 2004, Idais was approached by ICE agents while at
a Kensington Avenue convenience store and quietly arrested on federal criminal charges of lying on his visa application and then using
the visa to enter the country, both felonies. No bond was set, and
he was placed immediately in solitary confinement. Rrahime was
beside herself with worry. She could not speak with her husband.
She wasn't even sure where he was. Ghorab himself was placed in
solitary confinement at York County Prison. According to his wife, he
was punished for praying late at night. Others say it was because
he had become a respected figure among the many Muslim inmates
at the prison, acting as de facto imam; his new followers would step
in and do Ghorab's work, which violated prison regulations. Meriem
Moumen was not allowed to see or speak with him during the
months he was held in isolation.

The congregation at Ansaarullah was disintegrating. Rumors of
informants, terrorism, surveillance, and harassment began swamping the city's larger Muslim community. No one seemed willing to
step in and offer real help and funds. An imam from Al Aqsa did visit
Ansaarullah during the summer to offer encouragement, but the lay
leaders of that congregation kept their distance.

Marwan Kreidie, who acts as an unofficial spokesman for Al Aqsa
and has never met or spoken to Ghorab, said Ansaarullah and Al
Aqsa simply never had a relationship. He said he also had heard
some rumors claiming that Ghorab was a virulent anti-Semite,
something I heard from no one else, friend or foe of the sheik.

"All I heard was he was radical, and I don't know what that
means," Kreidie said. "But we never had a relationship with him

because he kicked my people out. I'm not going to worry about it. I was going to have a sit down and like 'I'm trying to help you.' But it wasn't worth it."

Kreidie said he had sent an AmeriCorps volunteer up to Ansaa-rullah in 2002 or 2003 to see if there were any viable projects that could be initiated.

"At one point we wanted to organize with the youth and provide social services, and I sent my AmeriCorps volunteer to that mosque, and it was a woman, a covered woman, and she met with this guy, and he just was like, 'You shouldn't be working. You should be at home.' He had a stick. 'And get out of here.' I'm like, 'I'm not gonna deal with those people.'"

While this seems out of character for Ghorab, he did have a temper. At one point, he and Moumen were fighting, and she sought a protection from abuse order from the courts. Ghorab's anger was a like a bad summer squall: It erupted, and then it was over. Moumen's temper was very much the same. Neither one paid any attention to the protective order, however, and indeed, it was forgotten. The storm had quickly passed. Later, however, when Ghorab was impris-oned and seeking bail, he was asked by the court if an order had been filed against him. He said no. Moumen said the order was filed against someone else. The hearing was held in secret.

"I said, 'Look, I can't do a whole lot for you guys,'" said their attor-ney, Anser Ahmad. "'If you're telling the judge there's no tension be-tween you guys and there is, then it's credibility. It goes to whether you're honest people or not.' And it was based on that that the judge said, 'Look, I can't trust that they're being honest about this, so I'm going to deny the bond.' And they couldn't understand why a small credibility discrepancy could cause the bond to be canceled. A judge can use whatever criteria she chooses."

GHORAB, WHEN HE WAS not in solitary confinement, would speak with Moumen and other members of Ansaarullah by telephone, giving directions and advice, offering encouragement and admonishment—even as some congregants passed along rumors that subverted the imam and the mosque. But when the sheik called, disgruntled congregants were momentarily transformed into dutiful supporters.

"He used to call here and talk to us, and they would change," said Siddique. "Change like they his sons. 'Well, why do we got to lock the doors now?' they'd ask him. 'You lock the doors because in Islam, you should tie your camel. You should always lock your door. You don't invite people anywhere to steal from you. You close the door.'

"Somebody took something out of the cash register before," Siddique continued, explaining why the question came up. "Small stuff had started happening. Nit-picking small stuff. So he said, 'You got to close this door. Keep this stuff locked.' This is him from prison trying to advise us on how to do things better.

"He loved this *masjid*. He lived and breathed the *masjid*. 'Who's doing lesson this week? Who's coming in? Who's doing this? Who's fixing the water? Who's cleaning the bathrooms? Who's doing blah-blah-blah-blah?' Because he hasn't got anything else in life to talk about, to worry about, to do about. The *masjid* that he opened and is trying to maintain, this is his life. It's easy for him to get frustrated.

"He'd call and ask these guys, 'Why don't you guys come visit me? You were like my sons.' He'd say this to these guys. And they be sitting there, 'Oh, we're sorry. We're sorry.'

"He say, 'No, you don't come visit me. You like my sons. And it's not only that you don't come visit me, you treat my wife bad. You treat my wife like a so-called second-class citizen. And I'm away in the slam, and most of you people, when you were arrested, me and my wife we went to your house, and we took food to you. We went to your house, and we gave money to your wife. We went to your house, and we raised this money to get these people out of prison. We raised this, and we did whatever, and now that I'm in these circumstances, you're talking bad to my wife.'

"And it's not him bragging about what they did; it's about him trying to raise their consciousness about what's going on around them, how easily we forget, how soon we forget. It's a cliché, but he said it because that's what happened."

ATEF IDAIS WAS NOT someone who forgot Ghorab. But Idais's own arrest left Ansaarullah effectively without anyone capable of leading prayer. He was detained in solitary confinement in the Philadelphia Federal Detention Center for about two months. Rrahime's life was becoming uncoupled from everything other than trying to cope with legal burdens. She now had two small children, and debt was piling upon debt as she sought to raise cash for attorneys and put food on the table. Idais's first lawyer, distracted by a high-profile murder case, failed to prepare Idais's case. The trial was postponed. Rrahime was out about $7,500 that she didn't have to begin with and that her parents didn't have. All she wanted was to be together with her husband and children. But events were moving so, so slowly. And congregants kept slipping away from Ansaarullah.

Not everyone in the Muslim community was unhappy with the unraveling of the mosque and its congregation. At some point prior to Ghorab's arrest, federal authorities latched onto to an informant who wanted legal citizenship. He already possessed a green card enabling him to stay in the United States. Agents paid him $200 to go into Ansaarullah, check out what was going on, dig up as much information as possible on Ghorab and everyone else, and bring it back to them. There was at least a tacit understanding that such help would facilitate this man's desire to become a naturalized citizen.

According to my sources, the man delivered the goods. After Ghorab's arrest and when the mosque was falling apart, he returned to check on the impact of his effort. He was pleased, one source said at a later date. "He was talking and laughing about how many people there were at the mosque before and how now there was hardly anyone." The man, however, had his own past—something turned up, some brush with the law, some immigration technicality violated, and federal authorities "wouldn't cut him a break." He did not get his citizenship. "He still has his green card, but he did not get his citizenship—even though he informed," I was told.

Another man, who was offended by Ghorab's opposition to the Iraq War, was concerned that he might be suspected by Ansaarullah congregants of informing to authorities. He insisted he had not, but told an odd story, which made the rounds.

The man, who was seeking U.S. citizenship, said he visited Ansaarullah in 2003, and Ghorab added "anti-Western sentiments" to his sermons. Several weeks later, at the end of Ramadan, this man visited again and fell into conversation with Jabi Khatut.

"Ghorab is wrong to speak against the West," the man said to Khatut. "We need to remove Saddam from Iraq. He is a bad, bad man."

Khatut disagreed. Even if Saddam is a bad man, he argued, the United States had no business invading Iraq. The conversation became heated.

"Why are you so pro-America? Why do you defend the U.S.?" Khatut supposedly said. The man, deeply angry himself, walked out of the mosque and never returned.

This incident had ramifications following the 2004 raid on Ansaarullah. The man who walked out said that his mother in Syria had been approached by two bearded men in the market of her town. They told her that if her son ever returned to Syria, he would be "in danger." The man, who was still using this incident in 2008 to support his citizenship effort, attributed the Syrian threat to his argument with Khatut. Khatut, of course, was no longer in the United States; he was in Dubai, where he was building his family business. Suspicions, like water, fill all available space.

ATEF IDAIS WAS REMOVED from solitary confinement about six or eight weeks after his arrest and was placed on a general cell block at the Federal Detention Center in Center City Philadelphia. His wife was finally able to get on his visiting list—something, she says, that was initially blocked—and she made the trip from Ormes Street to Center City for a visit every week.

She needed Atef, she said, but even more importantly, his children needed him.

"I feel so bad that Atef is not around," Rrahime told me one day. "He would spend more time with them. He left when the little one was very little, but with Tazkia, I really, really found him a very special parent. He was so attached with her. He would play with her, making her happy and satisfying her. They had a very, very strong bond together. Sometimes I really feel bad because when you're apart from each other, then that bond kind of weakens.

"I didn't want my daughter—I don't want that to happen. I wanted father and daughter to have a strong relationship. And the way he started it was wonderful! Every day he would take her out and buy her something. He was very special to her, and she was very special to him. It was a very strong bond between them."

Tazkia, the elder daughter, was born in August 2002. When her father was picked up the second time, she was two years old. When her father vanished, she knew there was a hole in her life.

"She was very capable of understanding that he's missing, that he's not around," said Rrahime. "And she was asking for him. 'Where's Baba?' Every time the doorbell would ring, 'Oh! Baba's coming!' And she'd run to the door, and it would be my parents or something, and she'd be so disappointed. And many times she'd cry, 'I want Baba!' Other times people would say, 'Put her to sleep.' And she'd say, 'I don't want to go to sleep with you! I want Baba!' And I talked to everybody who would listen and hear my pain, but nobody actually heard it. Maybe nobody feels it because nobody looks at my kids the way I look them, and nobody feels it. I don't know. So."

Baba did not come home. Rrahime dismissed his first attorney and decided to go with the federal public defender. At least that didn't cost any money. Not that she had any. (Because Idais faced criminal visa fraud charges, he was entitled to a lawyer, even if he could not pay. With straight immigration offenses, generally civil not criminal matters, there is no such right. An immigration defendant, if he or she wants a lawyer, must pay, and pay dearly.) Idais felt that he could not mount any kind of defense as long as he was in jail, but bond was repeatedly denied, his hearings kept being postponed, and nothing seemed to happen. He decided that if he pleaded guilty, since he had already served more time in jail than the sentencing guidelines called for in similar cases of visa fraud, he would be sentenced to time served and get out. Then he would only face immigration charges, and he had already been released on bond for those.

This was not a reasonable expectation, attorneys said, particularly since his case now had the word "Hamas" embedded in it. But Idais steadfastly denied he had ever been a member of Hamas, despite what Israeli court records indicated.

Those records, which federal prosecutors used to suggest that Idais was virtually incapable of telling the truth and was a terrorist anti-Semite, tell a somewhat less ominous story.

According to the sworn statements of Idais and his acquaintances rounded up by the Israelis, Idais was accused of joining Hamas in 1991 or 1992—at fourteen or fifteen years of age—and throwing stones at soldiers and eggs at "passenger buses in the Hebron area," according to English translations of the Israeli records. He was also accused of disturbing the peace by burning tires and garbage containers and blocking roads. Idais gave a statement to Israeli military authorities admitting these acts, but denied taking part in writing graffiti slogans because "his parents did not permit him to go out at night," one statement says.

U.S. prosecutors also had statements from other supposed Hamas members who identified Idais. One young man said his Hamas "unit" included Idais and two others. "I taught them the Koran but after a relatively short time we stopped our activities, because they were busy."

I read these records with amazement. Hamas is now the main political force in Gaza, winner of the 2006 Palestinian legislative elections, and support for or involvement in its activities is hardly unusual on the West Bank. Apart from that, Idais was a child accused of throwing stones and eggs. No specific incident was ascribed to him. How many thousands of dollars, how many hours of investigation and legal preparation had been poured into the federal effort to nail an adolescent who wasn't even allowed out of the house at night?

There are people I know who are now running some of the largest corporations in the United States, and running them well, who were deeply involved in antiwar, antigovernment activities during the 1960s and 1970s. Some blocked traffic. Some even threw stones. Are they subversives? Their corporations would be thrown into turmoil if they were removed. But the message of the Idais prosecution seemed to be once an egg-throwing, tire-burning "terrorist," always an egg-throwing, tire-burning terrorist. Even the U.S. criminal justice system treats convicted juvenile murderers more humanely. And that does not even address Idais's contention that his admissions were coerced by the Israelis.

In April 2005, Judge John R. Padova questioned Idais about his guilty plea in Federal District Court. The judge was trying to determine whether to accept the plea. It did not go well. Idais told him that he wanted to get out and that his lawyers were, in essence, making that impossible by not preparing for trial. His first lawyer was too busy. Hearings had been postponed. Judge Padova grew exasperated.

"I can accept your plea only if I am satisfied that you are guilty of what you're pleading to. Okay?" Padova told Idais. "And if you tell me that you're guilty to what you are pleading guilty to, and you're not guilty, then you have just committed perjury and that's a whole different other crime. I want the truth from you, sir. Nothing but the truth. Or else we're going to end this guilty proceeding right here and now."

"This," Padova continued, "is not a game."

The situation was this: Idais wanted to plead guilty and by so do-ing be released from prison. But if he made such a plea and was, in fact, not guilty, he could be charged with perjury for claiming guilt and thus be found guilty of falsely claiming to be guilty. (Ghorab, it should be remembered, was adjudged guilty of lying on his mar-riage residency application, and as a result all subsequent filings were deemed suspect. There is no end to the resourceful catches.)

Idais said he understood, and the proceeding continued.

He would agree that he threw stones, he would agree that the Is-raelis arrested him, but he would not agree that he was a member of Hamas.

Things quickly bogged down again, however, when Idais said he had been arrested by the Israelis but didn't know why.

"It is not my government, and I'm not in their country," he told Padova. "They are in my country. They arrested me. I don't know."

"Okay," said Padova.

"They just took me at the borders like they take any Palestinian," Idais said.

He then agreed that he had been arrested for throwing stones and membership in "an illegal organization."

But he would not agree that he had been convicted. Rather, he said, he had been "coerced" preceding his trial.

"I was tortured," he said.

At this point, Padova decided he had heard enough and started to call off the hearing in preparation for setting a trial date. He said he had no intention of playing "word games" with Idais. But Idais's public defender intervened, and the hearing continued. Through a long series of questions, Idais finally agreed that he had been ar-rested by the Israelis and convicted and that this had not been dis-closed on the visa application before the court. Then, when it was almost a done deal, he pointed out that the visa application that the government was using to prosecute him was unsigned.

"I'm sorry," said Padova, "I didn't hear that."

"I'm saying they also didn't see my signature on the application," Idais said. "The application is not signed." The application before the court, he said, was not the application he filled out in Jerusalem.

Nancy Winter, assistant U.S. attorney, dismissed this claim and argued that the lack of a signature was an immaterial "oversight." Not only that, she said, the application was filled out under oath, and false statements made on it amounted to fraud, signed or not.

Idais said he did not recognize the application—a point he had made to authorities months earlier—which consists mostly of a hand-printed name and address and checked boxes.

Winter argued that handwriting analysis would show that Idais filled it out. But the defendant said he did not, that he had filled out and signed another form—something he had maintained since his arrest. (Idais did not mention this to the judge, but he had told immigration authorities almost immediately after he was first detained that he had been arrested in Israel. That seemed to me an odd piece of information to pass on so quickly if someone had lied about the arrest to gain entry to the country in the first place.)

On the original application, Idais said, he had answered the questions as required, noting his arrest in Israel. It was in filling out this application that he reveled in thoughts of coming to the United States. "I was in love with my wife, and I wanted to come to this country and continue my education and meet a happy family, that's all."

Padova ended the hearing and refused to accept a guilty plea. Idais returned to prison. He dismissed his second attorney, public defender Catherine Henry.

Rrahime was thrown further into despair. She had set her hopes on having Atef home. But her hopes proved valueless, and her dream of going to college on scholarship had been utterly obliterated. Now any dreams she had at all were rapidly diminishing: Could she have her husband home for a day? Could her children hug their father for just an instant?

"It's a sad, sad situation," said Catherine Henry. "You can't get anything from the government. [They] say, 'There's a lot more to this, Cathy, than we can tell you.'" In the case of Idais, she said there has been a serious emotional and financial toll on the family.

"Retaining counsel with credit cards is a very difficult situation. It's sad, sad, and something we're seeing again and again."

Beyond that, Henry said, "no one in the case has a recollection" of Idais actually presenting his visa application, although prosecutors said they would produce such a witness from the embassy in Jerusalem. (They never did.) Henry also said that Idais's "file is missing."

"It's the most ridiculous case," she said, "brought for reasons we don't know."

But it was effective.

IDAIS HIRED A THIRD attorney, Robert Miller, and changed his plea to no contest. Miller said he was prepared to go to trial, prepared to argue that the government's version of the visa application was forged, and prepared to argue that Hamas was an organization not unlike civil rights groups in the United States in the 1960s.

When I talked to him, I asked how equating Hamas with the Southern Christian Leadership Council or SNCC would be an effective argument. Miller said Hamas was largely "a political organization," and stone throwing also took place during the civil rights movement. "I'm not attributing all this to some vast conspiracy," Miller said, referring to the Idais prosecution. "It just doesn't seem likely that all those diplomats missed that application not being signed all that time in that part of the world. It's not what [Idais] submitted, but that's what they're charging him with. The truth is that's not his application; he signed his application."

Nancy Winter, the prosecutor, said all that was nonsense. Idais, she said, was a liar. He lied about his visa application. He lied about college. He lied to two different colleges. He lied to the court.

"He was arrested, and he was convicted in Israel," she said.

Winter is a no-nonsense career prosecutor who at that point had handled the bulk of criminal cases related to terrorism in the Eastern District of Pennsylvania.

"His lies finally caught up with him," she told me after Idais was sentenced to a year in jail by Judge Padova. Idais had already served that time, less a few hours, and faced the prospect of being immediately taken into custody by immigration authorities, who would ship him to York County Prison in preparation for deportation proceedings.

"He threw stones at buses when he was a kid," I said. "So what? How many Palestinians have not done that?"

"That's what he admitted in court," Winter replied. "What was found in a court in Israel was that he was a member of Hamas, and I have sworn written statements to that effect from other people who were members as well as himself."

The statements, Winter said, were clearly not tortured out of anyone, but freely given.

"But he knows that if he admits he was in Hamas, even if he's no longer in Hamas, that will just absolutely kill any chance he has in immigration court," she said.

"He's dead in immigration court now anyway," I said.

"Well, but in his mind, that's the thing he knew was a problem. And he stated to agents that, 'Listen, I admire Hamas because they only kill Jews. Hezbollah—I've got a problem with Hezbollah because they kill tourists and others as well, whereas Hamas kills the Jews like they should be killed.' That's the kind of formal statement to an FBI agent."

That is not exactly what is in the FBI report. On January 9, 2004, Idais told FBI agents that Palestinians were unfairly treated by Israel and that he did not support any group "that hurts tourists or others that have not harmed them." He supported Hamas to the extent the group defended Palestinians. Again, in the many hours I talked to

Idais, I never heard him comment about "Jews"—only Israelis, a political distinction largely lost, it seems, on Americans.

As Ghorab was transferred from York County Prison to Pike County Prison, Meriem Moumen also hired a new attorney, Steven Morley, to appeal Sheik Ghorab's immigration case. The Immigration Board of Appeals had ruled that Ghorab was guilty of marriage fraud and his residency application was properly denied. Morley, highly regarded in the legal community, had a succinct take on the sheik's situation.

"The government can't find any real terrorists," he said, "so they're deporting my clients instead."

"I was a kid during the '50s," he said, "but from everything I've read about the Cold War and the hysteria around the Communists, the Red Scare of the '50s, this is just reminiscent of the same thing. Instead of the word 'Communist,' it's 'terrorist.' Which is not to say there probably weren't some grains of reality to be concerned about in the '50s as it started, and there is, to be sure, some grain of reality to be concerned about today. But it's being used way out of proportion to justify oppressive laws and abusive conduct by the government. It's scary."

Like Henry, Ahmad, Miller, and every other attorney I encountered in discussing cases growing from Ansaarullah, Morley was having difficulty extracting information from the government.

"They just decided they were not going to let this guy out. It's part of—I've seen this in other cases," he said. "It's my perception that what they're doing is putting pressure on people to withdraw their federal claims. What they can't win legally, they will put the squeeze on them in other ways to discourage people, keep them in jail a long time, which costs taxpayers inordinate sums of money, to no real purpose."

It also puts crushing financial pressure on the families of defendants. As Ghorab's case wore on and on, Meriem Moumen's ability to meet her debts and the debts of the mosque became problematic. By the spring of 2005, with maybe two dozen congregants showing up regularly, it became clear that the mosque would close. It was just a matter of time. But Moumen did not give up. She faxed a plea to mosques all over the country. Estimated debt at that time: $20,000.

"This *masjid* is trying to minister to all types of people, Muslim and non-Muslim alike, in a very depressed section of Northeast Philadelphia," she wrote in the plea. "We have helped many families in the past, but now we are struggling to keep our doors open and we are asking for your support. We feel that with hard work and faith in Allah, the mosque could become a safe haven for the poor and outcast of our society. We want to be able to open our doors to people who have nothing left, and renew their faith in God and belief in themselves. But we cannot do this without any money. We pray that you find it in your hearts to help us, and if you cannot, please pass this letter on to someone who can."

The letter, she said, elicited one reply.

"All I can say is what happens, happens," she said to me afterwards. "I've done all I can. It's in God's hands." By the time I met Moumen at Ansaarullah, Ghorab had been jailed for over a year. No charges had been filed against him. No bond had been set. Morley filed a habeas corpus petition to force the government to show why he was being detained. It was sitting in federal court.

The mosque was stifling on one muggy day I spoke to Meriem. She told me she did not want to talk about the past. She was done talking; there was no point to it. I said that no one in the wider community knew what was going on at Ansaarullah, no one had any idea.

"I can't say any more," she replied. "One year and two months my husband has been away. One year and two months. For what? What has he done? His little girl was born. She has begun walking. She has begun talking. And he has been away. They put him in shackles around his legs and handcuffs when I went to see him and two guards standing on either side of him. What has he done? They say he was praying in the middle of the night, and they put him in isolation for two months. For praying! He was praying at night. Is this what he has done?"

By this point, Meriem had worked herself up, and the words were flowing, and she was about to burst into tears. We were standing near the bay door of the mosque after Friday prayer, and I felt like a burglar breaking into her most private affairs. She turned away from me and went into a small vestibule to compose herself. She was wearing a grey *abaya*.

"I'm sorry," she said, returning a moment later. "I cannot talk about this. I begin crying. You can't understand."

I told her that no one apparently wanted to talk about Ansaarullah—something I had said to her several times in the past—because they were afraid.

"Yes," she said. "People are afraid. All of them are terrified. I blame ourselves. There was a Palestinian who was here two years ago who needed help, needed support. We didn't go down there."

Farouk Abdel-Muhti, Palestinian activist and broadcaster for WBAI, the Pacifica radio station in New York, was held for two years by immigration authorities, including over eight months in solitary confinement at York County Prison. Following his release, he embarked on a speaking tour, thanking supporters, detailing his prison and immigration experiences, and urging a focus on Palestinian issues. Abdel-Muhti collapsed and died of a heart attack after delivering a speech at the Philadelphia Ethical Society in July 2004. "He basically gave an inspirational message to the human rights community and the progressive community, giving them credit and, you know, for his release and telling them to continue the struggle, and he said thank you," Sharin Chiorazzo, Abdel-Muhti's fiancée, told a *Democracy Now!* television and radio audience the day after his death. "Then, as we saw on the tape, he collapsed."

Moumen felt the pain of this incident even as we spoke much, much later. It filled her not with remorse but with anger.

"We didn't help," she said. "People are afraid to do anything. Only the African Americans are unafraid. The Arabs are all terrified. Not one of them showed up to help my husband. Not one."

Siddique, with his calm presence and deep empathy, said yes, the Arabs and Middle Easterners at the mosque had been unhelpful at best. At worst, they had undermined and abandoned Ansaarullah to its fate, spreading rumors as they went.

I saw this one day as Moumen and I stood near the counter filled with cassette tapes of Sheik Ghorab's sermons.

It was, as usual, very hot, and Moumen was telling me she was having a particularly hard time. There was yet another expense— she had to find a mover to take her things out of the house and put them in storage. It was clear by then that the mosque would close soon. Her landlord was harassing her, she said, demanding rent, excoriating her. Where is the money? She had none. That week he had come into her house and would not leave. He wanted to be paid.

"I called the police," she said. "He sat on my couch screaming at me."

It was July 2005, and attendance at the mosque had dwindled to a dozen.

The mover she found wanted $700.

"For what?" she complained. "I should move it myself. I should leave it all. I don't want it."

As we were talking, a man came up and began speaking to her in Arabic. He was relatively young, in his thirties perhaps, neatly dressed in khakis and a short-sleeve, plaid cotton shirt.

Moumen turned to me and said, "He's asking me how much I'm paying for my lawyer," she said, turning back to the man and continuing in English.

"I'm paying $22,000," she said.

"These are blood-sucking lawyers," the man replied, adding a derisive comment about yet another lawyer who worked on the Ghorab affair.

"He made so many mistakes, so many," Moumen agreed.

"He screwed up the case from the beginning," the man said, turning very somber. "My lawyer looked at Mohamed Ghorab's case, and he said the FBI had a sealed file on him from Egypt. Very thick, a sealed file from security."

Moumen erupted at this remark.

"They have nothing on my husband!" she hissed. "That is a lie. There is nothing here. There is no file. They said they had nothing. This is only about immigration. The FBI in Washington said this is only about immigration. Who is your lawyer? Who is your lawyer? Because he is lying! Tell me his name, and I will go and tell him myself! You are lying."

The man said nothing, just watched Moumen becoming more and more agitated.

"They looked all through this mosque. They looked all through our home. There is nothing! Who is your lawyer?"

The man remained silent in the face of this torrent.

"Who told your lawyer this? Where does this come from? Why are you saying this in front of him?" she said, indicating me. "You don't know who he is. He could be anyone. A file? That is a lie!"

She turned away to compose herself. The man shrugged and walked off.

Moumen turned back to me.

"Why did he say that? There is no file. I never heard of any file. He used to come here, and then he was arrested. What is his name? I can't remember. He's just some brother who came around here. Now they've all gone away. One person says something like that, and it gets passed on and passed on, and people become afraid. They stop coming. What if you were thinking of joining the mosque and you heard something like that? Would you come here? Of course not. Secret file. You wouldn't want anything to do with that."

And then she began thinking about Ghorab, how it used to be.

"All that has nothing to do with my husband. He is a gentle, decent man. He was a businessman in Egypt. He studied engineering, and he was a businessman who sold cotton. He fell in love with his religion. That's all. Where is the crime? What do they want here? What is so special about this little mosque?"

Her tears came again, and she said she could not talk anymore.

So it is on the "Arab street," where rumors are passed along like burning embers from one person to another. There is no way to counter such rumors, no way to refute them, no way to stop them. Nothing Moumen could say to the man could possibly sway his belief in the ominous secret file or his intention to talk about it in front of a stranger. Nothing she could say could stop the story from spreading from one person to another to another, until Al Aqsa and the rest of the Muslim community in Philadelphia was filled with the certainty that Egyptian intelligence had compiled a massive dossier on Sheik Ghorab, the radical.

That is not to say that some kind of file does not exist. Ghorab himself had told U.S. authorities that he had been extensively interrogated on numerous occasions by Egyptian police and that his mosque had been closed down. But interrogation by the police—and the creation of a "secret file" that could indeed be provided to U.S. investigators—might well be virtually meaningless.

In any event, federal agents would not discuss the backdrop of the case, why they were spending so much time going after "this little mosque," what lists they were compiling, what lists contained the name Mohamed Ghorab, what other mosques were targeted for cleansing. Unofficially, investigators talked vaguely about Salafist groups in Morocco that were suspected of carrying out terrorist bombings there. They talked about Salafists in Algeria. Their Egyptian counterparts began arresting members of Dawaa Salafia in 2002. In 2003, Egyptian security forces began accusing the group of complicity in Moroccan bombings. Those arrests prompted Ghorab to seek asylum in the United States, claiming that the political situation in Egypt had changed drastically since his departure in 2000 and his application for U.S. residency in 2001. He argued that Dawaa Salafia in Egypt had no connection to any similarly named groups in

Algeria or Morocco or anywhere else, his attorney told me, yet its members were on lists compiled by Egyptian security forces and were in imminent peril.

None of these arguments seemed to matter. Ghorab was already entangled in what was a thick jungle of innuendo, association, and rumor.

Siddique could see this happening at the mosque, although he did not know the details of all the sects fragmenting and fracturing across North Africa. He understood that the dissolution of Ansaa-rullah was intensifying and that there would soon be no option but to close.

"Paranoia is existing in this," said Siddique.

"They was arresting these people, but after they released them, after they were bailed out, every time somebody got arrested here, everybody here came together as a family sentimentally and said, 'Let's get this one together, let's get these people out, let's come on, please.'

"A person put a hat or bucket on the ground, and people put in $20 or whatever. They would beg and scrape and scratch, keep trying to get this person out because the person has a wife and family and little baby," Siddique continued. "'What are we gonna do with the family? Let's try to help, let's try to help, let's try to help.'

"This repeated itself over and over and over. These people that we got out, most of them, 95 percent of them that we got out, they never come here any more, and the money to get them out was raised inside this *masjid* to get them out of jail and back to their family members.

"But they don't come here any more. Most of them say, 'Okay, the government questions us every day. I got to report to them once a week or every two weeks about what's going on or what's this, that, or the other. They ask me about this. They ask me about that.'"

Former congregants left and returned to pick up information, it seems, and, in the case of the man speaking about Ghorab's "secret file," to see what kind of response the story would elicit. And perhaps to get the story out into the rumor mill.

Siddique sighed. He tried to fathom what Meriem and her family were going through and explain it to me. When he first came to Ansaarullah, he had not expected any of this, and it hurt and saddened him. Siddique is a man with a strong sense of human frailties in the face of fate.

"The *masjid* belongs to God," he said. "This mosque belongs to God. We can't control it. If God wants it to exist, it's gonna exist."

But it is human beings who are dismantling the mosque, I said. Human foibles played on by state authority.

"Yeah," he said.

Moumen appeared at the door of the mosque as we were talking in the heat and darkness and asked if we would like some tea. Siddique said no thank you.

"Do we agree with our laws to be used against somebody who they have nothing on and against a lady and a little baby and a young seventh-grade student? Who has no breadwinner no more?" Siddique said. "No. Afraid. Police coming by the house at night, government coming around, disgruntled people from this mosque coming by the house at night, throwing threats at this lady, whatever the case may be, and she's just left in the dark! Left in the dark by herself!

"She comes and opens up the mosque in the morning and closes it at night or comes to sweep up this place to keep her sanity. To keep her sanity! This lady do stuff like this just to keep her worth! To come in and ask you and I do we want any ice tea in here. It gives her purpose. I should've said yeah. It gives her more purpose. Because she has nothing to surround herself with except her children, cleaning up the *masjid*, and just worrying about her husband, who is one year incarcerated for nothing. For nothing!"

EIGHT

Nobody Wants a Terrorist Case

DEAN BOYD, ICE SPOKESMAN in Washington, likes to talk about the "toolbox" that law enforcement authorities have at their disposal.

"One thing that's really changed since 9/11 is that immigration as a tool is being used and recognized as a pretty important tool for these joint task force, national security cases," Boyd said at one point when I spoke to him in 2006. "It really wasn't used before 9/11. But prosecutors, agents from INS, ICE look at all angles to attack these groups. It's another tool in the toolbox."

The cases of Atef Idais and Mohamed Ghorab "are examples of that," he said. Idais, for instance, was initially arrested on a visa violation.

"Further investigation showed he was a member of Hamas [and] lied on his visa application," Boyd said. "So what the public may perceive as throwaway charges really . . . prove very useful."

Boyd declined to comment directly on Ansaarullah and the focus of authorities and agents on that mosque, but he compared the

Philadelphia investigation of Ghorab and Idais to the investigation into a supposed terrorist cell in Lodi, California, to "help," as he put it, in understanding Philadelphia.

In June 2005, federal authorities arrested twenty-two-year-old Hamid Hayat, a U.S. citizen with a grade-school education living in Lodi, on charges that he attended al Qaeda–linked "jihadist training camps" in Pakistan and lied about it. Authorities also arrested Umer Hayat, age forty-seven, Hamid's father and also a U.S. citizen, and charged him with lying about his son's activities. At the same time, authorities arrested Muhammed Adil Khan, a Pakistani national and imam at the Lodi Muslim Mosque, and Shabbir Ahmed, also a Pakistani and an imam at the mosque, and charged them with immigration violations. The two imams were working to establish a Muslim school in Lodi and met with Umer Hayat shortly before his arrest. Hayat was wearing a recording device during the meeting, according to news accounts. He later told a reporter that agents assured him that recording the imams would help his son. "They did trick with me," Umer Hayat told a *Frontline* journalist.

Mohammad Hassan Adil, age nineteen, son of one of the imams, was also taken into custody, again on immigration charges.

The investigation did not stop there; it spread, seeming to absorb Lodi's small but not insignificant Muslim community, which included perhaps 2,500 Pakistanis. Agents fanned out through the agricultural town of 63,000, located ninety miles east of San Francisco, interviewing residents, conspicuously driving the downtown streets, watching. News reports said at least half a dozen Lodi Pakistanis were suspected of training in al Qaeda camps overseas. Some news outlets reported that federal authorities believed plans were afoot to attack area hospitals. The original criminal complaint referred to such plots, as well as to planned attacks on food markets. Those charges were subsequently disavowed by authorities as mistakes— after the "news" had spread through the media. There were also suggestions that money was being funneled to terrorist groups. No evidence of that ever turned up. News for a day; rumor forever.

Meanwhile, the Pakistani community in Lodi and the surrounding area felt under siege. Undercover agents and unmarked cars were everywhere, residents told reporters. FBI and ICE agents interviewed scores of people. One community resident told me the mosque had become "a nest of informers." Basim Elkarra, director of the Sacramento Council on American-Islamic Relations, said the mordant joke making the rounds was that Lodi Muslims now had their very own special agents. But it was not funny. "It's like a nightmare," Kay Khan, a nineteen-year-old Pakistani American told a reporter for the *Sacramento Bee*. "It's our country, too."

It also appeared that the arrests had something to do with feuding within the Muslim community that crystallized around construction of the new Islamic school backed by the two imams. Indeed, the lay president of the Lodi mosque, Muhammed Shoaib, said he told federal authorities that one imam, Muhammed Adil Khan, was not an imam and had overstayed his visa, according to local news accounts. Shoaib opposed plans for the school. The Lodi mosque had run through several imams in recent years—they clashed with the lay leaders over matters related to religious practice, women, and even economics; Khan, the imam, and Shoaib, the lay leader, fit into that pattern. Federal agents claimed that Shabbir Ahmed—the other imam supporting the school and a protégé of Muhammed Adil Khan—preached support for the Taliban when he was in Pakistan during the early days of the U.S. attack on Afghanistan. Ahmed said he urged his listeners to "pressure Americans to stop bombing" Afghanistan—nothing more, according to reports in the *Sacramento Bee*. Ahmed added that his visit to the United States had completely changed his views about this country.

The *Bee* itself became a subject of federal ire for its reports detailing terrorism charges. The FBI opened an investigation into how the newspaper obtained sealed court records.

Both imams, as well as the son of one, eventually cut deals with the government and left the country voluntarily in 2005 rather than fight deportation.

The Hayats went to trial in 2006, when it was revealed that virtually the entire framework of the federal case against them was built
on information supplied by an informant paid about $230,000 by
federal agents to infiltrate the Lodi Muslim community. The man,
Naseem Khan, age thirty-three, also a Pakistani, taped many meetings with the Hayats that suggested to some who listened that the
informant was haranguing a dithering younger Hayat for his passiv-
ity and urging him to get out there and commit some terrorist acts.
In addition, trial testimony revealed that Naseem Khan told federal
agents that some of the most wanted terrorists in the world—
including Ayman al-Zawahri, Osama bin Laden's personal doctor
and the number two man in al Qaeda—were walking the streets
of Lodi in recent years. That so-called information, which is what
caused excited federal agents to sign up Naseem Khan in the first
place, seemed at best fanciful to many terrorism experts and raised
credibility issues at the Hayat trials.

The case was multifaceted and deeply troubling for many reasons,
not the least being the dubious use of provocative informants; the
federal interpretation and use of remarks made by one of the imams
in Pakistan several years ago; the deep internal fissures in the Pakistani community that were exploited by investigators; the eager in-
sertion of Osama bin Laden's name into proceedings; the dramatic
announcement at the investigation's onset that a network of terrorist
plotters had been uncovered—followed by substantially less dramatic criminal charges and virtually no evidence of any plot offered
at trial; the money paid to Naseem Khan, the government's informant; the indiscriminate interrogations throughout the Pakistani
community; the prolonged videotaped interrogation of Hamid Hayat, who had no attorney, that led to his confession, which he later
disavowed; and the federal probe of the *Sacramento Bee*'s reporting
of sealed court documents—just to touch on the most obvious.

Despite these issues, Hamid Hayat was convicted in April 2006 of
providing material support for terrorism after a jury deliberated

eight days; on the same day, his father's trial, held separately, ended in a hung jury and mistrial.

The day after the younger Hayat was convicted, however, a distraught juror in his case filed an affidavit with the court saying she was badgered by other jurors into pronouncing Hamid Hayat guilty—something she did not believe. Moreover, she painted a deeply disturbing portrait of a racially charged jury room where jurors routinely brought in newspapers with accounts of the case and indicated plans to convict Hayat well before the end of the trial. The jury room itself, as described by this juror, seemed to reflect the nation's most diminished sense of itself after 9/11.

Prosecutors vowed to launch a new trial of Umer Hayat after the jury in his trial was unable to reach a verdict. But in August 2006, U.S. attorneys agreed to drop the case, and the elder Hayat agreed to plead guilty to a charge of lying to customs officials and bringing undeclared cash into the country from Pakistan. He was fined and placed on probation. His life ruined—with all of his possessions, including his house, sold to raise money to pay legal fees—and the health of his wife shattered, Umer Hayat left Lodi to find work in Stockton.

U.S. District Court Judge George E. Burrell Jr. denied Hamid Hayat a new trial in the wake of the juror's affidavit describing purported improprieties in the jury room, dismissing a host of issues raised by defense attorneys. In September 2007, he sentenced Hayat to twenty-four years in prison. At that point, not even prosecutors continued to maintain that the informer in the case had seen top al Qaeda operatives in Lodi. "I think it's a situation of a mistaken identification," U.S. Attorney McGregor W. Scott told a *Frontline* interviewer in 2006. The New York police were more direct in their characterizations of sensational claims coming from their informer in the Herald Square case: "It's bullshit."

"We will utilize every legal tool available to us to ensure we, our children, and our children's children never have to relive the horror of that day," Scott said at Hamid Hayat's sentencing, referring to the September 11 attacks.

The case, with all of its problems, was on appeal in 2009.

ALL OF THIS WOULD, of course, seem eerily familiar to Philadelphia Muslims, but not for the reasons Dean Boyd had in mind when he raised the Lodi case for comparative purposes. Boyd was citing the use of immigration law to eject the foreign-born imams from the United States and the criminal law to go after the U.S. citizens. It was an instance of the toolbox in use.

"You look at what you've got and how do you deal with it, what's the best strategy," said Boyd. "Prosecutors make these decisions based on evidence, based on strategy. What is the best strategy for dealing with these cases? And they're going to look at what tools are available. And there may be an immigration violation they can bring, maybe a money-laundering violation; maybe actually they can go with a terrorism violation. But just because terrorism is not charged doesn't necessarily mean you're not dealing with the problem."

Whatever works. It is almost inconceivable, however, that the federal government would allow prime terrorism suspects to leave the country—or walk the streets of Lodi—if there was even the slightest evidence that could detain them and put them behind bars. Meanwhile, secrecy in such cases prevents any kind of outside assessment of official action.

Nancy Winter, the U.S. prosecutor in the Eastern District of Pennsylvania, pointed out that the thrust of post–9/11 enforcement activities is to disrupt whatever may be developing before it happens. Preemptive strikes, if you will. This same point was made by U.S. attorneys in Lodi who were justifying their cases. And, not surprisingly, ICE spokesmen in California characterized their use of immigration law to deport the Lodi imams as an example of the "tool kit" at work.

"None of us want to have a terrorist case," Nancy Winter told me one day following her successful prosecution of Atef Idais. "We want to charge something short of that, shut whatever there is to be shut down, and get 'em out of here."

"Some of what we do, we can't let people know," she continued. "Sometimes we have informants who've told us stuff, and we have to protect those people, so we do something else to obstruct and interfere. Sometimes the information comes from a confidential source, meaning an overseas—say it's secret—a classified source. And you can't utilize the information in an open forum. So what you do is you get creative; you find another crime. So I get very frustrated by the criticism, 'Oh, we don't have any terrorism cases here.' We have a lot of terrorism cases. We just don't have a lot of terrorism prosecutions. But that's not something people understand or that I can cite an example of because to cite an example I'd have to tell you something that's off the record."

So, I asked, we have to take it on faith?

"I think we do," she said. "At a lot of levels you have to take it on faith that people prosecuting and investigating crimes are trying to do the right thing. To think the opposite is to think we . . . we don't want to be effective in fighting terrorism. I mean, we don't fabricate cases; we don't make cases up. The constraints on our ability to investigate—I know there's been this big thing about the PATRIOT Act. But can I tell you something? People need to get real. When we want to get some information, I have to jump through a trillion million hoops to get it. I have to get court orders, I have to get this, I have to get that. It is not easy to investigate people in this country, contrary to what people see on television. It's tough, and it's kept secret, and it's not revealed. So if we find out there's really nothing to it, the person being investigated isn't traumatized, isn't drummed out of their community."

Yet for every interrogation, every investigation, files are also created. And files have nine lives. Nassim Saghour was interviewed in 2001 about the visit of an acquaintance in 1998. Saghour was not charged with a crime. He was not a target. But a file existed. That file came into play again in 2003, when ICE agents picked up Faycal

Saghour, erstwhile Jersey Shore soda jerk. I told Winter that the Saghour prosecution—harboring an illegal immigrant—reminded me of all the nanny cases that have bedeviled politicians and celebrities in recent years. Yet I couldn't think of anyone else prosecuted for that particular crime.

"Well, if their nannies had been wanted international terrorist fugitives, I think we'd prosecute them for harboring them," she said.

"I don't think his brother was a wanted international terrorist," I replied.

"No, but the person he had previously housed was, showing a pattern of housing illegal stowaway immigrants from Algeria, one of whom was. We didn't know who he was housing this time. He says it's his brother. Again I have no reason to doubt that. But once it's on the table, we pull a thread, and then we follow it."

In the post–9/11 world, that thread leads Muslims, in particular, into criminal charges and deportation proceedings.

Winter acknowledged that law enforcement authorities pay special attention to certain ethnic and religious groups.

"There's a little common sense here, I mean," she continued. "The terrorists who've recently harmed our country and harmed England come from a certain background. You don't have Jewish suicide bombers. You don't have Catholic little old ladies—they don't do suicide bombs. There's only one culture that has suicide bombs that wants to kill innocents for the most part. So I think it's silly and naïve to think we aren't obviously going to pay more attention to the groups from which that ideology evolves. I don't know how to answer that without it sounding bad. But it would be foolish to look at groups that don't have a history of doing things like that and spend equal amounts of investigative time looking at them."

Foolish? I thought of the bombing of the Oklahoma City federal building; all of the deadly IRA attacks carried out over the last half century; the bombings of mosques, churches, and women's health clinics in the United States; the two hundred–plus bogus anthrax threats and powder-filled envelopes delivered to clinics and women's health workers in the wake of the anthrax deaths in the fall and early winter of 2001 to 2002. And, of course, the actual anthrax attacks, almost certainly the work of a non-Muslim American, investigators now believe. Potential threat is in the political eye of the beholder.

For the FBI, the focus is on counterterrorism, and for that focus to bear positive results, it is necessary to have the cooperation of the Muslim community. Brian Lynch repeatedly emphasized to me the importance of contacts between the Bureau and leaders of Al Aqsa mosque.

"At the end of the day, we both want the same thing," Lynch said. "We both want safety. We both want our kids to go to school without any concerns. And we can't accomplish that—the FBI and JTTF can't accomplish that ourselves. We have to have the community's input, help, and assistance, and that comes from a two-way communication between the FBI and the community, and I know we have that."

That communication, however, takes place within a new kind of investigatory environment. It is not a case of federal agents seeking help to arrest mobsters or drug dealers. It is not a case of authorities investigating a "crime." Agents are engaged in identifying and isolating those whom they believe might commit some act at some future date. Once one enters this world, there is a very fine line—if any line at all—between an upstanding Arab American and a potential threat.

Leaders within Middle Eastern and South Asian communities across the country have sought to work with law enforcement authorities, seeking to find a way to shed the taint. They sit down with the FBI and local police and immigration agents and talk about community concerns. They seek to demystify and to assert—repeatedly, it seems—the desire of Muslims for peace and justice. They repeatedly affirm their patriotism, and every time there is an incident somewhere, anywhere, they reaffirm that patriotism and love of America. Muslims in Lodi have worked this way with the current leadership of the FBI in Sacramento. Philadelphia residents have done the same. But these efforts often bear some bitter fruit. Marwan Kreidie, the prominent Philadelphia leader, has pointedly promoted efforts to work with the Philadelphia Police Department and the local office of the FBI. It hasn't all gone well.

"We are here in this country because we want to be here," Kreidie said, as we spoke in late 2008. "We love our country and support our country, and we want to make sure things go well. But we're not going to be the scapegoats. We're not going to let whatever happens with the shredding of the Constitution. We're going to do our best to say, 'Yes, we'll help protect America.' There's no group in the country that can be more effective than we are with this whole 9/11 thing. But that's not going to give an excuse to destroy the whole web of laws protecting civil liberties and civil rights that it's taken generations to build."

So there have been ongoing meetings with local police and the FBI.

"We've met regularly with the FBI and worked together on things like when they came to do the interviewing of Iraqis," he continued. "We sat down with them and made that a real program instead of a stupid knocking on doors and scaring the crap out of people and arresting people scenario. We worked with the FBI to say while we're against this, we're going to work to make sure this works and works to protect as much as we can the rights of the people they're going to interview and protect the concept of law enforcement. I've always said to the FBI that I want the illegal Arab immigrant, the Palestinian immigrant who's scared shitless, excuse my French, in some small house in North Philly, if he somehow hears about a bomb, some kind of nut coming in, something, I want him to feel comfortable in calling law enforcement or calling me, rather than saying, 'You know what? They're going to deport me; I'm not going to get involved.' We've always worked on that, and we've tried to protect people, do our best to try and protect people's rights."

Kreidie's efforts have earned him the enmity of right-wing extremists and professional anti-Muslims, like writer Daniel Pipes, head of the Philadelphia-based Middle East Forum, and have triggered not-inconsiderable suspicion among Middle Easterners in Philadelphia. He now faces the classic double-bind of a centrist in troubled times.

"I've been accused of being *mahabarat,* you know, secret police," he said. "And I've also been accused of being an Islamist. I think if you have people on the fringes of both ideologies challenging you, I think you're doing your job."

But trust within the community is essential to that job, and if the trust is frayed, for whatever reason, the job fails, and the community becomes a community outside the country's social core, uncertain of its leaders, uncertain of its members, isolated. This is one of the most destructive aspects of the war on terror: the corruption of civil society from the profound infusion of suspicion. Kreidie is more than aware that informers riddle al Aqsa and the neighborhoods of its congregants, even as law enforcement seeks to gain the trust of citizens.

"I'm sure. I'm sure. I'm sure that every sermon is taped. I'm sure there are people there all the time. I'm sure that exists. I think there's a line we've crossed. Our government has crossed the line. I don't know who they are. I don't know who puts them in there. But I don't have the time to be bothered. I'm going to do what I'm going to do. I'm going to fight it if I know about it. If I can prove it, I'm going to fight it. But I'm not going to run around, Chicken Little, saying, 'This is happening, this is happening, and this is happening.' If it doesn't go anywhere, I won't."

But suspicion rolls along the sidewalks and through cafés anyway.

"The group I've been with, we've been together since before 9/11, and I think there's a trust factor there," Kreidie said, echoing comments I've heard from former members of the Weather Underground and SDS, former antiwar activists, former Cold War leftists and political dissidents today. Long familiarity breeds trust.

"I also know there are all these newer members that I don't know. And I have not made that connection. And I think people have a tendency to just interact—this isn't scientific or anything, but the Moroccan community seems to hang together. This community hangs with its own people. I think people are a little more wary of others. Everybody is convinced there's something going on. Iraqis stick together. Reality is that the informers are going to come with that. If they are there, they are going to come from within their group. And hey, listen: It's very easy. Informers are very easy. What you do is you get someone who has an issue with the law, and you just say, 'Look, we're going to keep the case open until you do this for us. You have to do this for us. Or immigration.'"

I once asked Siddique if Arabs at Ansaarullah were afraid. He looked at me out of the corner of his eye, the way people occasionally look at a blind man on the subway. "They're terrified," he said. African Americans, he noted, don't face the immigration threat, and, at least in Philadelphia, they have a history of loudly objecting to perceived inequities. "You're not going to be deported if you say something is wrong," he said.

FEDERAL AUTHORITIES, OF COURSE, are charged with the enormous and virtually impossible task of prevention; avoiding social and political fragmentation is not part of their portfolio. In fact, fragmentation and suspicion are important tools in the toolbox: They generate tips and sources. "The paradigm has changed because it's not 'open a case, investigate a case, arrest, convict,'" said the FBI's Brian Lynch. "Our job is simply to prevent the next attack."

"This is not about convictions as much as it used to be," he went on. "It's about who are the five people out there who want to blow up a mall in King of Prussia. How do we take care of that issue? How do we resolve that threat? That's what it's all about."

The five people planning to blow up the giant mall may well not exist. But they might. Anything conceivable is possible and actionable. If someone expresses hostility to the United States, how would they react to a suggestion of blowing up a mall? Or the suggestion of attacking Fort Dix? Or the Sears Tower? In Ohio, a Somali resident pleaded guilty to a count of conspiracy in a plea bargain after being accused of plotting to attack a mall. No particular mall was ever identified. No bomb-making equipment was ever uncovered. Angry words spoken in a Caribou Coffee shop were reported to authorities by another federal terrorism target. (Prosecutors planned to introduce evidence of a $11.25 payment to the coffee shop at trial, according to the *Columbus Dispatch*.) "Other people are being looked at," a spokesman for the U.S. Attorney's Office said in 2007, following the sentencing of Nuradin Abdi, a Columbus cell phone salesman, to ten years in prison for the supposed mall plot. Many in central Ohio are now convinced an extensive Muslim terrorist network lurks in the heartland.

In Cherry Hill, New Jersey, across the Delaware River from Philadelphia, five Muslims were convicted in 2008 of ostensibly plotting to attack the army base at Fort Dix. They planned to use a two-by-three-foot laminated pizza-delivery map to carry out the plot, prosecutors argued. The jury was shown videos of Middle Eastern beheadings found on a computer belonging to one of the men. Conviction followed. Viewing beheadings was not important in reaching the guilty verdict, one juror told the *Inquirer*. Really, it wasn't, she insisted. In Miami, five impoverished black cultists went through two trials for a supposed Sears Tower bomb plot; both trials resulted in hung juries. In 2009, a third jury at a third trial finally brought in a conviction. Cases like these, all revolving around informers, fill the years since 9/11. Did prosecutors disrupt real plots? Or were informers simply tugging ragged threads in the poor and isolated parts of America? In each of the communities where these cases have unfolded, Muslim and Middle Eastern community members believe the government and the informers it uses have concocted the supposed plots and inflamed the supposed plotters. Much of the surrounding non-Muslim community is just as convinced that *something* must have been going on in the mosques and coffee shops.

THE PATRIOT ACT WITH its wide array of investigatory powers has been extremely important to the law enforcement effort, Lynch said. The Philadelphia office has made rich use, he said, of the Foreign Intelligence Surveillance Act, which provides for quickie warrants for wiretaps and secret searches. National Security letters, which give agents access to financial and other records, including library and business records, have been an important tool, often used. Lynch would not comment on whether his office has also benefited from warrantless National Security Agency wiretaps authorized by President Bush.

Better safe than sorry?

"I'm not sure I'd like to make a blanket statement about 'better safe than sorry' as much as, if something doesn't look right, we have to follow it," said Nancy Winter. "The thing that's very difficult is when our mission is to obstruct and impede and interfere. You do sometimes do the 'better safe than sorry.' . . . I don't think there are any easy answers, and the problem is that on an individual level, everything always seems to make sense and to be fair or unfair depending on the perspective of whomever you're speaking to."

Winter agreed that there has been an increase in the number of criminal cases growing from immigration charges—matters that ten years ago might have been generally ignored by authorities or handled as civil cases.

Not any more. A study conducted by TRAC, the Transactional Records Access Clearinghouse at Syracuse University, indicates that the increase is a national phenomenon and represents a fairly steady trend up since the September 11 attacks. While the study clearly indicates that the federal government is willing to turn immigration matters into criminal actions, what that means in terms of 9/11–related cases is less clear.

According to the 2005 study, the Department of Homeland Security (DHS) recommended prosecution of 65 percent more immigration cases in fiscal 2004 than it did in fiscal 2003: 37,765 versus 20,771. Most of that increase, however, can be attributed to one area along the Texas-Mexico border. The TRAC report says, "Overwhelmingly, the DHS is involved in the prosecution of traditional kinds of immigration cases that appear to have very little to do with intercepting bombers. In fact, only seven out of the 37,765 prosecutions filed arising out of its immigration enforcement were classified as involving international terrorism during FY 2004, and only one out of 20,771 prosecutions involved international terrorism during FY 2003."

The report does not analyze what nationalities were involved in various cases, although it is safe to say the vast majority of cases involve immigrants from Mexico. Nor does the report define "international terrorism." Would the case against Atef Idais fall under that heading? Probably not. Yet it seems not unfair to characterize the Idais prosecution as a product of 9/11.

If prosecutions are up, investigations are up even more. And once an investigation is started, it never seems to end. It just continues, traveling from one person to another and another, like a space probe heading on and on and on. Ansaarullah is a case in point. Lodi is another. Ohio. There are literally dozens and dozens of examples. Federal officials, no matter what the facts are that come out at trials, seem to stick to a preexisting script that reflects events like a fractured mirror. John Negroponte, the nation's first director of National Intelligence, told the Senate Select Committee on Intelligence in February 2006 that federal agents had uncovered an al Qaeda–related jihadist cell in Lodi, "a network of Islamic extremists" that "maintained connections with Pakistani militant groups, recruited U.S. citizens for training at radical Karachi madrassas, sponsored Pakistani citizens for travel to the U.S. to work at mosques and madrassas, and according to FBI information, allegedly raised funds for international jihadist groups." No evidence of any of this activity was presented at either of the Lodi trials. But it does serve to promote national anxiety and the counterterror mission.

Even with the Lodi trials over, federal authorities said their investigation into that community would continue. "Certainly there are people of interest to us" in Lodi, U.S. Attorney McGregor Scott told the

Associated Press in the immediate aftermath of the trials. Drew Parenti, the FBI agent in charge of the Sacramento office, said the same: "There are aspects of this [case] which remain under investigation."

Unending investigations in an unending war.

Another TRAC study at Syracuse University, using data obtained under the Freedom of Information Act from the Executive Office for United States Attorneys, speaks to the somewhat defensive responses of law enforcement authorities to the conduct of the war on terror. The 2006 study found that of 6,472 individuals referred to U.S. attorneys for terrorism prosecutions from 2001 to 2006, prosecutors found 64 percent of the cases not worth pursuing. Another 9 percent were dismissed, or the suspects were found not guilty. Convictions were obtained with 1,329 suspects, 27 percent—about 1 in 4 of those referred. Of those 1,329 convictions, 1 percent—14—received sentences of twenty years or more; 5 percent—67—received convictions of five or more years.

But 704 received no prison time, and 327 received sentences of a day to less than a year. Even though some of the prosecutions were still pending at the time it was completed, the study rammed the point home: "Thus, the median or typical prison sentence for them all was zero because the majority received no time at all in prison."

I HAD INITIALLY PERCEIVED the "toolbox" that law enforcement authorities refer to repeatedly in the way that agents and officials most likely perceive it themselves: a suite of laws and regulations whose purpose—no matter how used—is to repair and preserve a damaged nation. But the more I considered Ansaarullah and other similar situations across the country, I began to realize that the toolbox held instruments of demolition; what is labeled repair is, in fact, a dismantling. A once-thriving mosque in Frankford Valley, gone; Pakistani stores on Coney Island Avenue, Brooklyn, or South Seventh Street, Philadelphia, vacant; an Islamic school in Lodi, not built, and the surrounding community fearful and withdrawn. What was actually happening was disintegration across the American landscape, both the cultural and the physical landscape. Gap-toothed streets, empty lots, populations of migrants forced from place to place by federal law—these are as much a result of the war on terror as deportations and increased prison populations. Pakistanis have fled Brooklyn, just as much as they've fled Philadelphia. Some have left the country. Some have moved to more isolated areas. Those who remain in place, in Lodi, for instance, have become so fearful, feel so besieged, that they refuse to respond to the outside world at all, except in the most perfunctory way.

"No one wants to talk about it now," Taj Khan, a prominent Lodi resident, told me in 2009. "Everyone wants to hush it up. There is nothing more to say."

Two imams were arrested, he said, on false charges. They were imprisoned in shackles and finally left the country voluntarily. "You remove two leaders from the community; it had a very profound effect," Khan said.

Now in 2009, going on four years since federal agents first swept through Lodi, he said that the FBI is still knocking on doors, "visiting homes and asking people to cooperate and talk with them." Khan had been a supporter of construction of an Islamic Center when the massive investigation got underway. Fundraising stopped. The mosque was riven by disputes over the center, the imams, the investigation, the future of the community, he complained. A group left the mosque, refusing to return. A lawsuit was filed, further splitting the community. Efforts to collaborate and join with local synagogues and churches halted. "All because of the encouragement and support of the FBI," Khan said. Even so, local Pakistanis did not leave the Lodi area in significant numbers, he said. Many South Asians have Lodi roots going back to the early twentieth century. They see the hot farmland as their home. In a nation full of people who think nothing of picking up and moving every couple of years, Pakistanis in Lodi have embraced what can be called, in the deepest Old World sense, their homeland.

But at the North Penn mosque in Montgomery County outside of Philadelphia, Mohammad Mollah told me that there were congregants who had fled the city seeking a quieter area out of the spotlight. "We don't ask why they left. That's not something you ask. They are here." At the same time, he said, there were congregants of North Penn who fled that quiet area for Canada.

In the view of virtually every Middle Easterner or South Asian I spoke with, such migrations are a direct result of the government's "toolbox." People flee to escape the looming specter of preventive detention. If someone is not chargeable under one statute or regulation, he or she can be held accountable on something else. If that doesn't pan out, perhaps another regulation can be found. Taxes, marriage, suspicious associations, credit cards, misspelled nicknames, ill-timed charitable efforts, application deadlines violated—there's always something that can be used. My sense is that once a suspect is identified, authorities are reluctant to let go, no matter what.

"You never know, you never know what this guy or this girl you've got in custody is about to do that you don't know about," said John Kelleghan of ICE.

You never know. Better safe than sorry. That might be a rule of thumb to apply on the road from the airport to the Green Zone in Baghdad, but is it appropriate in Philadelphia? Or Columbus, Ohio? Or Brooklyn? Is there a difference? Or is it all war, the war on terror?

Was the country preserved and protected in 1970 thanks to surveillance of antiwar student groups and civil rights organizations? Did surveillance and infiltration in the 1950s serve the nation well? Does the surveillance of Muslims, antiwar dissidents, environmentalists, and animal rights activists now strengthen the nation and its social fabric? In the wake of Lodi and innumerable other cases, I'm still left with the fundamental questions: What is this war? Who is the enemy?

I asked Kelleghan if the country is at war here on American soil.

"I'd say yes," he said. "Maybe 'war' isn't the right word. We're still protecting the homeland. Every day we're learning a new way the criminal element is trying to back door us. You never know if the guy trying to gain entrance at the airport, what he is here to do. You never know if the guy that trooper has pulled over—is he on his way to crash into a building, or is he on his way to cut grass? There's no routine anymore."

"Aliens," said Kelleghan, "have the capability to hurt the homeland." Since September 11, "you're that much more cognizant and focused on the nonroutine things. How can they beat us here? How can we protect this realm at the airport or at the seaport? How do we close that loophole?"

I asked Brian Lynch the same question.

"Well, we are at war, and our job is to protect the citizenry of this [FBI] division and globally, the United States and its citizens, and we take that very seriously every day," he said.

"Who is the enemy?" I wondered.

"Whoever it is who wants to make a statement or injure our citizens, make a statement by injuring our citizens," Lynch said. "The events of 9/11 have certainly changed our focus of having counterterrorism as our number one priority, as indicated by Director Mueller."

What are we being protected against?

"Well, we're being protected against the events that occurred on 9/11," Lynch said. "We're protecting against those events that occur worldwide that we all see on Fox and CNN. We're protecting against those things. There are people out there who would like to do us harm, and we're protecting against that."

Joseph O'Connor, the head of counterterrorism for the Philadelphia Police Department, had a similar, if more baroque response.

Do you consider this a war? I asked.

"I do, but many people don't," he said. "If you look at the old Caliph, all those countries that we're involved with, Syria, Iran, Iraq, all those countries were all part of the Caliph, to include the 'Stans—Kazakhstan, Uzbekistan, all those little 'Stan countries that are above Afghanistan."

O'Connor then proceeded to muse on Stalin's Russoization of that area, the persistence of mosques in the Soviet territories, Constantine at the Council of Nice, the nature of the pre-Byzantine Sun God, and the relationship of Christianity and the late Roman Empire.

"If we're at war," I wondered, "why don't people feel we're at war?"

"Because there's no country," he said. "In other words, during the Second World War, we could certainly dehumanize the Japanese. We could certainly dehumanize the Germans. You can't dehumanize everybody from all the different countries because we're not sure—there are only elements within certain countries. How big they are, who knows?"

"But who is the enemy?" I persisted.

"The enemy is anybody who comes under the umbrella of the Muslim Brotherhood, which is a philosophical stance with regard to basing each government on a theocracy, as opposed to a democracy. And anything Western is considered foreign and perverted, and anybody that subscribes to anything Western in nature is considered *Jahiliyah*. . . . They can be killed and executed just as infidels can."

"The philosophical umbrella of all these movements," he said, "regardless of what label they put on them, is the Muslim Brotherhood, which were the people responsible for the assassination of Sadat. So it's the radicalized, militarized type of Islam that's preached in some of these mosques, subscribed to by some of these Muslims."

No matter how it is parsed, the threads that tie the war on terror together are the same: religion and ethnicity. Yet the federal government is officially on record to this day as opposing use of religion or ethnicity in pursuing the "war." Given the extent of the federal effort at Ansaarullah, however, it seems reasonable to wonder if federal officials were indeed using it as a test case for the "toolbox." What would be the best way to remove the "threat" of this mosque?

O'Connor said he was not aware of such an effort. Winter, the U.S. attorney, said the same.

"The other thing you have to understand is once we start looking at something, when things come across our plate that otherwise might not have, we have to deal with it," she said. "So it's kind of like that mosque appears to have had the bad luck of having had these guys as members because then it brought attention to the mosque, and when [agents] are there, they look and they see and they find there's a whole bunch more illegals. And they have to then deal with the issue."

For Meriem Moumen, that rings hollow.

"They went after my husband; then they went after Atef and Jabi Khatut," she said—the spiritual leader of the mosque, his successor at prayer, and the president of the mosque. "It is a simple tactic: Cut off the head, and the body will die."

A man familiar with the mosque, but not a congregant, said exactly the same thing. "First they took out Sheik Ghorab," he said. "Then they arrested Atef, who had taken over leading the prayers. It was an experiment. How do you do it? What is the most effective way to knock it out?"

No organization nor the federal government has statistics on the matter, but culling through thousands of news stories from across the country suggests that at least 1,000 imams have been interrogated, arrested, detained, or deported from the United States since 9/11. The number could be much higher.

John Kelleghan at ICE would not discuss the specifics of the Ghorab case, but he said his agents followed up on leads, plain and simple. "If it's against the law, we're going to do our job," he said.

Brian Lynch at the FBI said he would not discuss anything that was not already in the public record.

"It was a JTTF investigation run through the JTTF, and we used the tools of the toolbox to address that case," he said.

Are you satisfied by the outcome of the investigation? I asked.

"Yes," he said.

NINE

What's the Use of Me?

A<small>FTER</small> J<small>UDGE</small> J<small>OHN</small> P<small>ADOVA</small> sentenced Atef Idais to a year in jail
for lying on his visa application and entering the country
fraudulently, the prisoner—who had already served the entire sentence less about six hours—asked if he could "hug my family."
Padova responded that the matter was outside of his jurisdiction.
Idais was in the custody of U.S. marshals now.

Two marshals stood on either side of Idais, placed handcuffs on
him, and led him away. Tazkia, sitting in the back of the courtroom,
blew kisses at her father as he turned and wanly smiled at her before disappearing through a side door. Rrahime looked down at her
hands.

"I am so, so tired," she said to me a few minutes later, out on the
street. "When Atef was arrested before and got out, he was ready to
leave right then.

"'What is the point?' he said.

"I said, 'No, this is the United States. People here have rights.
There is justice here. That's what this country is about.'

"And he said, 'Alright, I hope you are right.'

"I said, 'You haven't done anything. Why would anyone want to do anything to you?'

"Then he was arrested again, and we didn't know where he was for five weeks. Five weeks!"

He was in York? I asked.

"No. He was in the hole here in Philadelphia. We couldn't see him. Couldn't talk to him. Couldn't write to him. Tazkia was so upset. She misses him so much. It's destroyed my family, wrecked us financially. Why are they doing this? Why are they spending so much time, so many resources on people who have done nothing? Why don't they go after the real terrorists? Why are they going after little people who just want to live their lives? If we have to leave . . ."

She stopped for a moment, thinking. Tazkia wrapped herself around her mother's leg.

"I don't believe there is justice anymore in this country," Rrahime finally said. "If we have to leave, if he's deported, I'll have to give up my education. That's the one thing. I will never be able to finish my education. I will follow him, follow my husband. But that has always been my dream."

In November 2005, Idais had an immigration hearing before Judge Grace Sease at the York County Justice Center. The matter before the court was whether he had lied on his visa application—the same issue that had come before the criminal courts.

Rrahime drove out to York for the hearing and spent the day waiting outside a closed courtroom. She was not allowed to attend the hearing. She was not allowed to testify on her husband's behalf. And, in fact, Idais was not allowed to testify himself.

"Finally he had a merit hearing on the issue of whether his student visa was fraudulent in any sense and he failed to report his incarceration back home in Palestine," said Idais's attorney, Anser Ahmad. "The judge ruled that the government had met its burden and in that respect granted their request that he be found deportable. She ordered him removed, and after a full day hearing he pretty much said, 'This is not worth fighting. If I appeal it, I'll be in jail six more months, and if I lose that, I'll probably be deported anyway, so I'd rather go home and have my family move out there.' So that's how we left, and he did not want to appeal the process. And so he took the final order."

Idais, in essence, gave up.

"He foresaw what was coming, which was another six or nine months in jail," said Ahmad. "And the way the judge handled the matter, she pretty much didn't even want to hear his side of the story and ruled in favor of the government on all counts. He just got frustrated with the system."

I spoke with Idais early in 2006 as he awaited deportation.

"No one was allowed in during the hearing—it was closed," he said. "They brought in some guy from Jerusalem to testify by phone. I never heard of him before. Everything he said was totally different from what I experienced in Jerusalem. I wanted to testify, and my lawyer argued that I was the only one there who knew what actually happened. But the judge said, 'No, they made their case.' My lawyer was angry. Unbelievable. I've never seen such stupid games. You're telling me throwing rocks at the Israelis is a terrorist act? They're just doing whatever they want."

Rrahime was crushed. It was incomprehensible to her. She was now working at any temporary job she could get, dropping her children off at her parents' house in the morning. Her mother, at least, could look after them.

"Money is unbelievable now," she said. "Why wouldn't they listen to Atef's side of the story? This is justice? This is happening here in America? Why won't anybody listen? That's what hurts."

She sighed.

"Atef called last night. He was very sad, very hurt. I know the truth will come out. I don't know how long or when. I know it will. I told Atef to hang in. They have so much more power than we do. I'm here, broken financially, here with two kids. As time passes, there are more and more pressures. It's unbelievable."

For Rrahime, hope was gone. The truth was gone. Dust and grime, she said, would never be cleansed from the surface of their story to give a clear, true picture.

"Since nobody's been able to tell the truth about us or allow us to defend ourselves, or to defend us of these charges, that makes me say sometimes, 'Well, nobody is going to be able to light up the truth,'" she said.

Ansaarullah proved to be all a bitter illusion, she said, a mistaken involvement that destroyed her family and wrecked her future and that of her children. People there were not what they seemed. They were, at best, hypocrites. Disappointment is too small a container to hold Rrahime's feelings about the congregants at the mosque.

"I don't want to have anything to do with them," she said. "I don't know why they would say anything bad about my husband. We were going to the mosque. We were praying. We were going to meetings. I was going there, and I used to think everybody was very nice. I thought everybody connected to the mosque was wonderful, had wonderful qualities. Now it looks as though people there were acting nice, but it seems they had other plans for us. We used to laugh with them. Now I don't know who would want to do us harm."

There are, she said, "no more hopes.

"I am so, so tired."

Idais was deported to Jordan in January 2006. An ICE press release cited his arrest and prosecution as one of "25 public examples in which ICE has used immigration authorities to address terrorism-related threats since January 2004."

MERIEM MOUMEN AND HER children were evicted from their home at the end of the summer in 2005.

"The landlord changed the lock, changed everything," she told me later. "He even took my clothes. He took two bedroom sets, living room table, a bicycle, my baby's stuff. The crib. Took a lot of our belongings. A lot of stuff. I called the cops that day when I went to the house and I found the locks, they were changed. Basically, they told me there's nothing they can do. So I stayed at my mom's apartment for a week or so. Tried to get another place. Thought we'll get a fresh start. I'm going to move to New Jersey. We only stayed in New Jersey one month, and then the deportation, he got deported. One month. I was having a lot of financial problems, a lot—the lawyers and the children. It was *way* too much for us to handle. Way too much. My husband was supporting us, and the next thing you know he's not there any more. Your income is gone, and all your savings are gone. Bye."

In the weeks leading up to the closing of Ansaarullah, Meriem had been alternately angry, weepy, stoic, proud. A whole sheaf of emotions would wash over her in a single conversation. One day, toward the end, she was standing on Wakeling Street in the afternoon, her gray *abaya* flapping in the hot wind.

"I have nothing against this country," she said. "I have nothing against this government. Really, nothing at all. What really makes me angry is my own people. The brothers who wear beards. The sisters who wear this," she said, touching her veil. She stopped for a long moment.

"They just ran away," she said. "They let this happen. They are cowards. Sheik Mohamed made sure that this mosque was open. Everyone could come here. Anyone from the neighborhood was welcome. It didn't matter if you were a Muslim or a Jew or a Christian. This was for the neighborhood. These are poor people! And so when the time for charitable gifts came, he insisted it go out to the neighborhood. We went door to door with food.

"Now Atef's little children are suffering. And these brothers we helped, they just stopped coming here, and they passed on this rumor and that rumor, rumors of all kinds until no one would come here. Informers? Without a doubt."

What about Sheik Ghorab—how is he? I wondered.

"How do you think he is?" she shot back. "His family is being thrown out on the street. He's in jail for nothing. He can't do anything. And I am like any wife fighting for her husband."

Now, she said, it is out of their hands.

"It is in Allah's hands. It is all so sad. This was home for two years—for my husband, three years. Everything he worked so hard to build. We worked so hard. It is so sad to see it go right down the toilet. My husband built this up from nothing.

"When you accept what's happening, it's a lot easier," she continued. "It's a test, like my husband always tells me. I have to pass this test. I have to. I know we will be together somewhere. The main thing is to be together. If not in this country, then someplace else. I've given it up to God. It is in his hands. If God didn't put me in this situation, then I couldn't pass this test."

At first I took Meriem's reluctance to speak with me as a reflection of her fear. That certainly was the case with any number of Ansaarullah congregants who flatly refused to say anything about the mosque or Sheik Ghorab. If they had a potential immigration problem, they did not want to draw any attention to themselves whatsoever. If they had no problem, they didn't want to create one. But Meriem's reluctance was also rooted in an intense fatalism. Nothing she could do could affect the outcome of events. Nothing she could do could sway God's will. When prison authorities refused to allow Sheik Ghorab to have a civil marriage ceremony at York County Prison—a common practice for inmates—yes, she saw it as the act of officials seeking to undermine Ghorab's case for remaining in the United States, but it was, just as much, God's will. When Rrahime's citizenship papers were delayed and delayed and delayed for more than a year, until after Idais was criminally charged, yes, that was bureaucratic manipulation aimed at disrupting his case, but it was also God's will. When Ansaarullah finally closed, it was not simply the act of federal law enforcement agents seeking to weaken part of the Islamic community and get rid of "bad guys"; it was very much God's will. And when Ghorab was finally deported back to Egypt, it was not just an act of the government engaged in the war on terror; it was God's will.

Even Rrahime, an impressive young woman with a clear understanding of and a love for the United States, succumbed to a fatalistic view of events. She began to see her family as propelled by forces completely beyond her control. She could no longer resist—even if it meant deportation to one of what she called the "creepy countries" she and Atef came from. She was so tired. God's will.

SIDDIQUE IS BACK AT the mosque on Walnut Street. He is at peace with himself about Ansaarullah. He did what he could to keep the mosque open for God. What happened was God's will. He misses friends. The man who sat down with him the first time Siddique arrived at Ansaarullah in 2002 stopped attending when the heat became too much to bear. Siddique misses him.

"He's a beautiful man," Siddique recalled. "I'd go to his house, and we'd just sit down and watch *National Geographics* for hours about fishing. This guy was fantasizing about fishing. 'That's some beautiful fish,' he'd say. 'In my country I used to go scuba diving.'"

But the man turned away from Ansaarullah.

"We don't communicate anymore," said Siddique. "One time his wife asked my wife, 'Let's all sit down together.' Told me to make the date, and I made the date, and they never showed up. They just never showed up, and I don't know why. I lost a friend. I don't hold nothing against nobody. I'm quite sure his friendship for me was genuine. I'm quite sure there was a pain for him like it is to me."

Others Siddique knew from the mosque have occasionally resurfaced in his life briefly, perhaps out of guilt over abandoning Ansaarullah to fate.

"There's another guy who used to come to the *masjid*—he called me one time, and then he called me again," said Siddique. "I never returned the phone call. And then one day he called—he sounded like we used to sound when we was ten years old or something like that, calling a friend that you might've had a fight with, just calling to see how you doing, calling to see how you was doing, just calling to see how you doing. That's all he's saying. I understood where he's coming from. So I called him back. I called him, and the conversation went much better.

"I called. He said, 'How you doing? How you been? How's your family? I just called to see how you was doing,' and stuff like that.

"I said, 'Good, man, good to hear from you, glad you called. How's everything else? Everything cool? Ok, man, well, take care.' That was the end of the conversation."

THE NORTHWEST CORNER OF Wakeling and Aramingo was empty until 2009—no business, no tenant in the white cinder-block building where Ansaarullah once held its services. For rent. The threat became a more familiar one to an old city neighborhood: yet another vacant property. (In 2009, the mosque building returned to its roots, in a manner of speaking: It became a used car lot.)

ICE put out a press release on the day Mohamed Ghorab was deported, December 8, 2005:

> "Arresting and deporting those who violate the terms of their visas is a critical part of ICE's efforts to restore integrity to the nation's immigration system," said Thomas Decker, the Field Operations Director for ICE Detention and Removal Operations in Philadelphia. "The removal of Mr. Ghorab represents the latest in ICE's effort to ensure that there are consequences for violations of U.S. immigration laws."
>
> In the past two fiscal years, ICE has removed more than 293,500 illegal aliens and immigration status violators from the United States.

There were no press releases on the days other former congregants were expelled from the United States. They were shipped out silently. Or left before what they believed was the inevitable.

Nor was there a press release issued the day that Hassan Saddiq Faseh Alddin left the United States in the summer of 2004—more than a year before Ghorab. Alddin was not a member of Ansaarul-lah, but he was arrested in San Diego the same day that Mohamed Ghorab was arrested in Philadelphia, in May 2004, the day after Attorney General Ashcroft and FBI Director Mueller held their "Seeking Information Alert" press conference. Ghorab and Alddin were tied together at the time of their arrests in news accounts, the two American residents picked up in the cause of seeking information.

Alddin had been a resident of San Diego since 1994. He was married to a Wisconsin-born nurse, Pamela, who converted to Islam, and the couple had a little boy and girl. Alddin was accused of having 9/11 "ties," but officials refused to disclose any information on the case for "national security" reasons. What were those ties? How was Alddin related to 9/11? Was this a significant break in the case? Another cell uncovered? Another plotter unmasked?

The ties proved less than formidable. In 1994, as a student, Alddin roomed for one month with someone who, years later, became friends with two 9/11 hijackers living for a time in San Diego. Alddin had not seen his former roommate in several years, and he freely told government agents all of this in the fall of 2001. Nevertheless, three years later, in May 2004, it suddenly became a significant issue. He was arrested immediately. But rather than pursue a protracted legal fight—as Ghorab and Idais sought to do on the East Coast—Alddin chose to leave the country voluntarily, despite being a permanent resident. It appears that agents wanted more and more information from him. And when more information wasn't forthcoming—because, perhaps, there was no more to say about the unknown friend of a friend from years far in the past—they arrested him. Seeking information.

"If we apply six degrees of separation, anybody could be affiliated with the hijackers," Alddin's attorney, Randall B. Hamoud, told a San Diego reporter. Then Alddin's friends rallied around him—only to find themselves visited and questioned by federal agents.

"I find that information to be very disquieting because I'm wondering whether innocent people are being targeted merely because they show up at public hearings to lend moral support to someone who is caught up in the judicial process," Hamoud told a reporter for the *San Diego Union-Tribune*. "That's not what America is about."

Alddin left the country and his family in July 2004, returning to Saudi Arabia. His wife, Pamela, was utterly devastated by the situation, her life shattered. Should she follow her husband to a country not known for freedoms allowed women? Should she remain in the United States and deprive her children of their father? What should she do? According to her mother, she began drinking to kill the emotional pain and loneliness, the *San Diego Union-Tribune* reported. She stopped working. Finally, in October 2005, as she was about to be evicted from her home, Pamela Faseh Alddin had had enough. She took her children and left the United States for Saudi Arabia. In the autumn of 2006, Pamela's mother, Patricia Schreiner, said the couple had settled down. "She said she likes it over there," Schreiner told Kelly Thornton of the *Union-Tribune*. "She said they're treating her well."

In the neighborhood of Frankford Valley, former members of Ansaarullah have all moved. A "for rent" sign was placed in the front window of Rasheed's house. Youssef's house has the blinds drawn. It is empty as well. Ghorab's house has been rented. Used cars for sale now fill the mosque parking lot. The city has scabbed over the pain and confusion that bubbled out across the urban battlefield.

This is a close-knit neighborhood, as Kathleen Zoladek from the state representative's office told me. "The majority of these people die here," she said. "They raise their children, they stay in their homes, and the majority of them—either they go away to nursing homes, or they die here. That's the way it really is."

But not for Ghorab or Atef or Rasheed or Nassim. Not for any of those even marginally connected to Ansaarullah. These empty streets are closed to all of them now. They have been excluded.

As I stood looking at the old mosque one day, I thought of Hajrah Alakbar, Ghorab's first wife, an African American who knew, like all African Americans, the essence of exclusion in America. When I was talking to her at one point, she put Ansaarullah squarely into that experience.

"Why didn't they go after me?" she wondered. "I don't know. But I can tell you, brothers were being shipped back. This brother, that brother. Anybody that had anything to do with Mohamed was being shipped back. What did they have to do with anything?

"But that's the way this country was founded—going after people. It's the way things has always been. African Americans know all about it. My parents experienced it. My grandparents experienced it. Their parents. That's what this country was founded on."

So many more ghosts.

***

FOR MANY MONTHS FOLLOWING the deportations of Ghorab and Idais, I tried to locate them. Federal authorities were not helpful. The two were deported, Ghorab to Egypt, Idais to Jordan. That's all U.S. officials said they could tell me. Rrahime's phone ceased to work. The Ormes Street house was empty. Neither the Jordanian nor the Egyptian governments responded to inquiries. Human rights workers in Egypt were swamped with increasing numbers of disappearances and detentions and could not help locate a single lost soul. So many detentions, so few rights workers.

Finally I contacted every nongovernmental organization working in the Middle East to see if I could find Atef Idais, at least. Al Haq, an independent rights group working on the West Bank, came to my aid, and I was finally able to locate him. He had landed a job working with former Ansaarullah president Jabi Khatut's company in Dubai. But all was not well—Idais's family had made the profound decision to remain in the United States.

"I wish they had tortured me or killed me, rather than what they did to me, really," he said by phone from Dubai. It was a sigh audible 10,000 miles away.

At his last immigration hearing, which was closed, Idais said, Grace Sease, the immigration judge, ruled that Idais's rock throwing at the age of fourteen was "a terrorist act."

"Why are they calling this terrorism?" he wondered. "What they are doing to me is terrorism. They accepted nothing I said. Nothing I wrote. They didn't want to listen to me. They denied all my motions. I stood up and said, 'Okay, I will just leave.' My wife is crying behind me. And they deported me. They put me on an airplane with two agents on my left and on my right all the way to Jordan. We stopped for nine hours in transit in Amsterdam, and they kept me in a little room. There was no toilet. No water. Nothing. They kept me there for nine hours. When we walked through the airport, they blocked me off from people. They made me take my shoes off. It was search, search, search.

"I said to them, 'Why are you doing this? You've been with me the whole time.' They introduced me to people at the airport as 'the deportee.'"

When they finally arrived in Jordan, Idais was handed directly to Jordanian intelligence authorities, he said.

"They didn't detain me, thank God, but every two days, for one week, I had to go to different interrogations, different departments. They wanted to know why I was deported. I don't blame them. The Americans bring in this guy with two agents, they want to know why. I told them the whole story."

The Jordanians were not impressed with the case. They let Idais go.

Far worse was his family situation. Rrahime, in the end, could not bring herself to leave the United States. She could not face the prospect of life on the West Bank or in Albania. She could not bring herself to give up the dream of an education or put her children into what seemed like a future of no future.

"She said, 'Forget about me,'" Idais said. "I couldn't believe after all that was done to me, she was doing the same thing. She refused totally to come. I became like a robot."

I was shocked to hear this, but on reflection, I could see how torn Rrahime had been. She had lived her whole life dreaming of escaping the legacy of the Albanian peasantry. She had dreamed of college.

I finally located her, in Philadelphia, and asked her what had happened. She could not respond to me. She said she could not leave the United States. She just could not. Rrahime would say absolutely nothing more.

"This is Atef's story," she said. "I can't go through it again. I just cannot."

Life is messy; its entanglements are infinitely surprising and often contradictory. Despite the fact that her husband had been seized and thrown out of the country, despite the fact that she lost her home, despite the fact that she was swamped with debt and guilt, Rrahime could not give up the American possibilities that still danced in her head, no matter how fantastic they seemed in a time of war: an education, a job, maybe some measure of freedom at some point. That she was smothering in guilt was something she just had to suffer through. God's will. Rrahime responded to all of this by rejecting at least the trappings of Islam. She is no longer covered. She works. She attends college. She remains determined to get her education.

Reeling from this turn of events, Atef rebounded into another marriage in Dubai. His new wife became pregnant. Then, he said, Rrahime brought their two children over for a visit with their father. And she was impressed by Dubai herself. She admitted that maybe she had made a mistake, he said, maybe a decent life was possible in Dubai. But not if there was another wife on the scene.

Atef was in heaven with his two little girls, but he could not set his new wife adrift. Rrahime and children returned to the United States.

"It tore my heart," he said. "And I keep having this dream. I'm chasing the shadow of my kids. I run into the street, and I reach that spot, and they're somewhere else. And I go there, and they vanish. I want to see them. But they are in a country that I'm not allowed into. I think about my daughters and how they are going to grow up, and I never thought this would happen. I never conceived that my children would face this. It's evil. It's bad. It's an absolute calamity."

"Why?" he pleaded. "Why? Why did they do this to us?"

I HAVE NOT BEEN able to communicate directly with Sheik Ghorab, but by sheer luck, I managed to track down Meriem Moumen several months after Ghorab had been deported. She had returned to the United States to try to reestablish a relationship with her elder daughter, the young girl who been utterly humiliated by the swarming arrest of her stepfather before all of her classmates in the street in front of her school in 2004.

When the family was evicted from their home and Meriem was preparing to move to Egypt, her elder daughter refused to go. Flat-out refused. And who could blame her, really? She had been forced out of school, forced from her home, and now she was being forced from her country. Her home. Her homeland. That's where she drew the line. No more. Her anger, not surprisingly, turned on her mother and stepfather and on Islam.

Ghorab was deported in December 2005. He was accompanied to Cairo by immigration agents, who handed him off to Egyptian internal security authorities. He was held and questioned for a few days and then released, forbidden to preach, forbidden any religious work at all. Penniless, out of work, Ghorab was compelled to bring his American wife and young baby back to his elderly mother's small apartment in Alexandria.

It was, said Moumen, a nightmare. She found Egyptian society difficult, to say the least, and she found her husband's situation—unemployed and living with his mother—humiliating for him. Ghorab felt the same way. The pressure proved too much for Moumen, who had a series of breakdowns.

When I met with her in the wake of these disasters, she had returned to this country to try to work things out with her elder daughter and perhaps make a little money. She was living temporarily on the living-room couch in an apartment of an old Ghorab friend in a very poor East Orange, New Jersey, neighborhood. Homeless men sat in doorways in the immediate area and haunted the vestibule of the local Dunkin' Donut shop; crack vials freckled the curbside. Moumen had again fallen into deep depression.

"My house situation is not very good," she said. We were sitting in the back kitchen behind a restaurant owned by an old Ghorab acquaintance. Boxes were stacked all around us, and a black and white cat wandered in and out of our cramped area.

"There are days when I don't get up at all. What's to get up for?" Ghorab, she said, is not in a good emotional state either. His one joy is their baby girl, but now Moumen found herself in the United States trying to work with one daughter, while her second daughter was half a world away providing some measure of joy to a trapped man whose life lay in ruins. She had even feared arrest herself when they first arrived in Egypt and he was detained.

"Seriously, I was thinking, 'Are they going to arrest me as well?' Who knows? I'm in Egypt. I don't know. But after he comes out, he's very depressed. Two years in prison, my husband is not the same. My husband as of this day is not the same. Not the same. He's not the same. He's not the Mohamed Ghorab I used to know. A friend of mine told me this—she's from Syria—and she told me her husband was detained for three years, and when he came out, he wasn't the same. But right now I know what she's talking about. My husband is not the same. He wears glasses right now. He can't see very well. He doesn't sleep. My husband never sleeps. He doesn't sleep until seven o'clock or eight o'clock in the morning. He'll sleep for three hours or four hours. That's it. I couldn't have a job over there. I tried. I actually ended up at the hospital like three or four times. Egypt was very, very, very tough for me. What's the use of me?"

"And he felt embarrassed. He felt, 'What's the use of me as a man? I can't provide for you and my daughter.' You know how depressing that is for him? 'I can't even get an apartment for my wife and my child.' And we had to go back, and we had to live with his mom. Here is a man who was a businessman, and even in United States we were doing okay. We were doing more than okay. We went out. We took our children to the park. We went out to little restaurants once a week. We had friends. We were doing okay. Imagine the next thing—nothing. No friends. No car. Nothing. Nothing. Nothing. Your life is gone. They took your life, and they flush it down the toilet. Bye. Good-bye.

"What's the chance for somebody who's forty-seven years old? Where's he going to start at in Egypt? Where? Where? And you're wondering, 'Well, is he going to get arrested in Egypt?' If he goes out with his friends, I stay up until he comes back. I'm so afraid that something is going to happen to him. Something is going to happen to him."

And then there is the problem with her daughter. I promised Meriem I would protect her daughter's privacy, but I think it is safe to say that she blames her mother, stepfather, and Islam for all that has befallen the family. She has rejected the religion. Rejected all of its strictures. She will not leave the United States. She did not even want to see her mother.

The situation was as intractable as they get. Moumen was faced now with precisely the same choice that Pamela Faseh Alddin faced or that Rrahime faced: husband or children. It is the *Sophie's Choice* of contemporary America, unremarked on in the media, disregarded by the government. The antithesis of all that, when I was growing up, was said to be good about this country, a place that brought families together and held them closely.

How many Muslim families have been faced with the dilemma? It is virtually impossible to say. Since 9/11 thousands of Middle Easterners and South Asians have been deported. Most have families. It is impossible to know with any precision how many families have been fractured. Several thousand have been deported, but what happens in the wake of deportation is exceedingly difficult to track. Since 1997, according to a Human Rights Watch report issued in July 2007, almost 700,000 legal immigrants convicted of even minor crimes had been deported, separating "an estimated 1.6 million children and adults, including U.S. citizens and lawful permanent residents, from their non-citizen family members." The deportations are mandatory under 1996 laws.

Obviously not all deportations represent, as officials like to say, a "nexus" of terrorism. That makes criminal deportations a very broad brush for use in determining the impact of terror prosecutions on families—though the wrenching result for children is the same. Syracuse University's Transactional Records Access Clearinghouse reported in 2007 that "a claim of terrorism was made against only 12 (0.0015%) out of 814,073 individuals" by Homeland Security Department immigration officials in immigration courts over the three preceding years. The TRAC report was based on an analysis of millions of records obtained under the Freedom of Information Act from the immigration courts, supplemented by additional records obtained from the Executive Office for U.S. Attorneys that document criminal prosecutions in U.S. federal district courts. The TRAC report also maintains that an additional examination of a broader group of immigration court cases dealing with "what are called 'national security' charges" shows that from fiscal year 2004 to 2006 only 114 such charges, 0.014 percent of over 800,000-plus individuals, were brought in court. Actual removals, the study says, amounted to 37 cases in the three-year period.

The report states that "as a result of investigations by all federal agencies—primarily the FBI—the Justice Department data show that during the FY 2004–2006 period a total of 620 prosecutions were filed against individuals categorized by the prosecutors as international terrorists, domestic terrorists or terrorism financiers."

Government officials discount these studies as indicative of anything, largely because they neglect to take into account "pre-crime" efforts. Ghorab, for instance, would not fall into the terrorism category, although Idais might. Other Ansaarullah congregants might or might not. Neither of the Saghour brothers, for instance, would probably be considered a terrorist prosecution for statistical purposes, yet both were expelled from the country as a direct result of the war on terror.

Clearly, significant statistical work needs to be done to map the impact of what has been happening, but statistics hardly begin to measure the powerful human effect of the war on terror. Nor do they begin to suggest how the landscape has been scarred by battle after battle. How does one measure the decimation of community in Lodi, California? How does one begin to calibrate the destruction of community on Seventh Street in South Philadelphia or on Coney Island Avenue in Brooklyn? A handful of mosques have closed, including at least one in Brooklyn and one in Philadelphia. Seven charities have been shut down. Money sent by those seeking a better life in America to family and community left back in the Old World has dried up. These are the tangible results of the war on terror.

How is fundamental trust restored to communities and neighborhoods all across the country that are filled with informers? How define what has not happened and is not seen into a victory over "the terrorists"?

None of this matters to Meriem Moumen.

"What do I do?" she asked. "Go back and take care of the little one? But what is there in Egypt? I want my family back. I want my family back. I want my family back! I want the whole thing back. And the decision: Who needs me the most? I know my daughter— she's fifteen years old; I know she needs me. And the baby. You tell me. Or my husband, who's going through this crisis. Tell me what to do. And tell me, what did we do? They didn't just punish him. You know how many people? The whole family. What did we do? Again and again and again I think about it. What are the charges? What are the charges? Overstayed visa? They've destroyed my family."

By 2008 CHOICES HAD been made. Atef had a falling out in Dubai, quit his job, and moved to Amman. Rrahime, struggling still, brought their daughters to him. She returned to the United States alone. She continued to decline to speak with me. Atef was overjoyed to be reunited with his children. He could not, or perhaps would not, explain his former wife's motivations.

"She changed," he said. "I don't understand it."

Amman also brought another surprise—Atef ran into his old friend Mohammad, a Saudi-born Palestinian, longtime U.S. resident, and former Ansaarullah congregant. Mohammad had been in the United States since 1993. He had married a U.S. citizen but ultimately ran afoul of malleable immigration regulations—like so many connected with the mosque. He was arrested in early 2004 and charged with lying on his residency application. He had failed to note he had been employed.

I spoke with Mohammad's lawyer, a seasoned immigration attorney, who told me "the charge is completely unique."

"This kind of arrest never happens," he said. "There are always mistakes [on applications], so part of the process when you go in to review is to go over it. He had worked and said he hadn't. . . . He didn't realize that [the work requirement] is waived if you're married."

The attorney said there were other reasons for Mohammad's problems.

"He wore the beard. He looked the part, and he came from the mosque they were convinced was a bad-guy hang out."

Mohammad, father of three American-born children, was eventually jailed. Meanwhile, his wife found her application for citizenship delayed and delayed for more than two years because, federal officials kept saying, "background checks" had not been completed. Mohammad told her to persevere. But as the couple's bureaucratic problems deepened, her attitude toward citizenship changed with it.

"You should get your oath and go home a U.S. citizen," Mohammad told her, after he had finally decided to leave the United States rather than fight immigration authorities.

"She said, 'I don't want to be a U.S. citizen,'" her attorney recalled. "'I want to leave. Why are they doing this to us?' She didn't want to become a citizen—even though her kids were U.S. citizens. . . . She didn't want anything to do with it. I was begging her: 'If your kids want to come back to college, you can come back too.' She was disgusted."

Mohammad was delighted to reconnect with Atef in Amman in 2007. He told him that he had watched Sheik Ghorab's fight, Atef's fight, and the futile efforts of many others and simply decided that he could not prevail.

"I learned from you," Mohammad told Atef. "I told them: 'I don't want to spend the rest of my time in jail. Just deport me.'"

MOUMEN HAS ALSO MADE her choice. She pulled herself together and reconciled with her daughter, brought the little one back to the United States in 2008, and plans to fight for her husband from this country. He has decided to return to school for a postgraduate degree. Something will happen, she says, God willing. He is barred from the United States for the decade following his expulsion.

"I am working," Moumen told me in 2009. "I will bring my husband back. My daughter is doing much better. I am here." She said she no longer felt the old anger toward other Muslims and immigrants who had abandoned Ansaarullah.

"At first I got very upset: 'How come you didn't stay? You didn't support my husband. Why were you scared? My husband didn't do anything wrong. He helped all you guys. He was like a father to you.' And I had an anger. I was very angry: 'Why don't you support what's right?' I was a woman. A baby born. I was at the *masjid* every day opening and closing, and I wasn't afraid because I believed I didn't do nothing wrong. Absolutely nothing wrong. 'How come you didn't stay by me?' Now I understand it. I forgive them. They were scared. They had families. They had babies and wives. [Federal authorities] took a beautiful thing and just crushed it."

IN THE MEANTIME, Sheik Ghorab still has no job and no money. He desperately misses his small daughter. And she misses him.

"She's gone through a lot," Moumen said as we sat in a coffee shop in the summer of 2009. She had just returned from a visit to Ghorab in Alexandria. His circumstances had not changed.

"The little one is breaking my heart," Moumen continued. Ghorab's daughter is now five. "She is asking about him all the time. I'm tired of making up stories. I'm tired of making up stories."

"Why isn't he here?" her daughter asks.

"He's waiting for his green card. Daddy doesn't have a green card."

"And why doesn't he have a green card?"

Meriem sighed deeply.

"I'm out of answers. I'm out of answers. I'm out of answers."

She thought for a moment, looking back over the broken land-scape stretching years into the past.

"When I lived in Egypt, my husband and the little one used to sit on the balcony for hours and talk to the moon. He would tell her stories and read for her. And he would make this play, pretend he's talking to the moon. And until this day, she is so affected by the moon!

"The other night, we're driving; she says, 'Hi, moon! Say hi to my daddy.' I broke in tears. She still remembered. 'Hi, moon. Say hi to Daddy.'"

WAKELING STREET REMAINS HAUNTED, although people are gone, houses are empty, and the morning light flickers, as it always has, up over the girders and billowing steam of Allied Chemical. There is nothing unusual on the street, only the quick shadow of something not seen.

Acknowledgments

I AM GRATEFUL TO all those named in the text of this book who spoke with me. Many helped and spoke who cannot be named, and I am grateful to them as well. Finding sources and information was difficult, and my gratitude extends to those who assisted; there are so many that I'm afraid of attempting to list all for fear of missing one. Know that I appreciate all the help and time. That said, there are some people and organizations who were exceptionally helpful. I thank Adeeba al-Zaman, Joe Stork, Larry Fiebert, Larry Frankel, Patty-Pat Kozlowski, Mark Rudd, Bob Feldman, Mohammed Mollah, Bill Chadwick, Susan Braudy, Firooz Namei, and Mohamid Ibrahim, as well as numerous staff members of the New York, Washington, Philadelphia, Denver, and San Francisco offices of the American Civil Liberties Union, Al Haq, the American Friends Service Committee, and the Broward County Anti-War Coalition. I want to thank members of the Philadelphia Police Department and the Philadelphia offices of the FBI and Immigration and Customs Enforcement for making time available to speak with me. I also owe an enormous debt to colleagues all over the country, particularly the talented reporters and editors at the *Philadelphia Inquirer*. I thank them all for difficult work in difficult circumstances. My agent, Michael V.

Carlisle, has been unfailingly supportive and, when warranted, critical. I thank him and his associate Ethan Bassoff, who helped wrestle this project into shape. My editor at Nation Books, Carl Bromley, found manuscript holes a mouse could not slip through and stitched them up. I'm deeply indebted to him. Beth Wright did a terrific job copyediting. Meredith Smith at Perseus Books kept things moving through thick and thin. Many thanks for their efforts. Given all this assistance, if there are any errors in the text, the fault is my own entirely. Lastly, I want to thank my wife, Jennifer Baker, whose critical judgments, support, curiosity, and questions have made *Mohamed's Ghosts* much more than it would have been otherwise. For that, I am deeply appreciative and dedicate this book to her.

A Note on Sources

THE BULK OF THIS book is based on original reporting I conducted from 2005 to 2009. I interviewed hundreds of people, including government and law enforcement officials, attorneys, community and political activists, scholars, officials of American and foreign social agencies, human rights workers, and ordinary citizens. Comments by top federal officials in press conferences and speeches are drawn from transcripts, except where noted. In the case of federal officials in charge of investigations, the interviews were conducted on the record for attribution. I adhered to the same rule with local police, although I allowed some flexibility to better portray tensions embedded within the law enforcement universe as a whole. With all other sources, particularly those engaged with the immigrant community, as well as immigrants themselves, I often agreed to provide anonymity in an effort to overcome widespread fears. Even so, many declined to speak with me. In the case of Mohamed Ghorab, his imprisonment, deportation, and lack of English proved difficult barriers; his wife, Meriem Moumen, served as a conduit of information. The names of children have been changed for the sake of privacy.

I have tried to keep the text as uncluttered as possible with source references, but in addition to my own direct interviews, I have obviously relied on the reporting and assistance of many exceptional journalists around the country. For the most part, I have indicated use of published material in the text. In this note I am listing major sources. I often directly checked information myself to determine its reliability. I have sought to make clear in the text if information is based on my own interviews or readily available published material. I have also attempted to show when a particular interview took place. Following are some key published sources.

INTRODUCTION

"There is a continuum . . . ": *San Jose Mercury News*, October 19, 2002. "You don't really know what a terrorist looks like . . . ": *The Power of Nightmares: Shadows in the Cave*, written and produced by Adam Curtis, BBC 2, November 3, 2004.

CHAPTER ONE

Some information about the events surrounding the mosque raid was derived from published accounts in the *Philadelphia Inquirer*, May 27 and 28, 2004, and the *Philadelphia Daily News*, May 28, 2004. On usage of the word "homeland": William Safire, *New York Times Magazine*, January 20, 2002. On Tom Ridge's complaints: *USA Today*, May 10, 2005; *Washington Post*, August 21, 2009.

CHAPTER TWO

A sense of the anti-Muslim hostility following the Oklahoma City bombing can be found in *A Rush to Judgment: A Special Report*, Council on American-Islamic Relations, 1995. The account of incidents following the Trade Center attacks is drawn from many sources, including my own interviews. Several large reports and compilations portray the sweep of reprisals. These reports include: *The Status of Civil Rights in the United States: Stereotypes and Civil Liberties, 2002*, Council on American-Islamic Relations, 2002; *Report on Hate Crimes and Discrimination Against Arab Americans: The Post September 11 Backlash*, ed. Hussein

Ibish, American Arab Anti-Discrimination Committee, 2003; William J. Haddad, *Impact of the September 11th Attacks on the Freedoms of Arabs and Muslims*, Chicago Bar Association, 2004; *Caught in the Backlash: Stories from Northern California*, American Civil Liberties Union of Northern California, 2002; *America's Challenge: Domestic Security, Civil Liberties and National Unity after September 11*, Migration Policy Institute, 2003; *Witness to Abuse*, Human Rights Watch and American Civil Liberties Union, 2005; Department of Justice, Office of the Inspector General, *The September 11 Detainees: A Review of the Treatment of Aliens Held on Immigration Charges in Connection with the Investigation of the September 11 Terrorist Attacks*, June 2003, *Supplemental Report*, December 2003, and *Analysis of Response by the Bureau of Prisons*, March 2004. On concerns over suspects not talking: *Washington Post*, October 10, 2001. On Gul Mohammad Shah and Azmath Javed: Newsindia-times .com, January 25, 2002; Salon.com, June 19, 2002; BBC, January 1, 2003, February 10, 2003. On Higazy: CNN, January 11, 2002, November 26, 2002, December 17, 2002; *Higazy v. Millennium Hotel* (05-4148-cv) 2005. On survey of college registrars: *Washington Post*, December 25, 2002; www.aacrao.org/transcript/index.cfm?fuseaction=show_view&doc_id =43t4. On detention center videotapes: Department of Justice, *Supplemental Report*. On the FBI losing control of its list of interview prospects: *Wall Street Journal*, November 11, 2002. On secret Justice Department memos directing detention of immigrants: *Detroit Free Press*, November 27, 2001; CNN, November 29, 2001.

CHAPTER THREE

Several significant studies of the government's special registration program have been issued, including Paul M. Sherer, "Targets of Suspicion: The Impact of Post-9/11 Policies on Muslims, Arabs and South Asians in the U.S.," Immigration Daily, 2004, www.ilw.com/immigdaily; Louise Cainkar, "The Impact of the September 11 Attacks and Their Aftermath on Arab and Muslim Communities in the United States," *GSC Quarterly* 13 (Summer/Fall 2004); "Special Registration: Discrimination and Xenophobia as Government Policy," Asian American Legal Defense and Education Fund, January 2004. On Nadir Khan's mistaken arrest: *Philadelphia*

City Paper, July 12–18, 2002; *Philadelphia Inquirer*, May 13, 2002, May 12, 2003; *Urdu Times*, April 24, 2003, as translated for Independent Press Association (IPA) New York, Voices That Must Be Heard. On special registration problems in Philadelphia: *Philadelphia Inquirer*, November 25, 2003. On mass LA arrests: *Los Angeles Times*, December 19, 2002; Sherer, "Targets of Suspicion." Mujahid estimates of deportations: "In a Virtual Internment Camp: Muslim Americans Since 9/11," 2003, www.soundvision .com/info/muslims/internment.asp.

CHAPTER FOUR

The four volumes of the Church Committee report, plus supplementary staff reports and caches of COINTELPRO documents, remain an important source on past domestic intelligence operations. The bulk of this material may be found online at www.icdc.com/~paulwolf/cointelpro. I have made use of additional police and FBI memos found in the Susan Braudy Papers, Bryn Mawr College Library Special Collections (which contain Ted Gold's FBI file), and the Harrison E. Salisbury Papers, Columbia University Rare Book and Manuscript Library. On the father of a busted ex-student: James K. Davis, *Assault on the Left: The FBI and the Sixties Antiwar Movement* (Westport, CT: Praeger, 1997). "I mean the idea sounds great . . . ": M. Wesley Swearingen interview for the National Security Archives, November 1, 1998. An account printed in the *Berkeley Barb*: Red Mountain Tribe, "Larry Is . . . Fucked Up," *Berkeley Barb*, August 21, 1970, quoted in *Weatherman*, ed. Harold Jacobs (Berkeley: Ramparts Press, 1970). Grathwohl on Ali Baba: Larry Grathwohl as told to Frank Reagan, *Bringing Down America: An FBI Informer with the Weathermen* (New Rochelle, NY: Arlington House, 1976). "By way of information . . . ": FBI memo, WEATHFUG, December 22, 1972 (Bob Feldman's FBI FOIA file). Police memo listing seventy-plus "closed hearing" attendants: NYPD BSS memo, From [Redacted], To Commanding Officer, Bureau of Special Services, March 15, 1967, Subject: Anti-C.I.A. Activity at Columbia University, Subsequent University Action. On Mamaroneck break-in: Salisbury Papers, Columbia, Boxes 249, 250; Harrison E. Salisbury, *A Journey for Our Times: A Mem-*

oir (New York: Harper & Row, 1983); Harrison Salisbury letter to Mark
Lynch, Salisbury Papers, Columbia, Box 250; FBI memos concerning
Harrison Salisbury's political views and behavior, Salisbury Papers, Columbia, Boxes 174, 249, 250. Ted Gold placement on Security Index: FBI
memo, From Supervisor, To SAC NY, November 30, 1967, Braudy Papers, Box 3, Bryn Mawr.

CHAPTER FIVE

On Infragard Network: *Orlando Sentinel*, October 7, 2001; "'InfraGard'
Lets FBI Disclose Sensitive Information to Select Few," *News Media and
the Law* (Winter 2002); see also the group's website, www.infragard.net.
"How does a supposedly democratic country . . . " statement made
through DRUM (Desis Rising Up and Moving), New York City, January
24, 2007. On man with shotgun aimed at Ansaarullah: *Northeast Times*
(Philadelphia), June 12, 2002.

CHAPTER SIX

Details of Saghour case: *U.S. v. Nassim Saghour* (2:04-cr-00738-SD),
March 7, 2005.

CHAPTER SEVEN

Khalil indictment: *U.S. v. Khalil et al.* (SDNY 03-CR-289), March 10,
2003, quoted extensively in Janice L. Kephart, "Immigration and Terrorism: Moving Beyond the 9/11 Staff Report on Terrorist Travel," *Connections: The Quarterly Journal* 5, no. 2 (Fall 2006); see also Associated
Press, February 6, 2003. On "cesspool of fraud": Associated Press, September 23, 2004. On Khalil's supposed views of Osama bin Laden and
terror attacks: Associated Press, February 6, 2003; *Newsday*, February 7,
2003; *New York Times*, September 24, 2004. On Khalil and "massive"
visa fraud: "ICE Uncovers Elaborate Scheme to Exploit Religious Worker
Visas," press release, Department of Homeland Security, September
2005. Idais court hearing: *U.S. v. Idais* (2:04-cr-00543-JP), May 31, 2005.

CHAPTER EIGHT

The *Sacramento Bee* reported the Hayat arrests and trials in detail throughout 2005 and 2006. I have made use of those accounts, as well as accounts in the *Los Angeles Times*. The *Frontline-New York Times* documentary *The Enemy Within*, October 2006, provides an in-depth look at the issues raised by case.

Index

ABC News, 19
Abco Body Shop, 5, 11, 30
Abdel-Muhti, Farouk, 241
Abduh, Mohammad, 44
Adil, Mohammad Hassan, 248
Afghanistan war, 48, 90, 188, 249
Ahmad, Anser
  as Atef Idais's attorney, 217,
    270–271
  as Ghorab's attorney, 48–49,
    131, 228
Ahmad, Ibrahim, 65
Ahmed, Abdo Ali, 75
Ahmed, Ayman, 58
Ahmed, Fatima, 75
Ahmed, Shabbir, 248, 249
Airport security, 100
Alakbar, Hajrah
  on African American Muslims,
    279
  as Ghorab's first American wife,
    51–54, 57

  sons destroy Ghorab's
    immigration status, 193–195
Al Aqsa Islamic Society mosque
  cooperates with law
    enforcement, 54–55, 171
  FBI connection required for
    counterterrorism, 255
  Ghorab's imam contract not
    renewed, 56–57, 118–119
  infiltrated with informers, 257
  Philadelphians support
    members, 95
Albasti, Tarek, 91–95
Alddin, Hasan Saddiq Faseh, 40,
  277–278
Alddin, Pamela Faseh, 277–278, 284
Al Farooq mosque, 180, 181
Al Haq human rights group, 279
Alien Absconder Apprehension
  Initiative, 98
Almansoop, Ali, 76
Al Noor mosque, 180

Al Qaeda
  and Ashcroft's Seeking
    Information Alert, 38–39
  informer reports operatives in
    Lodi, 250, 251
  perceived as tied to U.S.
    Muslims, 40, 100, 189
  training camps, 248
Alter, Jonathan, 83
American Friends Service
    Committee, 60. *See also*
    Quakers
Amin, Qasim, 44
Anderson, Ray, 9
Andrews, Stephen, 179–180
Angari, Abdullaziz Al, 80–81
Ansaarullah Islamic Society
    mosque
  congregants arrested, detained,
    deported, 13–14, 17, 177,
    203–214
  congregants compared to '60s
    activists, 139–140
  congregants raise bonds for
    detainees, 189, 193, 207–208,
    210, 245
  described, 11–15, 112–116,
    119–122
  informers, surveillance, sow
    distrust, fear, 58–59, 137–138,
    178, 206, 211, 230–231
  raided, 32–37
  struggles, disintegrates, closes,
    15–17, 225–230, 275–276
  systematically dismantled by
    JTTF, FBI, ICE, 266–267
  threatened by armed drive-by
    stalker, 201
  as training, test case, for
    intelligence gathering, 22–23,
    28, 266–267
Anthrax attacks, 90, 254–255

Anti-Communism Red Scares
    of '20s and '50s, 14,
    104–105, 239
Anti–Vietnam War movement
  effects of surveillance,
    informers, 264
  FBI protestors' files, 142,
    166–168
  with freedom as core of
    politics, 8
  government intrusion as fact of
    life, 7
Aqsa mosque. *See* Al Aqsa Islamic
    Society mosque
Arson attacks in post-9/11 period,
    66, 72
Ashcroft, John
  accuses critics of supporting
    terrorists, 105–106
  announces Seeking Information
    Alert, 37–39, 277
  on immigrant visa violations, 101
  issues name list with alert,
    90–91
  on PATRIOT Act powers,
    96–98
  preemption policy against pre-
    crime, 25–26
  "this new war" press conference,
    18–19
Attack stages, 175
Awed, Zabat, 76
Ayers, Bill, 148
Ayesh, Nabil, 71

Baltimore Sun newspaper, 76
Bangladeshis, 74, 124, 129, 132
Baptist Worship Center on Wakeling
    Street, 4, 29–30, 112
Baugh, Carolyn, 91–92
Baugh, Mary Francis, 93, 95
Baxter, Matthew, 190–191

Bay Ridge Islamic Society mosque
    fear, distrust in community, 185,
        219–220
    infiltrated by informers,
        including Eldawoody, 180,
        184–185
BBC report, 84
Berkeley Barb newspaper, 149
Berkeley radical street politics in
    1969, 145
Biddle, Francis, 166
Bin Laden, Osama, 25, 221,
    222, 250
Black Panthers, 139, 142, 143, 144
Boyd, Dean, 247–248, 252
Bridge photography as suspicious,
    175–176
Burrell, George E., Jr., 251
Bush, George W.
    on Arab sleeper cells, 19
    on general threat on
        America, 91
    and notion of crusade against
        terror, 107–108
    on tenets of Islamic faith, 96
Bustleton (Philadelphia
    neighborhood), 35
Butt, Muhammed, 104

California Anti-Terrorism
    Information Center, 24, 25, 27
CBS News, 65
Central Intelligence Agency
    (CIA), 83
Charitable giving of Islamic
    organizations
    of Ansaarullah mosque, 120, 273
    eradicated from communities, 58
    targeted by informers,
        investigations, 21–22, 185
    undermined by law enforcement
        scrutiny, 21–22, 185

Cheney, Richard "Dick," 106, 108
Chinese Cultural Revolution,
    106–107
Chiorazzo, Sharin, 241
Civil liberties, 105–107, 256
Civil rights movement
    Birmingham church
        bombing, 61
    with freedom as core of
        politics, 8
    with government intrusion as
        fact of life, 7
    infiltrated with informers,
        surveillance, in '60s, '70,
        141, 264
Clark, Mark, 143
CNN news broadcasts, 65, 81
COINTELPRO
    described, 139–143
    informant activities, files, in '60s,
        158, 166
Columbia University
    in '60s, 1, 7–9
    FBI, police, informers,
        135–137, 138
    1968 demonstrations, strikes,
        134–135, 153
    See also Anti–Vietnam War
        movement
Council on American-Islamic
    Relations, 66, 78–79, 85,
    101, 249
Counterterrorism
    Ansaarullah serves as FBI
        training ground, 22
    FBI requires Muslim community
        cooperation, 255
    files, lists, become permanent,
        172
    mission promoted by endless
        investigations, 261–262
Cunniff, Kenneth L., 92–93

Daily Oklahoman newspaper, 66
Dar Ehya Essunnah mosque,
    220–222
Dar-Ui Islam mosque, 53
Dawaa Salafia religious
    organization, 45, 216
Democracy Now! program, 241
Demonstrations
    antidraft, 9
    anti–Vietnam War, civil rights, of
        '60s, 134–135
    Bastille Day, Berkeley, 145–146
    in Oakland protesting
        Iraq War, 23
    over Ansaarullah mosque raid,
        59–60
Deobandi branch of Islam, 220
Dershowitz, Alan, 83
Dhamat Houmet Daawa Salafia,
    131, 217
Disappearances
    Albasti case, 92–95
    into detention centers, 103
    of Iranians detained by INS, 126
    of Middle Eastern Muslims in
        U.S., 84, 88, 129
    in nightly sweeps, 122–123, 127,
        131–132, 191
    reported, 105
    vanishings discussed, 127
Dissent expressed, linked to acts of
    terrorism, 23–25
Dohrn, Bernardine, 144, 148

Education Department, U.S.,
    Project Strikeback, 97
Egypt
    disappearances, 279
    Ghorab persecuted by security
        forces, 45–46
    Ghorab's U.S. deportation,
        282–286
    Salafist traditions, 44

security forces arrest Dawaa
    Salafia members, 244–245
and torture, abuse, human rights
    violations, 45–47
Eldawoody, Osama, 178–184
Elkarra, Basim, 249
El Mftah Mosque, Alexandria,
    Egypt, 42
Elshafay, James, 180, 183
Emerson, Steven, 65
Enemy in the post-9/11 period
    difficulty of identifying, 108, 185,
        264–265
    as invisible, lurking within, 13,
        18–19, 26
    Muslim Brotherhood, 266
    as the unknown, 40
Erroneous arrests, detentions, and
    tortures
    discussed, 88–89, 102
    of Nadir Khan, 122–124

Falwell, Jerry, 107
Faseh Alddin, Hasan Saddiq. *See*
    Alddin, Hasan Saddiq Faseh
Faseh Alddin, Pamela. *See* Alddin,
    Pamela Faseh
Fear
    fractures communities,
        Ansaarullah, 185, 241, 257, 258
    generated from big arrests,
        sweeps, 191
    as government policy, 106–108
    and NSEERS registration, 125, 128
Federal Bureau of Investigation
    (FBI)
    counterintelligence program (*see*
        COINTELPRO)
    harrasses Khatut out of U.S.,
        226–227
    and Higazy case, lawsuit, 86–88
    informant-driven investigations
        of Muslims, 50–51, 133–134

investigates universities and
students, 97, 136–137, 162
lists, files, ordered destroyed are
renamed, 166, 167
PENTTBOM (*see* PENTTBOM)
secretly seizes, detains Albasti,
91–93
uses harboring illegal alien
charge, 213–214
uses material witness warrants,
80–81, 86, 92
See also Erroneous arrests,
detentions, and tortures
Feldman, Bob, 134, 136, 162, 166
Felt, W. Mark, 150
Fine, Glenn A., 103–104
Fire Dancer film, 78
Fitzgerald, Patrick, 93
Foreign Intelligence Surveillance
Act, 260
Fort Dix attack plot prosecution, 259
Frahm, Charles E., 129–130
Frankford Valley community, 5–7,
278–279
Freedom of Information Act
(FOIA) requests, 161, 163,
262, 285
Free Speech Movement, 145
Fresno Bee newspaper, 75
Frontline television program, 251
Fuentes, Thomas, 93

Gale, Stephen, 63
Gallup polls, 100
Gamble, Kenny, 56
Gardner, Richard N., 154–155
Gerassi, John, 155–156
Ghetto Informant Program, 142
Ghorab, Mohamed
early background in Egypt, 41–48
(*see also* Salafism)
early experiences in U.S., second
marriage, 51–57

described as husband, father,
12–13, 29
arrested, jailed without charges,
31–32, 187–189, 227–230,
239–246
prosecuted for immigration
marriage fraud, 194–196
deported by U.S. to Egypt, 276,
282–286
teachings as Muslim, imam, 30,
54–55, 109, 115–116, 119–120,
197, 222–225
Gill, Victor, 64
Ginsberg, Tom, 57–58, 96
Gold, Ted
FBI files compiled, 167–168
killed in Weatherman bomb blast
(1970), 148, 166
Goldfield, Steve, 157–158, 162
Grathwohl, Larry, 147–152, 178
Greeman, Richard, 153–154
Greenberg School, Bustleton,
Philadelphia, 31–32, 59
Greenwich Village townhouse
explosion (1970), 148–149, 167
Guelzo, Alan, 108

Hamas as issue for Idais, 217, 226,
233–234, 237–238
Hamid, Abdul, 31, 222
Hamoud, Randall B., 277–278
Hampton, Fred, 143
Hassan, Durreshawar, 74
Hassan, Waquar, 74
Hayat, Hamid, 248–252
Hayat, Umer, 248, 251
Herald Square subway station
bombing plan, 182–183
Higazy, Abdallah, 86–88
Hoeffel, Joe, 85
Holt, Rush, 74
Holy Land Foundation,
22, 185

Hoover, J. Edgar
  on COINTELPRO preventing rise
    of messiahs, 141
  compiles Custodial Index/
    Security Index, 165–166, 167
  creates target lists of Americans,
    142–143
Human Relations Commission of
    Philadelphia, 69
Human rights
  conditions in Egypt, 46–47, 279
  monitored in U.S. with
    detentions of Iranians, 126
Human Rights Watch, 46, 76,
    104, 285
Hussain, Iftekhar, 85

Ibershof, William C., 152
ICE. *See* Immigration and Customs
    Enforcement Bureau (ICE)
Idais, Atef
  replaces Ghorab in leading
    prayers, 17, 58–59, 225
  arrested, imprisoned, in solitary
    confinement, 116–119,
    121–122, 126, 203–210, 227,
    237–238, 269–270
  and disparities in agents' reports
    with truth, 215–216
  alleged Hamas association, 217,
    226, 233, 235, 237–238, 247
  Israelis torture, coerce,
    admissions, 209–210, 234, 235
  prosecuted for Israeli arrest, 215,
    226, 234–237
  deported, 269–272
  later life in Jordan, Dubai,
    Amman, 279–282, 287
Idais, Rrahime, 117, 284
  struggles with Atef's arrest,
    detention, 205–207, 230–233,
    269–272, 275

  in U.S. upon Atef's deportation,
    279–282, 287
Idais, Tazkia, 204–205, 232,
    269–270
Immigrants of Middle Eastern
    backgrounds
  fearfulness, 10–11, 258
  fleeing or deported (statistics),
    128–129
  prejudice expressed from general
    public (polls), 100
  required to register under
    NSEERS, 124–127, 128
  targeted for violence post-9/11,
    70–72
  visa violations used for arrests,
    detention, torture, 81–83,
    188–189
  See also Disappearances
Immigration and Customs
    Enforcement Bureau (ICE)
  arrests, interrogates, Ghorab,
    188, 276
  arrests are justified in
    themselves, 170, 187,
    260–261
  arrests Moumen, Ghorab, in
    front of daughter's school, 34
  and Atef Idais, 207, 272
  charges as tool by JTTF, INS, ICE,
    49, 247
  raids, intimidates, deports,
    Ansaarullah congregants,
    13–14, 17, 185–186
Immigration and Naturalization
    Service (INS)
  interviews under PATRIOT
    Act, 98
  nanny cases, 213, 254
  prosecutions vs. international
    terrorism cases, 260–261,
    272, 285

refuses information about heart
attack victim, 104
secrecy surrounds abuse,
detention, deportation, 81, 82,
84–85
uses informers for investigations
of Muslims, 133–134
Indians and Indian Sikhs
attacked by arsonists, 72
elderly visitors abused, detained,
deported, 84–85
murdered, 73–74, 76–77
news dealers detained for having
box cutters, 81–82
targeted for violence, 70–71
Information/databases
based on leads from public, paid
informants, 173–174
as evidence withheld from
defendants, lawyers, 170
gathered on suspicious persons,
169–171, 177
Informers
in Ansaarullah mosque, 58–59,
206, 211, 230–231
at Columbia University in '60s,
61, 135–137
effects on communities, 137–139,
219–220
Eldawoody, for NYPD, 178–184
Grathwohl, with Weatherman,
147–152
within mosques, 132, 133, 180,
220, 257
motives, 148–149, 178, 180
paid with green cards, U.S.
citizenship, 17, 130,
230–231
produce culture of mistrust, fear,
137–138, 160–161, 185
used extensively by FBI in '60s,
135–143

used to build case against Hayats
in Lodi, 250
See also Undercover police
INS. *See* Immigration and
Naturalization Service
Internal Revenue Service (IRS)
raids Ansaarullah mosque,
Ghorab's home, 6, 33–34, 49
International Muslim Brotherhood
mosque, 86
Iranians, 126
Iraq war
opposed by Ghorab, 58,
188–190, 231
opposed by Oakland protestors, 23
Islam
Ghorab's teachings, 115–116,
222–225
Salafi beliefs described, 42–44
Wahhabism, 43–44
Islamic charities. *See* Charitable
giving of Islamic organizations
Israel, 207, 209–210, 226, 238
Iyman, 191–193

Jamal, Omar, 76
Jason the Cop, 135–136, 137, 138,
146, 160
Javed, Azmath, 82, 84
Jim (former Columbia University
student), 160–163
Joan (nervous Frankford Valley
neighbor), 200–201
Joint Terrorism Task Force (JTTF),
60, 169, 173
agents receive cultural sensitivity
training, 172
arrests Ghorab, 6
described, 171
raids Ansaarullah mosque, 6, 37
requires Muslim community
cooperation, 255

Jordan, 280
Jordan, Howard, 26
JTTF agents. *See* Joint Terrorism
    Task Force

Karas, Adel, 75
Kelleghan, John, 185–187, 206,
    264–265, 267
Kerry, John, 39
Khalil, Muhammad, 220–222
Khan, Ahsanullah "Bobby," 122–123,
    132, 221
Khan, Ayub Ali, 82, 84
Khan, Kay, 249
Khan, Muhammed Adil, 248, 249
Khan, Nadir, 122–124
Khan, Naseem, 250
Khan, Taj, 263
Khatut, Jabi
    argues with informer, 231
    as friend, employer of Idais, 204
    harassed by FBI, ICE, INS, out of
        U.S., 215, 226–227
    home is raided, ransacked,
        32, 35
    raises bail for Ghorab, 189
    as U.S. citizen, businessman,
        119, 120
King, Martin Luther, Jr., 134, 140,
    141
Kreidie, Marwan
    on Aqsa mosque–
        Ghorab/Ansaarullah relations,
        56–57, 58, 227
    efforts to protect Muslims
        post-9/11, 67, 69
    on lack of advocates for
        Pakistanis, 124
    on morning of 9/11, 64–65
    on NSEERS, 126
    on trust/distrust within groups,
        255–258

Leahy, Patrick, 106
The Liberation of Women (Amin), 44
Lindsay, John V., 10
Lodi, California, 248–264
Lodi Muslim Mosque, 248, 249, 263
Lowe, Kimberly, 77
Lynch, Brian, 169–172, 258, 265, 267
Lynch, Mark, 163

Majlis Ash-Shura coalition of
    mosques, 59
Mall bombing plot, 258–259
Manavian, Ed, 24
Manieri, Rich, 37
Marriage fraud case of Mohamed
    Ghorab, 48–49, 193–196,
    226, 239
Masjid Ibrahim mosque, 53
Masjid Taha Islamic Society
    mosque, 53
Mason, Mike, 99
Mateen, Isa Abdul, 59–60
Material witness warrants, 80–81,
    86, 92
McCaffrey, Shannon, 38
McCarthyism of 1950s, 7
    similar to anti-immigrant
        government activities, 7, 102
    surveillance, infiltration of
        informants, 264
    See also Anti-Communism Red
        Scares of '20s and '50s
McCurdy, David, 65
McVeigh, Timothy, 25
Metropolitan Detention Center in
    Brooklyn
    abusive conditions of, 83–84,
        103–104
    detainees held in solitary
        confinement, 82
    detainees held without being
        charged, 71

Miami Herald newspaper, 89

Mohammad (friend of Atef Idais), 287–288

Mollah, Mohammad, 264

Morley, Steven, 239

Mosques
 affected by government investigations, 21
 with business conflicts of lay leaders, 54–56
 clandestinely monitored for radiation levels, 99
 infiltrated with informers, 132, 133, 180, 220, 257
 See also Al Aqsa Islamic Society mosque; Ansaarullah Islamic Society mosque; *under specific mosques*

Moumen, Eliza, elder daughter of Meriem Moumen, 29, 246, 286
 humiliated by parents' arrest in front of school, 31, 34, 59
 and reconciliation with mother, 288
 refuses to leave U.S., 12, 282–284

Moumen, Meriem
 described, 12–13, 16, 197–198, 274–275
 on dismemberment of Ansaarullah by JTTF, 267
 and elder daughter, 12, 31–32, 59, 282–284, 286, 288–289
 evicted from her home, 18, 272–273
 on Ghorab's deportation, exile, 282–286, 288–289
 JTTF raids her home, 33
 struggles to keep mosque, home, going, 225–227, 239–244, 246

Moussaoui, Zacarias, 82

Mueller, Robert S., III, 19, 23, 38, 39, 51, 265

Muhaimin, Anwar, 86–88

Muhaimin, Nafeesah, 86–87

Mujahid, Abdul Malik, 128

Murders and shootings in post-9/11 period, 73–79, 104

Muslims
 effects of efforts to work cooperatively with FBI, 255–256
 families in wake of deportations, 284–285
 native-born U.S. citizens from Ansaarullah mosque, 14–15
 perceived as sympathetic to al Qaeda, 100
 perceive selves as under siege, 189
 in Philadelphia on 9/11, 67–70
 threats, violence against, following Oklahoma City bombing, 65–66
 U.S. polls reveal antagonisms, 100

Muwsawi, Sahar Al-, 65–66

Nannies, illegal immigrant, 213, 254

National Education Statistics Act, 206

National Security Agency (NSA), 3, 89
 refuses FOIA requests, 163–164
 warrantless wiretap program, 102, 172, 260

Native American Digest, 77

Native Americans, 77

Negroponte, John, 261

Newark Star-Ledger newspaper, 74

New Left, 149, 158–159

Newsday newspaper, 181

New York Times newspaper, 8–9, 157, 165

Nimer, Abdullah Mohammed, 77

9/11. *See* September 11, 2001
    attacks
1993 World Trade Center bombing,
    67, 80, 188
North Penn mosque, 264
NSEERS registration, 124–127,
    187, 191

Oakland Port protest and police
    shootings, 23–26
Oakland Tribune newspaper, 24, 25
O'Connor, Eileen, 81
O'Connor, Joseph, 173–178,
    265–267
Oklahoma City bombing, 25
    followed by violence, threats,
      against Muslims, 65–66
    initial blame placed on Middle
      Easterners, 64–66
Olexa, Mark, 188
O'Neal, William, 143
Oughton, Diana, 149
Ouldali, Samir, 58

Padova, John R., 117, 234–238
Pakistanis
    flee from NSEERS
      registration, 124
    jailed, disappeared, deported,
      or flee U.S., 122–123,
      128–129, 131, 191
    of Lodi, 248–264
    murdered, 74
Palestinian immigrants, 241
Parenti, Drew, 262
Parveen, Shahina, 179
Patel, Vasudev, 74
PATRIOT Act
    effects on law enforcement, 260
    measures described, 96–98
    powers and congressional
      oversight, 105–106

    provides access to student
      information, 206
PENTTBOM
    becomes institutionalized, 122
    described, 80
    and Higazy case, 86–88
    initial dragnet, 103, 191
    orchestrates information about
      suspects, 169, 221
Philadelphia
    in aftermath of 9/11, 67–70, 95
    anti-Muslim violence, 66,
      70–72
    efforts to support/protect
      Muslims, 67, 95
    neighborhood cleansed of
      Muslim South Asians, 63–64
Philadelphia Inquirer newspaper,
    15, 33–34
Philadelphia Police Department
    on 9/11, 67–70
    collaborates with Kreidie, 256
    with JTTF, 171, 173
Powell, Nathan Chandler, 78
Pre-crime efforts, 26, 285–286
Presser, Stefan, 126
Prevention or preemptive law
    enforcement activities, 25–26,
    252–253, 255, 258–259
Prosecutions of terrorism suspects
    to be taken on faith, 253
    convictions low or zero, 125, 172,
      262, 285
    vs. immigration violation
      prosecutions, 260–261,
      272, 285
Protests. *See* Demonstrations

Quakers, 18, 27

Rabble Rouser Index of Names,
    142–143

Radiation monitoring of
  mosques, 99
Rahman, Omar Abdel, 188
Raid of Ansaarullah mosque, 6, 12,
  32–37, 40–41
Reagan, Ronald, 145
Refugees (internal) or displaced
  persons
  emigrate to Canada, less visible
    parts of U.S., 131–132, 264
  flee U.S. government, 127
Reichbach, Gus, 154–155
Reid, Richard, 43, 100
Ridge, Tom, 39, 40
Riley, Bill, 125
Rimawi, Zein, 184–185
Robertson, Pat, 107
Rosenthal, Willow, 26
Rudd, Mark, 139–141, 143–144, 146,
  154, 156–157, 168
Rumors
  about Ghorab, 222, 227–228
  in Ansaarullah, 227–228, 242,
    245–246
  as basis for Hoover's lists, 165
  in chaos following 9/11, 79, 80, 89
  gathered, planted, spread, by
    informers, 273
Rumsfeld, Donald, 14

Sacramento Bee newspaper,
  249, 250
Saghour, Caterina, 210, 214
Saghour, Faycal, 210–213, 253–254
Saghour, Nassim, 210–214, 253–254
Said, Edward, 154
Said, Soima, 42
Salafism
  as Dawaa Salafia religious
    organization, 45
  discussed by federal
    investigators, 244

distinguished from Wahhabism,
  42–44
Saleem, Pervaiz, 129
Salem (Ghorab's mentor), 41–42
Salisbury, Harrison
  background and philosophy,
    2–3
  discovers false FBI personal files,
    163–166
  in Soviet Union, 8–9
Samra, Davinder, 77
Samra, Surjit Singh, 76–77
San Diego Union-Tribune
  newspaper, 278
San Francisco Chronicle
  newspaper, 75
San Francisco Golden Gate Park
  police station bombing
  (1970), 148
Sarsour, Linda, 185, 219
Savio, Mario, 145
Sawyer, Diane, 19
Schreiner, Patricia, 278
Scott, McGregor W., 251–252,
  261–262
SDS. *See* Students for a Democratic
  Society
Sears Tower conspiracy scenarios,
  92, 94, 259
Sease, Grace, 207, 270, 280
Seeking Information Terror Alert
  (Ashcroft), 38–40, 277
Seever, Brent David, 76
Seidel, Jonathan, 95
Senate Select Committee on
  Intelligence, 140, 261
September 11, 2001 attacks
  followed by violence against
    Middle Easterners, 70–72,
    73–79
  hijackers' Wahhabist beliefs,
    43–44

September 11, 2001 attacks
(*continued*)
Philadelphians' accounts of
events, 64–65, 67–70
SEVIS. *See* Student and Exchange
Visitor Information System
Shah, Gul Mohammed, 82
Shelby, Michael, 124
Shoaib, Muhammed, 249
Shoe bomber (December 22, 2001),
45, 100
Siddique
on Atef Idais, 214
describes Ansaarullah, raid,
disintegration, 35–37,
111–116, 244–246, 275–276
on Ghorab's religious, ethical,
teachings, 222–225
on ICE arrests, detentions of
congregants, 185, 191–193
Siddiqui, Aafia, 33–34, 39–40
Sikhs. *See* Indians and Indian Sikhs
Singh, Jagajit, 128
Siraj, Matin, trial and conviction of
Herald Square bombing plan,
178–185, 219
Society El Shariaa mosque in
Egypt, 42
Sodhi, Balbir Singh, 73
Sodhi, Lakhwinder, 73–74
Sodhi, Sukhpul Singh, 73–74
Somali immigrants, 75–76
Soviet Union, 8–9, 10
Star Tribune (Minneapolis)
newspaper, 75–76
Stolar, Martin, 183–184
Street, John F., 69–70
Stroman, Mark, 74
Student and Exchange Visitor
Information System
(SEVIS), 206
Students for a Democratic Society
(SDS)

convention (1969), 144–145
FBI, police, files from '60s,
166–167
and law enforcement
pressure, 141
surveillance and informers, 158
Suicide bombings, 254–255
Suspicious persons and behavior
Ashcroft warns of terrorists
within borders, 6, 18, 38, 90
citizens urged by government to
report, 39, 91, 171
defined as any lead from public
to FBI, JTTF, 169–171
as Middle Eastern visitors or visa
violators, 101
Swearingen, M. Wesley, 142
Sweeps conducted by INS,
police, FBI
create chaos, disappearances,
for Pakistanis, 122–123, 127,
131–132, 191
injustice of, 191, 221
led by ICE-NSEERS data, 187
of Mauritanians, 79
in PENTTBOM dragnet,
102–103
revitalize fear of 9/11, 108

Taliban
in Afghanistan, 189, 249
used for accusations against U.S.
Muslims, 57, 58, 221
and Wassel murder, 78
Taylor, John J., 32, 199
Templeton, Michael, 87
Terrorists. *See* Prosecutions of
terrorism suspects
Tessie (suspicious Frankford Valley
neighbor), 32–33, 199–200
Timoney, John
as Philadelphia police
commissioner, 64

post-9/11 efforts to protect
Muslims, 67–70, 95–96
Toolbox of laws and investigatory
techniques
immigration used as tool,
247, 252
as instruments of demolition,
forced migrations,
262–263, 264
results in visa violation
deportations, migrations,
170, 264
as tools of fragmentation,
suspicion, 258
used to dismantle Ansaarullah,
266–267
Torture and abuse of detainees
in Egypt, 47
in Israel, 209–210, 234, 235
in Metropolitan Detention
Center, 83–84, 103–104
as post-9/11 policy, 83–88
See also Disappearances

Uddin, Rais, 74
Undercover police
in '60s, 9–10, 144, 157–158
allegedly Frank Ferrara, 157
Kamil Pasha, 180
lead march against police
violence, 26
in mosques, 132
See also Informers
United Nations High Commissioner
on Human Rights, 47
Universities and colleges
collude with police and FBI
about students, 97, 136, 153
culture of surveillance,
informing, described,
137, 159
U.S. News and World Report
magazine, 99

Valentine, Linda, 185–187
Van Winkle, Mike, 25
Vietnam Veterans Against
the War, 142
Vietnam War
Harrison Salisbury on, 2
as motivator for New Left and
FBI informers, 148–149
Phoenix program, 83
See also Anti–Vietnam War
movement
Vigilante revenge attacks for 9/11.
See Arson attacks in post-9/11
period; Murders and
shootings in post-9/11 period

Wahhabism, 43–44
Wahid, Khurrum, 130
The War of the Worlds movie, 68
War on terror
based on enemy-within concept,
26, 40
as Bush's crusade against
evil, 107
and decimation of families,
communities, 284–286
as informant-driven, infused
with suspicion, 133,
178, 257
investigations based on
immigration status, 262
questions defining war on U.S.
soil, enemy, 264–266
Washington Post newspaper, 82
Wassel, Jawed, 78
Weatherman, 144, 145, 147–152
Williams, Jerri, 37, 169
Winter, Nancy Beam
on criminal cases from
immigration charges, 260
dismisses unsigned visa
application claim, 236
nanny cases, 254

Winter, Nancy Beam *(continued)*
    on post-9/11 law enforcement,
        252–253
    preemptive enforcement
        activities against Muslims,
        252–253
    prosecutes Idais, 210, 215,
        237–238
Wiretapping
    illegalities cause dismissed
        indictments, 152
    under NSA, 102, 260
    U.S. polls sanction bugging of
        mosques, 101

World Trade Center and Pentagon
    attacks. *See* September 11,
    2001 attacks
World Trade Center bombing in
    1993. *See* 1993 World Trade
    Center bombing

York County Prison, Pennsylvania,
    12, 48, 104, 188, 191, 205,
    211, 227

Zawahri, Ayman al-, 250
Zero tolerance, 190
Zoladek, Kathleen, 32–33, 199–200